Doctrines of the Great Educators

Robert R. Rusk
and
James Scotland

FIFTH EDITION

MACMILLAN

First edition 1918
Reprinted 1922, 1926, 1930, 1937, 1941, 1948, 1952
Second edition 1954
Reprinted 1955, 1956, 1957, 1962
Third edition 1965
Reprinted 1967
Fourth edition 1969
Reprinted 1971, 1972, 1974, 1976
Fifth edition 1979
Reprinted 1981, 1982, 1985, 1987

Published by
MACMILLAN EDUCATION LTD
Houndmills, Basingstoke, Hampshire RG21 2XS
and London
Companies and representatives
throughout the world

Printed in Hong Kong

British Library Cataloguing in Publication Data
Rusk, Robert Robertson
Doctrines of the great educators. — 5th ed.
1. Education — Philosophy — History
I. Title   II. Scotland, James
370.1   LA21
ISBN 0-333-23220-8
ISBN 0-333-23221-6 Pbk

Doctrines of the Great Educators

Contents

Preface to the Fifth Edition

Dr Robert Rusk died in 1972, at the age of ninety-three, his energy undimmed. This book went through four editions and seventeen impressions during his lifetime, and it has been reprinted three times since his death. It is a classic of educational exposition.

For this new edition I have made some alterations, omissions and additions. I have dropped three of Rusk's chapters, those on Elyot, Milton and Whitehead. The first two were included as representative of English educators in the period of the Renaissance and Reformation, but they do not seem to me to satisfy all the criteria Rusk adopted for a 'Great Educator': few students, even specialists, would claim much currency for their educational doctrines today. Some of these doctrines, especially Elyot's, I have added to the beginning of the chapter on Loyola. Whitehead did not make his appearance in the book until its fourth edition, and in the event his philosophy has proved to be less influential than it promised. Nevertheless his ideas still have power, and they have been given their place in the last chapter.

That chapter is itself an addition. The outstanding educators of the seventeenth, eighteenth and nineteenth centuries virtually select themselves; but after Dewey, who?* There have been many writers of stature in the last half-century, perhaps too many. Piaget would have his supporters, and detractors; so would Neill, Bruner and Illich. There is a good case for suggesting that the ideas of Marx and Freud (and for that matter Nietzsche) have had more influence in our education than those of any educational specialist. But fashions change: today's Peter the Apostle looks tomorrow

---

* Dewey himself did not make his appearance until the second edition.

like Peter the Hermit. The last chapter is my attempt to discern patterns in the spate of recent ideas.

To smooth continuity I have introduced a little extra material into each chapter – at the beginning a short biographical sketch, with some suggestions concerning influences at work on the educator concerned; at the end a few remarks on his impact in schools, colleges and educational systems. For students I have rectified an omission Rusk himself intended to repair, by adding short bibliographies. And, as is fitting in a new edition, I have amended the text in places to take account of a decade of recent scholarship.

This last task has not been onerous. Generally it has amounted to providing alternative readings and fresh emphases, seldom to introducing corrections. This is because Rusk worked habitually from the original texts or the best translations; what we have is his interpretation of the author's own statements, not his summary of another critic's commentary. In consequence many pages of the last edition he revised appear unchanged in this. One would expect no less of a book going into a new edition after sixty years. It is a measure of Robert Rusk, who was my own master, over thirty years ago, in the University of Glasgow.

James Scotland

September 1977

1

'The Great Educators'

MOST people concerned in education will tell you that there is no such creature as a 'Great Educator' nowadays; some will contend there never was. The concept is seen as part of the hero myth, now widely and enthusiastically discredited, the fantasy that an individual with a message is capable of changing the course of human affairs. In a world of 'superpowers' and international combines, it has become increasingly difficult to imagine an individual exercising any significant influence at all. The hero has been converted into an abstraction, an image required by ordinary men and women to see them through the confused, messy business of daily living. In war he is Douglas Haig, Foch, 'Monty', Rommel; in politics Churchill, Stalin, Fidel Castro, Che Guevara; in education the 'Great Educators'. The image exists because we want it to exist. We live in chaos, but continue to believe that somewhere someone holds the key to order. We are all educational alchemists, in quest of the Educator's Stone.

The evidence to support this is that the anti-hero men are as enthusiastic in their quest as everyone else; only their Educator's Stone is to be found in committees, working parties, soviets, the Democratic Process, the Good of the Nation or the People's Will. We have travelled from the age of the prophet into the age of the expert, and although many, probably the majority, still hanker after their prophets, the experts will see that they do not have them. There are famous and fashionable names today as there were in previous ages, Piaget and A. S. Neill, Whitehead and Skinner and Illich, but fashions change, and few observers would risk forecasting which of them will be a Great Educator tomorrow.

Nevertheless, as Whitehead pointed out,[1] 'education never reverts to its old position after the shock of a great philosopher'.

There have been some deeply influential thinkers in educational history; faced with our present problems, we may still profit by reading and reflecting on their ideas. That seems reason enough to call them Great Educators. That is certainly what they were thought to be, some in their lifetime, all by succeeding educators.

There are five common features in those whose ideas are considered in this book. First, each contributed theories or new emphases to the process of education. These may relate to the psychology of the pupil or his teacher, as when Rousseau and Froebel chart the stages through which a child matures, and Locke or Pestalozzi describes the properties of an 'ideal educator'. They may be concerned with general or specific methods of teaching and learning. This is the field of Comenius, with his 'one sure way', of Loyola and the Jesuits, constructing a carefully articulated system, of Dewey, the main begetter (whatever he himself said) of the 'Project Method', and Herbart, whose 'Steps' were developed into the lesson plans of countless courses in pedagogy. The new directions pointed by these pioneers may be in the content or locale of the educational experience. We find Rousseau and Locke agreeing that the best place for teaching is the home, but disagreeing violently on what ought to be taught. On the other hand Pestalozzi accepts much of Rousseau's curriculum, but transfers it to a classroom. Both Froebel and Montessori concentrated their attention on the learning processes of very young children, but the divergencies of the elaborate systems they produced have led their followers into bitter feuds.

Most commonly, the men we shall study have novel ideas on the proper relationship of education and society. Here above all we turn to Plato, who formulated with total clarity the problems which still beset us in the competing claims of individual fulfilment and community satisfaction. Here we see the contrast of Rousseau, for whom the task is to protect his pupil from social corruption, and Locke, whose aim is to educate men capable of making a rich contribution to the society in which they live:

> 'Here and here did England help me: how can I help England? – say.'

Out of this conflict of individual and social demands rises the perennially troublesome question of discipline. It is one on which most of the Great Educators have something to say. Quintilian regards the whipping of children as 'mean and servile'; Rousseau puts his trust in the controlling effect of natural consequences; others as unlike as Plato, Pestalozzi and Montessori are all prepared to compel their charges to concentrate. The problem, as any student in training will witness, is as pressing today as ever it was.

The second feature distinguishing our Great Educators is that they were all, in greater or less degree, philosophers. Their ideas are invariably rooted firmly in a definite philosophical position, a conception of the nature of human beings and their place within their world. This is why it is never difficult to identify their educational aims. Plato is concerned, he tells us, with enquiring into the true meaning of 'justice'; this leads him to examine the kind of state in which justice may be expected to flourish, and so the kind of education necessary to produce and preserve that state. Comenius, Loyola and Froebel see the perfection of man only in a world beyond ours; their educational systems are therefore designed to bring him as near as possible to a full understanding of God's will on earth, and to prepare him for a better life hereafter. Herbart considers the ends of education to be ethical, its means psychological. Dewey's pragmatism commits him to a belief that thinking arises out of practical needs, and that actions must be tested by their practical effects, both concepts having important consequences for his theory of education. The author of this book, Dr Robert Rusk, was himself a philosopher; it was the educational philosophers who interested him.

On the other hand, this is not a formal history; it makes no attempt to recount or criticise the march of educational ideas. Each Great Educator, except perhaps Loyola, has been placed at the dead centre of his chapter, and although I have added some linking material, hoping to identify some of the factors which may have influenced an individual's thought, I have remained with Rusk in making no special effort to discern 'cosmic' movements. No special effort, that is, until the last chapter, in which Rusk had little part. As additional evidence of this individual approach, each Educator appears in his chronological place, although the speed with which they made an impact on international thought varied widely: Dewey and Montessori were International Grand Masters in their lifetime, Comenius virtually vanished from Western eyes for a century and a half.

The third feature of these thinkers is the novelty of their ideas. Each was advocating a critical departure from the norms of his day. Even those, like Quintilian and Loyola, whose aims were acceptable to their contemporaries made proposals so systematic as to require a transformation in emphasis. Others, like Rousseau and Pestalozzi, were frankly revolutionaries, and were so regarded.

Fourth, to find a place here their work must have emerged effectively in practice. It is in classrooms and studies, in high schools, nurseries and orphanages, in relations with real children, sometimes recalcitrant, sometimes 'underprivileged', all comparatively untouched by philosophy, that the truth and validity of the ideas proposed were confirmed. The practice need not have been that of the Educators themselves. In fact, from such evidence as we have, comparatively few have left a name as brilliant teachers – Quintilian and Montessori, it would seem, probably Comenius and Plato, though the latter is more renowned for *describing* a master teacher. Herbart and Dewey were essentially lecturers: they had devoted disciples, but in the university world students have been notoriously willing to place matter above manner, and from first-hand accounts neither was a compulsive teacher. Pestalozzi too commanded respect through the inspiration he gave and the sweetness of his personality; in his classrooms something like chaos often ruled. Rousseau taught with his pen. But their ideas were capable of being put into practice by many different teachers in many different situations. They therefore remained alive long after the death of the men who proposed them.

That is the final point of qualification: their work must have continued effective for a notable period. Ideally, it ought to be effective still: a truly great Educator should have something to say to us in our present predicament. His influence need not have been continuous, for educational theories are as vulnerable as any other to the vagaries of fashion. Dewey, who was 'out' for a number of years because some of the more melodramatic excesses of educational revolution were fathered upon him, is now coming back 'in'. Montessori has been in, out and in again during the five editions of this book. The Educators' systems may also have changed with the world for which they wrote. The followers of Loyola and Froebel, by adapting their ideas, have rejuvenated them. And where their worlds – Plato's, Quintilian's, that of

Locke and Comenius – have altogether vanished, it is the fundamental ideas that remain. Dr Rusk was right to choose philosophers: more than psychology and much more than sociology, philosophy stands independent of the philosopher's daily world. The problems that occupied Plato and Rousseau still occupy us; their answers may be adapted to become ours.

Thus we define a 'Great Educator'; what do we mean by 'Doctrines'? In fact the title of the book may mislead. A doctrine suggests something systematic, but not all the Educators treated here intended to establish, or even sketch out, a complete educational system. The *Ratio Studiorum*, the foundation of the Jesuit system, was composed almost half a century after Loyola's death. Locke's work was exactly what its title denoted, *Some Thoughts Concerning Education*. Pestalozzi's ideas, set down first in a romantic novel, and later expanded and altered in the light of his experience, remained tentative and experimental to the end. Herbart's contribution was largely psychological: he never produced a comprehensive scheme for the education of youth, or even, as Froebel and Montessori did, for the fostering of one age-group. In short the 'doctrines' proposed may be narrow in compass.

On the other hand, as we have already noted, they must be rooted in a coherent philosophy. There is no place here for men concerned only with methods or psychology, nor, of course, for purely descriptive writers. Moreover, there are no studies of 'Great Philosophers' unless they dealt directly with education. However powerful their influence, they appear only through the impact they made on educators: we see Kant and Hegel, for instance, only through the eyes of Froebel. This point takes on substantial importance in the final chapter, when we must look closely at the influence in our schools of Marx and Freud.

The question remains, why these and not others? Is Aristotle not a 'Great Educator', or Benjamin Franklin, or Robert Owen? The answer is in the original plan of this book. Although it is not a comprehensive history of educational ideas, its form is essentially historical. It surveys the field of Western education since the days of the Greeks, and ends by attempting to place our modern problems in their historical context. The Educators chosen are there for two reasons. First, their ideas can be demonstrated to have had major influence in the schools of the West: some, like Quintilian and Herbart, principally in their own time; some, like Loyola, in a comparatively narrow but significant area; some, like Plato and Rousseau, over centuries. Second, some of them, especially the earlier, are in a sense representative. Before concentrating on Plato, the next chapter briefly considers his predecessors in Greek education. Aristotle's most distinctive ideas had their impact mainly in medieval times; Plato is more relevant today. Similarly, Quintilian stands for Roman education, Loyola for the Renaissance and the Counter-Reformation.

This individual approach has one great advantage: each Educator, as we study him, appears as a man rather than an abstraction, struggling as we do, though much more powerfully, to find answers to continuing problems. His insights dazzle, but his mistakes are also instructive. This is the classical benefit of the teaching process, when the student not only learns new facts or discerns new horizons, but draws unfailing sustenance from another, livelier mind.

2
Plato

IT is to Greek thought that we first turn when we wish to consider any of the problems of ethics, education or politics, for in Greece we find the beginnings of Western culture. Although every day is disclosing that the Mycenaean, Minoan and Egyptian civilisations have all contributed to Greek development, yet the boast of Plato was not an empty one that whatever the Greeks acquired from foreigners they subsequently developed into something nobler.[1]

Greek thought has, in addition to its originality, a surprising universality, not a mere municipal fitness. The principles of logic, ethics and politics which Plato and Aristotle enunciated are generally regarded as universally valid; the writings of the Greek poets are still read; the Greek tragedies are acted before modern audiences; and the surviving works of Greek art are appreciated by the untutored.

Greek thought has likewise a simplicity which enables us to focus the problems involved more easily than under modern complex conditions. It is accordingly both natural and necessary to begin our study of the doctrines of the great educators with a consideration of the Greek thinkers.[2]

About the fourth or the third century before the Christian era, at a time of intellectual unrest in Greece, a new school of teaching came into being. The enlargement of the intellectual horizon resulting from the unrest that ensued demanded a class of men who could impart quickly every kind of knowledge; and to satisfy this demand all sorts and conditions were pressed into the service of education and classed under the general title 'Sophist'. 'Is not a sophist one who deals wholesale or retail in the food of the soul?' it is asked in the *Protagoras*.[3] Fencing masters like Euthydemus and his brother Dionysodorus, Prodicus with his stock of philological subtleties,[4] and Protagoras 'the wisest of all living men'[5] declared themselves 'the only professors of moral improvement'.[6]

The teaching of the sophists was unsystematic; it was also limited to the few who could pay for it,[7] and we find Socrates, for example, saying: 'As for myself, I am the first to confess that I have never had a teacher; although I have always from my earliest youth desired to have one. But I am too poor to give money to the sophists, who are the only professors of moral improvement.'[8] The fact that they accepted payment for their services created a certain prejudice against the sophists, for this enabled those who could afford their instruction to acquire a definite superiority over their fellow-citizens. In consequence, they taught not what was best but what their pupils wanted to hear. Their lectures were intended for entertainment rather than education, the use of words for example rather than the exploration of values.[9] The popular attitude towards them may be inferred from the violent outburst of indignation with which Anytus received the suggestion of Socrates that Meno should go to the sophists for his education. 'The young men', says Anytus[10] 'who gave their money to them [the sophists] were out of their minds, and their relations and guardians who entrusted them to their care were still more out of their minds, and most of all the cities who allowed them to come in and did not drive them out, citizen or stranger alike. . . . Neither I nor any of my belongings has ever had, nor would I suffer them to have, anything to do with them.'

The prejudice against the sophists was intensified by the fact that they degraded knowledge by making its aim direct utility. Education was with the Greeks a training for leisure, not for a livelihood. In the *Protagoras*.[11] for example, it is asked: 'Why may you not learn of him in the same way that you learned the arts of the grammarian or musician or trainer, not with the view of making any of them a profession, but only as a part of education and because a private gentleman ought to know them?'

Socrates recognised the unscientific nature of the methods of the sophists, and his own method, although superficially resembling theirs, was essentially systematic and founded on general principles.[12] 'There are', according to Aristotle,[13] 'two things which we may fairly attribute to Socrates, his inductive discourses and his universal definitions.' Inductive reasoning was his method of arriving at a definition. The result attained by his method could not in many instances be regarded as satisfying the requirements of scientific exactness, but this did not disturb Socrates, for he himself continually and emphatically disclaimed the possession of any knowledge, except perhaps the knowledge of his own limitations. 'He knows nothing', the intoxicated Alcibiades says of him in the *Symposium*,[14] 'and is ignorant of all things – such is the appearance which he puts on.' Although not possessing knowledge himself, Socrates claimed to have the gift of discerning its presence in others, and of having the power to assist them to bring it to light.[15]

His first task was to arouse men from that false self-satisfaction which was by him believed to be the cause of their misery, and to lead them to self-examination and self-criticism. 'Herein', he says,[16] 'is the evil of ignorance, that he who is neither good nor wise is nevertheless satisfied with himself: he has no desire for that of which he feels no want.' The mission which Socrates conceived himself as charged to fulfil was to make men feel this want, to teach others what the utterance of the Delphic oracle had taught him – his own ignorance; to imbue them with a divine discontent; to make them feel, as Alcibiades puts it,[17] 'the serpent's sting', 'the pang of philosophy'. And in his defence Socrates neither disowned his mission nor his method: 'I am that gadfly', he tells his judges,[18] 'which God has attached to the state, and all day long and in all places am always fastening upon you, arousing and persuading and reproaching you.'

A characteristic of the method of Socrates was the necessity for having a companion in the pursuit of truth. Anyone sufficed for this purpose, and Socrates had many devices for alluring men into this search, though not infrequently they were unwilling companions who soon discovered that for the onlookers 'there is amusement in it'.[19] In the *Protagoras* Socrates is represented as saying: 'When anyone apprehends alone, he immediately goes about and searches for someone to whom he may communicate it and with whom he may establish it.'[20] The principle implied is that if one other can be convinced, then all others can likewise be persuaded, and consequently the belief in question is universally valid. Carlyle expresses the same idea when he cites the statement: 'It is certain my conviction gains infinitely, the moment another soul will believe in it.' The dialogue is thus a necessary and essential feature of the method of Socrates.

In the Socratic discourses three stages can generally be distinguished: first, the stage called by Plato 'opinion', in which the individual is unable to give valid reasons for his knowledge or assumed knowledge; second, the destructive or analytic stage, in which the individual is brought to realise that he does not know what he assumed he knew, and which leads to contradiction and a mental condition of doubt or perplexity; third, a synthetic stage for the results of which Plato would reserve the term 'knowledge'. When this last stage is attained, the individual's experience is critically reconstructed and he can justify his beliefs by giving the reasons for them.[21]

The possibility of applying a method similar to that of Socrates in the teaching of school pupils has frequently been questioned and sometimes even denied. Pestalozzi is probably the most vigorous opponent of what he terms 'Socratizing'. In one passage[22] he says: 'Socratizing is essentially impossible for children, since they want both a background of preliminary knowledge and the outward means of expression – language.' If, however, the teacher adequately recognises the limits of his pupils' experience and adapts his terminology to their vocabulary, the method can be applied quite successfully.[23]

We see Socrates only in the accounts of his followers (and their followers), and of these the greatest was Plato. Born in 428 B.C. into a family of aristocrats on both sides, he grew up during the strains and alarms of the Peloponnesian War, and at one time contemplated a military career. In his twentieth year, however, he became a friend of Socrates, and remained under the great man's influence for several impressionable years. The execution of his friend turned him away from state affairs, and for a decade he is thought to have travelled widely in the civilised world of his time, visiting Egypt, Cyrene, Sicily and southern Italy. During these years, too, he took his part, with Xenophon and other Socratic disciples, in perpetuating their master's memory in a series of dialogues of which he was the hero; examples are the *Apology* and *Crito*.

About 389 B.C. Plato returned to Athens and began teaching at a *gumnasion* near the city, in the grove dedicated to Academus; his school came to be known as the Academy. His aristocratic bent of mind led him into increasing mistrust of popular democracy, and confirmed his disinclination for public life. Of his teaching we have little record, only a clue in the works of his pupil Aristotle; in all probability it was largely mathematical, for he came to regard mathematics as indispensable to the would-be philosopher. At the same time he wrote many dialogues, of which a high proportion has survived, and it is in these that he emerges as one of the most influential philosophers and educationists in history. As he grew older the ideas in the dialogues were increasingly his own rather than those of his revered master, even when Socrates figured as the principal character. He died about the year 347 B.C.[24]

Education was a subject to which Plato attached the greatest importance.[25] In the *Republic*[26] he reckons it with war, the conduct of campaigns and the administration of states as amongst 'the grandest and most beautiful' subjects, and in the *Laws*[27] he repeats that it is 'the first and fairest thing that the best of men can ever have'. In the *Laches,*[28] which is professedly a treatise on education, he asks: 'Is this a slight thing about which you and Lysimachus are deliberating? Are you not risking the greatest of your possessions? For children are your riches; and upon their turning out well or ill depends the whole order of their father's house.' Again in the *Crito*[29] he says: 'No man should bring children into the world who is unwilling to persevere to the end in their nurture and education.' The extent and elaborateness of the treatment of education in the *Republic* and in the *Laws* likewise testify to the importance of the subject in Plato's mind.

The type of education which was then current in Greece we can gather from several references in the dialogues. In the *Crito*[30] it is asked: 'Were not the laws which have the charge of education right in commanding your father to train you in music and gymnastic?' and the answer of Socrates is: 'Right, I should reply'. In the *Protagoras*[31] it is stated: 'I am of opinion that skill in poetry was the principal part in education and this I conceive to be the power of knowing what compositions of the poets are correct, and what are not, and how they are to be distinguished and of explaining, when asked, the reason of the difference.' In the *Timaeus*[32] there is a reference which gives us an interesting side-light on ancient Greek education. Critias there says: 'Now the day was that day of the Apaturia which is called the registration of youth, at which, according to custom, our parents gave prizes for recitations, and the poems of several poets were recited by us boys, and many of us sang the poems of Solon, which at that time had not gone out of fashion.'

An idealised education of a Greek youth is sketched in the *Protagoras*:[33] 'Education and admonition commence in the first years of childhood, and last to the very end of life. Mother and nurse and father and tutor are quarrelling about the improvement of the child as soon as ever he is able to understand them; he cannot say or do anything without their setting forth to him that this is just and that is unjust; this is honourable, that is dishonourable; this is holy, that is unholy; do this and abstain from that. And if he obeys, well and good; if not, he is straightened by threats and blows, like a piece of warped wood. At a later stage they send him to teachers, and enjoin them to see to his manners even more than to his reading and music; and the teachers do as they are desired. And when the boy has learned his letters and is beginning to understand what is written, as before he understood only what was spoken, they put into his hands the works of great poets, which he reads at school; in these are contained many admonitions, and many tales and praises, and encomia of ancient famous men, which he is required to learn by heart, in order that he may imitate or emulate them and desire to become like them. Then, again, the teachers of the lyre take similar care that their young disciple is temperate and gets into no mischief; and when they have taught him the use of the lyre, they introduce him to the poems of other excellent poets, who are the lyric poets; and these they set to music, and make their harmonies and rhythms quite familiar to the children's souls, in order that they may learn to be more gentle and harmonious, and rhythmical, and so more fitted for speech and action; for the life of man in every part has need of harmony and rhythm. Then they send them to the master of gymnastic, in order that their bodies may better minister to the virtuous mind, and that they may not be compelled through bodily weakness to play the coward in war or any other occasion. This is what is done by those who have the means, and those who have the means are the rich; their children begin education soonest and leave off latest. When they have done with masters, the state again compels them to learn the laws, and live after the pattern which they furnish, and not after their own fancies; and just as in learning to write, the writing-master first draws lines with a style for the use of the young beginner, and gives him the tablet and makes him follow the lines, so the city draws the laws, which were the invention of good law-givers who were of old time; these are given to a young man, in order to guide him in his conduct whether as ruler or ruled; and he who transgresses them is to be corrected, or, in other words, called to account, which is a term used not only in your country, but also in many others.'[34]

Xenophon's *The Economist*[35] furnishes the complementary education of the Greek maiden. 'Ah, Ischomachus, that is just what I [Socrates] should like particularly to learn from you. Did you yourself educate your wife to be all that a wife should be, or when you received her from her father and mother was she already a proficient well skilled to discharge the duties appropriate to a wife? – Well skilled! (he replied). What proficiency was she likely to bring with her, when she was not quite fifteen at the time she wedded me, and during the whole prior period of her life had been most carefully brought up to see and hear as little as possible, and to ask the fewest questions? Or do you not think one should be satisfied, if at marriage her whole experience consisted in knowing how to take the wool and make a dress, and seeing how her mother's handmaidens had their daily spinning-tasks assigned them? For (he added) as regards control of appetite and self-indulgence [in reference to culinary matters], she had received the soundest education, and that I take to be the most important matter in the bringing-up of man or woman.'

It is in the *Republic*,[36] Plato's major work and the most sustained practical statement of his philosophy, that his chief treatment of education is to be found.[37] Rousseau has said:[38] 'If you wish to know what is meant by public education, read Plato's *Republic*. Those who merely judge books by their titles take this for a treatise on Politics, but it is the finest treatise on Education ever written.' Edward Caird has likewise affirmed of the *Republic* that 'perhaps it might best be described as a treatise on Education, regarded as the one great business of life from the beginning to the end of it'.[39]

The *Republic* is professedly an inquiry into the nature of justice, that is, morality or righteousness.[40] But justice is essentially a social virtue;[41] consequently to determine the nature of justice Plato is driven to construct in thought an ideal state wherein he hopes to find justice 'writ large'.[42] His reason for constructing such a state is to provide a society within which, since all men are equally entitled to happiness, arrangements can most effectively be made for the happiness of all men.[43]

Because of the multiplicity of human wants and of the insufficiency of any one individual to satisfy these by his own efforts, the state, in Plato's view,[44] is necessary. He found the states of his own time suffering from the strains of a social revolution in which individual demands came into conflict; to solve the problem he saw no alternative to a justly constructed state whose welfare must be placed above the welfare of any individual.[45] Such a state is likewise advantageous since by reason of the diversity in the natural endowment of the individuals constituting the state the greatest efficiency can only be attained by the application of the principle of the division of labour and by co-operative effort.[46] These two principles are implied in the oft-quoted statement of Aristotle:[47] 'The state comes into existence originating in the bare needs of life, and continuing in existence for the sake of a good life.'

The application of the principle of the division of labour results in the separation of the citizens of the state into two classes – the industrial or artisan and the guardian class, the duty of the former being to provide the necessaries of life;[48] the duty of the latter being to enlarge the boundaries of the state[49] – a proceeding which involves war – that luxuries may be available for the citizens and the state be something more than 'a community of swine'.[50] The guardian class Plato further subdivides into the military and governing classes, representing respectively the executive and deliberative functions of government.

After the division of the citizens into the three classes – the industrial, the military and the ruling – has been established, the state assumes the nature of a permanent structure, and this has caused Plato's constitution to be designated 'a system of caste'.[51] To give sanction to the divisions in the state thus constituted Plato would bring into play 'a seasonable falsehood';[52] and the myth which he suggests is as follows: he would tell the people,[53] 'You are brothers, yet God has framed you differently. Some of you have the power of command, and in the composition of these he has mingled gold, wherefore also they have the greatest honour; others he has made of silver, to be auxiliaries; others again who are to be husbandmen and craftsmen he has composed of brass and iron.' The barriers between the classes are not, however, absolute, nor is the hereditary principle in legislation regarded as infallible, for Plato immediately adds: 'But as all are of the same original stock, a golden parent will sometimes have a silver son, or a silver parent a golden son. And God proclaims as a first principle to the rulers, and above all else, that there is nothing which they should so anxiously guard, or of which they are to be such good guardians, as of the purity of the race. They should observe what elements mingle in their offspring; for if the son of a golden or silver parent has an admixture of brass and iron, then nature orders a transposition of ranks, and the eye of the ruler must not be pitiful towards the child because he has to descend in the scale and become a husbandman or artisan, just as there may be sons of artisans who having an admixture of gold or silver in them are raised to honour, and become guardians or auxiliaries. For an oracle says that when a man of brass or iron guards the state, it will be destroyed.'[54]

For each of the three classes of the community – the producing, the military and the governing – Plato ought to have provided, we should imagine, an appropriate form of training; but although the education of the soldier and that of the ruler or philosopher are treated at considerable length, no mention is made in the *Republic* of the education of the industrial class.[55] The education of the members of this class, had Plato dealt with it, would doubtless have been of a strictly vocational nature, not, however, a state scheme of vocational training but something resembling rather 'the constitution of apprenticeship as it once existed in Modern Europe'.[56] There would be no specific training in citizenship, for these members of the community have no voice in the government of the state; their characteristic virtue is obedience, technically 'temperance' – to know their place and to keep it.[57]

Plato lays down stringent qualifications for guardians – high intellectual calibre, moral concern, disinterestedness to the extent of deriving no gain from their guardianship, a constant desire for the happiness of all.[58] Nevertheless, however well intentioned the scheme, the fact that a large element in the community is denied the benefits and privileges of citizenship, the communistic scheme being confined to the guardian class, must be regarded as a serious defect in Plato's ideal state. It has been attributed to Plato's aristocratic prejudices, and to the Greek contempt for the mechanical arts. Aristotle regards the artisans as of even less account than the slaves, and maintains[59] that they can only attain excellence as they become slaves, that is, come under the direction of a master. If, however, the constitution is to be stable, or be 'a unity', as Plato phrased it, all must share in the government.[60] Contrasting the Greek with the modern ideal of virtue, T. H. Green says:[61] 'It is not the sense of duty to a neighbour, but the practical answer to the question Who is my neighbour? that has varied.' This explains the defect in Plato's scheme, and helps us to appreciate the increased difficulty of our present-day ethical, social and educational problems.

The first phase of Plato's curriculum,[62] the training of the guardians including the military and ruling classes, is a general education governed mainly by the principle of imitation. Its two main divisions are the current forms of Greek education, namely, music[63] and gymnastic, but as Plato again warns us:[64] 'Neither are the two arts of music and gymnastic really designed, as is often supposed, the one for the training of the soul, the other for the training of the body. I believe that the teachers of both have in view chiefly the improvement of the soul.'

Remembering this, and likewise mindful of Plato's general idealistic position, we are not surprised when at the outset of his treatment of education he asserts that we should begin education with music and proceed thereafter to gymnastic;[65] mental is thus to precede physical education. The mothers and nurses are to tell their children the authorised tales only: 'Let them fashion the mind with such tales, even more fondly than they mould the body with their hands.'

Education for Plato cannot begin too early; he recognises the importance of first impressions in forming the right attitudes. 'The beginning', he says,[66] 'is the most important part of any work, especially in the case of a young and tender thing.' Consequently consideration of the tales to be told to infants he does not assume to be beneath the dignity of a philosopher.[67]

Music includes narratives, and these are of two kinds, the true and the fictitious.[68] Somewhat paradoxically Plato maintains that the young should be trained in both, and that we should begin with the false; fables, he implies, are best suited to the child mind. He thus recognises the truth of art as well as the truth of fact. But not all fables should, according to Plato,[69] be taught, 'for a young person cannot judge what is allegorical and what is literal; anything that he receives into his mind at that age is likely to become indelible and unalterable; and therefore it is most important that the tales which the young first hear should be models of virtuous thoughts.'

Here we have formulated Plato's guiding principle – that nothing must be admitted in education which does not conduce to the promotion of virtue. For 'true and false' he substitutes the standard 'good and evil'. Plato declines to take upon himself the task of composing fables suitable for children, but using as a criterion the principle just enunciated, he assumes a moral censorship over the tales then current. 'The narrative of Hephaestus binding Hera his mother, and how on another occasion Zeus sent him flying for taking her part when she was being beaten, and all the battles of the gods in Homer – these tales must not be admitted into our state, whether they are supposed to have an allegorical meaning or not.'[70] Such a prescription does not endear him to liberal critics, but, as has been pointed out,[71] 'if people are not suggestible to the influence of fictional characters, it is difficult to see how much of advertising has any effect'.

Plato proceeds to pass in review the stories about the gods and formulates the following theological canons: (1) 'God is not the author of all things, but of good only' – and the poet is not to be permitted to say that those who are punished are miserable and that God is the author of their misery.'[72] (2) 'The gods are not magicians who transform themselves, neither do they deceive mankind in any way.'[73] The tales to be told to children must conform to these principles, and others are not to be told to the children from their youth upwards, if they are to honour the gods and their parents, and to value friendship.[74]

After having considered the fables dealing with the gods, Plato proceeds to consider those relating to heroes and the souls of the departed. To make the citizens free men who should fear slavery more than death, the other world must not be reviled in fables but rather commended. All weepings and wailings of heroes must be expunged from fables; likewise all descriptions of violent laughter, or a fit of laughter which has been indulged to excess almost always produces a violent reaction.[75]

In the tales to be recited to children a high value is to be set upon truth; 'if anyone at all is to have the privilege of lying, the rulers of the state should be the persons; and they, in their dealings either with their enemies or with their own citizens, may be allowed to lie for the public good. But nobody else should meddle with anything of the kind.'[76] Temperance, implying obedience to commanders and self-control in sensual pleasures, is to be commended, while covetousness is to be condemned. The fables concerning heroes and others must accordingly be amended to agree with these principles.

The use is likewise to be forbidden of such language as implies that wicked men are often happy, and the good miserable; and that injustice is profitable when undetected, justice being a man's own loss and another's gain.[77]

Having thus discussed the matter of the narratives to be used in education, Plato addresses himself to a consideration of their form.[78] In compositions he distinguishes between direct speech, which he calls 'imitation', and indirect speech, which he calls 'simple narration'. 'Imitation' is only to be allowed of the speech and action of the virtuous man: the speeches of others are to be delivered and their actions described in the form of narration. The reason Plato gives is that 'imitation beginning in early youth and continuing far into life at length grows into habits and becomes a second nature, affecting body, voice and mind'.[79]

With regard to music in its limited and modern sense Plato maintains that all harmonies which are effeminate and convivial are to be discarded and only such retained as will make the citizens temperate and courageous. The rhythm is to be determined by the nature of the words, just as the style of words is determined by the moral disposition of the soul.

So must it be with the other arts and crafts, and not only the poets, but the professors of every other craft as well must impress on their productions the image of the good.[80] Here we have the origin of the old quarrel between poetry and philosophy, or between art and morality. Plato will not entertain the idea of 'art for art's sake'; the only criterion he will recognise is the ethical.

The reason of Plato's solicitude for a good and simple environment for the children who are to be the future guardians of the state is his belief in the efficacy of unconscious assimilation or imitation in the formation of character. As evidence of this we may cite the following:[81] 'We would not have our guardians grow up amid images of moral deformity, as in some noxious pasture, and there browse and feed upon many a baneful herb and flower, day by day, little by little, until they silently gather a festering mass of corruption in their own soul. Let our artists rather be those who are gifted to discern the true nature of the beautiful and graceful; then will our youth dwell in a land of health, amid fair sights and sounds, and receive the good in everything; and beauty, the effluence of fair works, shall flow into the eye and ear, like a healthgiving breeze from a purer region, and insensibly draw the soul from earliest years into likeness and sympathy with the beauty of reason.'

'And therefore', Plato continues, 'musical training is a more potent instrument than any other, because rhythm and harmony find their way into the inward places of the soul, on which they mightily fasten, imparting grace, and making the soul of him who is rightly educated graceful, or of him who is ill-educated ungraceful.' That the result of a musical education should be the production of harmony and grace in the individual is repeated in the introduction to Plato's treatment of higher education or the education of the philosopher. There,[82] he says, 'music was the counterpart of gymnastic, and trained the guardians by the influence of habit, by harmony making them harmonious, by rhythm rhythmical.' The end throughout was the Greek ideal of manhood, a life which in itself was a work of art.

Plato's treatment of gymnastic in the *Republic* is decidedly brief;[83] he contents himself with indicating no more than the general principles. 'Gymnastic as well as music should begin in early years; the training in it should be careful and should continue through life', he says, adding, however, 'Now my belief is, not that the good body by any bodily excellence improves the soul, but, on the contrary, that the good soul, by her own excellence, improves the body as far as this may be possible.'

Plato prescribes a simple moderate system such as would be productive of health and the utmost keenness of both eye and ear.[84] Of the habit of body cultivated by professional gymnasts he disapproves as unsuitable for men who have to undergo privations in war and variations in food when on a campaign. Abstinence from delicacies is also enjoined. The whole life, however, is not to be given up to gymnastics, for everyone who does nothing else ends by becoming uncivilised: 'he is like a wild beast, all violence and fierceness, and knows no other way of dealing; and he lives in all ignorance and evil conditions, and has no sense of propriety and grace'.[85]

Such then is, in outline, Plato's scheme of early education with its training in music and gymnastic. The dances which will be in vogue, the hunting and field exercises and the sports of the gymnasium and the race-course, he adds,[86] must correspond with the foregoing outlines.

There is one omission from this early education to which attention ought to be directed, for the omission is intentional on Plato's part; it is the absence of any reference to a training in the manual arts. The reason for the omission is incidentally disclosed by Plato in a later section of the *Republic*:[87] 'All the useful arts were reckoned mean.'

There are other omissions evidently unintentional at this time. He later came to recognise that the subjects of higher education must be begun in youth. Hence, when he goes on to deal with the education of the ruler or philosopher, we find him stating:[88] 'Calculation and geometry and all the other elements of instruction, which are a preparation for dialectic, should be presented to the mind in childhood; not, however, under any notion of forcing our system of education.'

The principle of teaching method here implied he elaborates by adding: 'Bodily exercise, when compulsory, does no harm to the body; but knowledge which is acquired under compulsion obtains no hold on the mind. . . . Then do not use compulsion, but let early education be a sort of amusement; you will then be better able to find out the natural bent.' In the *Laws* the positive significance of play in education is emphasised. Thus, as has frequently been pointed out, we do not have to come to modern times, to Herbart, Froebel or Montessori, to find the child's interest or his play taken as a guiding principle in education: it is formulated in Plato.

Those who are to undergo the early education and become guardians of the state are to unite in themselves 'philosophy and spirit and swiftness and strength'.[89] Throughout their education they are to be watched carefully and tested and tried in various ways;[90] and those who, after being proved, come forth victorious and pure are to be appointed rulers and guardians of the state, the others remaining auxiliaries or soldiers.

The qualities required for the higher education[91] or for the philosophic character Plato frequently enumerates. Preference is to be given to 'the surest and the bravest, and, if possible, to the fairest; and, having noble and generous tempers, they should also have the natural gifts which will facilitate their education'.[92] Another account runs:[93] 'A good memory and quick to learn, noble, gracious, the friend of truth, justice, courage, temperance'; again,[94] 'Courage, magnificence, apprehension, memory'.

The aim of the higher education is not a mere extension of knowledge; it is, in Plato's phrase,[95] 'the conversion of a soul from study of the sensible world to contemplation of real existence'. 'Then, if I am right', he explains,[96] 'certain professors of education must be wrong when they say that they can put a knowledge into the soul which was not there before, like sight into blind eyes. Whereas, our argument shows that the power and capacity of learning exist in the soul already; and that just as the eye was unable to turn from darkness to light without the whole body, so too the instrument of knowledge can only by the movement of the whole soul be turned from the world of becoming into that of being, and learn by degrees to endure the sight of being, and of the brightest and best of being, or in other words, of the good.'

Such is the aim of the higher education, the education of the philosopher or ruler.[97] Plato, having determined the aim, next proceeds to consider the scope of higher education. It includes number or arithmetic, plane and solid geometry, astronomy, theory of music or harmonies, all preparatory to the highest of the sciences, namely, dialectic. 'Through mathematics to metaphysics' might be said to sum up Plato's scheme of higher education.

The principles that decide the selection of the studies of the higher education are that they must lead to reflection rather than deal with the things of sense;[98] they must likewise be of universal application.[99] The first subject that satisfies these requirements is number, hence Plato concludes:[100] 'This is a kind of knowledge which legislation may fitly prescribe; and we must endeavour to persuade those who are to be the principal men of our state to go and learn arithmetic, not as amateurs, but they must carry on the study until they see the nature of numbers with the mind only; nor again, like merchants or retail traders, with a view to buying or selling, but for the sake of their military use, and of the soul herself; and because this will be the easiest way for her to pass from becoming to truth and being.' The main function of number is thus to afford a training in abstraction.

The value which Plato assigns to number, as a subject in the training preparatory to philosophy, strikes the modern mind as somewhat exaggerated. This can be explained, however, by the fact that philosophers had then only begun the search for universal or conceptual notions, and the science of number presented itself as satisfying their requirements in a remarkable degree. The Pythagoreans had indeed maintained that number was the rational principle or essence of things, and it is generally agreed that Plato, who probably visited their school in southern Italy during his lengthy travels after the death of Socrates, was for some time under Pythagorean influences; in fact, by some it is maintained that by 'Ideas' he understood at one stage in the development of that doctrine nothing other than numbers themselves. At the time of writing the *Republic*, however, he had outgrown the naïve identification of numbers with things themselves, for we find him asserting:[101] 'Yet anybody who has the least acquaintance with geometry will not deny that such a conception of the science is in flat contradiction to the ordinary language of geometricians. They have in view practice only, and are always speaking, in a narrow and ridiculous manner, of squaring and extending and applying and the like – they confuse the necessities of geometry with those of daily life; whereas knowledge is the real object of the whole science.' If the Greeks, as is implied in Plato's statement, were at times in danger of ignoring the purely conceptual nature of number, we of the present day are in danger of disregarding the practical needs which brought the science into existence and the concrete bases in which numbers were first exemplified.

In insisting on the value of number as a means of training in abstraction Plato gives expression to a statement which implies the doctrine of formal discipline or transfer of training, that is, that a training in one function results in a general improvement of the mind, which in turn favourably influences other functions. Thus he asks: 'Have you further observed, that those who have a natural talent for calculation are generally quick at every other kind of knowledge; and even the dull, if they have had an arithmetical training, although they may derive no other advantage from it, always become much quicker than they would otherwise have been?'[102] When in the same section he adds: 'and indeed, you will not easily find a more difficult subject, and not many as difficult', he approximates to the doctrine that the more trouble a subject causes the better training it affords, the fallacy of which is evident in its enunciation by a modern paradoxical philosopher, namely, it matters not what you teach a pupil provided he does not want to learn it.

In dealing with geometry[103] Plato also remarks that 'in all departments of knowledge, as experience proves, any one who has studied geometry is infinitely quicker of apprehension than one who has not.'

These views must nevertheless be qualified by the statement[104] occurring in the discussion of the relation between mathematics and dialectic. 'For you surely would not regard the skilled mathematician as a dialectician? Assuredly not, he said; I have hardly ever known a mathematician who was capable of reasoning.' This qualification, it has been contended,[105] acquits Plato of the responsibility of initiating the doctrine of formal training, but if it does so, it is only at the cost of consistency. In his defence, however, it may be said that in Plato's day little was known of, although much was hoped from, the science of number; and no objection could have been urged against him had he said that a knowledge of number 'broadened' rather than 'quickened' the mind. Number, like language, affords us an invaluable means of mastering and controlling experience, and does not require to be defended on the ground of some hypothetical influence on the mind in general.

As number is the first subject, so geometry is the second, selected for inclusion in the curriculum of the higher education. Its bearing on strategy is acknowledged, but what Plato is concerned about is whether it tends in any degree to make easier the vision of the idea of good.[106] This, he believes, geometry does accomplish; 'geometry will draw the soul towards truth, and create the spirit of philosophy',[107] consequently those who are to be the rulers of the ideal state must be directed to apply themselves to the study of geometry.

Astronomy is the next of the instrumental subjects of the higher training, and in enumerating its practical advantages to the agriculturist and navigator Plato remarks:[108] 'I am amused at your fear of the world, which makes you guard against the appearance of insisting upon useless studies; and I quite admit the difficulty of believing that in every man there is an eye of the soul which, when by other pursuits lost and dimmed, is by these purified and re-illumined; and is more precious far than ten thousand bodily eyes, for by it alone is truth seen.' 'Then in astronomy, as in geometry, we should employ problems, and let the heavens alone if we would approach the subject in the right way and so make the natural gift of reason to be of any real use.'[109]

The last of the studies preparatory to dialectic is music, not, however, music as an art as dealt with in the early education, but the theory of music, harmonics, the mathematical relations existing between notes, chords, etc., or what we should now probably term the physical bases of music[110] – 'a thing', Plato affirms,[111] 'which I would call useful; that is, if sought after with a view to the beautiful and good; but if pursued in any other spirit, useless'.

If a common basis for the mathematical studies just enumerated could be discovered, Plato believes that it would advance the end in view, namely, preparation for the science of dialectic.

Dialectic is, for Plato, the highest study of all. It is as far removed from the mathematical sciences as they are from the practical arts. The sciences assume certain hypotheses, or make certain assumptions; geometry, for example, assumes the existence of space and does not inquire whether it is a perceptual datum, a conceptual construction or, as Kant maintained, an *a priori Anschauung*. Philosophy, or dialectic as Plato calls it, tries to proceed without presuppositions or, at least, seeks critically to examine their validity and to determine the extent of their application.

'I must remind you', says Plato,[112] 'that the power of dialectic can alone reveal this [absolute truth], and only to one who is a disciple of the previous sciences.' 'And assuredly', he continues, 'no one will argue that there is any other method of comprehending by any regular process all true existence or of ascertaining what each thing is in its own nature; for the arts in general are concerned with the desires and opinions of men, or are cultivated with a view to production and construction, or for the preservation of such productions and constructions; and as to the mathematical sciences which, as we were saying, have some apprehension of true being – geometry and the like – they only dream about being, but never can they behold the waking reality so long as they leave the hypotheses which they use unexamined, and are unable to give an account of them. For when a man knows not his own first principle, and when the conclusion and intermediate steps are also constructed out of he knows not what, how can he imagine that such a fabric of convention can ever become science?'

'Then dialectic, and dialectic alone, goes directly to the first principle and is the only science which does away with hypotheses in order to make her ground secure; the eye of the soul, which is literally buried in an outlandish slough, is by her gentle aid lifted upwards; and she uses as handmaids and helpers in the work of conversion, the sciences which we have been discussing.'

Dialectic then is the coping-stone of the sciences;[113] no other science can be placed higher; it completes the series. All who would be magistrates in the ideal state must consequently address themselves to such studies as will enable them to use the weapons of the dialectician most scientifically.

Having determined the subjects which the philosopher or ruler must study, Plato proceeds to consider the distribution of these studies.[114] For three years after the completion of the early education, that is, from seventeen to twenty years of age, the youths are to serve as cadets, being brought into the field of battle, and, 'like young hounds, have a taste of blood given them'. The course is largely that undertaken by the *ephebi* of Athens in Plato's time, the one he himself had served.

During these years of bodily exercises there is to be no intellectual study, 'for sleep and exercise are unpropitious to learning'.

At the age of twenty the choice characters are to be selected to undergo the mathematical training preparatory to dialectic. This training is to continue for ten years, and at the age of thirty a further selection is to be made, and those who are chosen are to begin the study of dialectic.[115] Plato deliberately withholds the study of dialectic to this late age, giving as his reason that 'youngsters, when they first get the taste in their mouths, argue for amusement, and are always contradicting and refuting others in imitation of those who refute them; like puppy-dogs, they rejoice in pulling and tearing at all who come near them'.[116] This study is to be prosecuted for five years, every other pursuit being resigned for it. For the next fifteen years, that is, from thirty-five to fifty years of age, the philosophers or rulers are to return to practical life, take the command in war and hold such offices of state as befit 'young men'. After the age of fifty the lives of the rulers are to be spent in contemplation of 'the Good', so that when they are called upon to regulate the affairs of the state, their knowledge of this will serve as a pattern according to which they are to order the state and the lives of individuals, and the remainder of their own lives also; 'making philosophy their chief pursuit, but when their turn comes, toiling also at politics and ruling for the public good, not as though they were performing some heroic action, but simply as a matter of duty; and when they have brought up in each generation others like themselves, they will depart to the Islands of the Blest and dwell there'.[117]

Such is Plato's scheme of education as set forth in the *Republic*, and he warns us in conclusion that it is an education for women as well as for men; they are to have the same training and education, a training in music and gymnastic, and in the art of war, which they must practise like men, 'for you must not suppose', he adds,[118] 'that what I have been saying applies to men only and not to women as far as their natures can go'.

Plato dismisses as irrelevant the ridicule which would be excited by his proposal that women should share with men the exercises of the gymnasia, maintaining that the question should be decided on principle. The principle, he argues, which applies in this case is that each member of the state should undertake the work for which he is best fitted by nature, and while admitting that physically the woman is weaker than the man, he nevertheless maintains that with regard to political or governing ability the woman is the equal of the man. Had he affirmed that with regard to intellectual ability the woman is *on the average* the equal of the man, he would have anticipated the conclusions of modern research.

His coeducational proposal arouses distrust, not so much on its own account but because the second 'wave', the community of wives and children, results from it.[119] To secure and preserve the unity of the state Plato was forced to destroy the family as the social unit; the family with its bonds of kinship and ties of natural affection was the only institution which he feared might challenge the supremacy, or lead to the disruption, of the state, and the pains he displays to eliminate every trace of family influence are witness to its power. Plato can only secure the unity of the state at the cost of sacrificing all differences; he makes a wilderness and calls it peace. This is the great defect of his ideal state, and on this ground his communistic scheme has been effectively criticised by

Aristotle.[120] A similar criticism has been applied by Rousseau,[121] who says: 'I am quite aware that Plato, in the *Republic*, assigns the same gymnastics to women and men. Having got rid of the family, there is no place for women in his system of government, so he is forced to turn them into men. That great genius has worked out his plans in detail and has provided for every contingency; he has even provided against a difficulty which in all likelihood no one would ever have raised; but he has not succeeded in meeting the real difficulty. I am not speaking of the alleged community of wives which has often been laid to his charge; . . . I refer to that subversion of all the tenderest of our natural feelings, which he sacrificed to an artificial sentiment which can only exist by their aid. Will the bonds of convention hold firm without some foundation in nature? Can devotion to the state exist apart from the love of those near and dear to us? Can patriotism thrive except in the soil of that miniature fatherland, the home? Is it not the good son, the good husband, the good father, who makes the good citizen?'

In the *Laws*, the work of his old age, Plato readdresses himself to the subject of education. The dialogue commencing with a consideration of the laws of Minos drifts into a consideration of the perfect citizen-ruler and how to train him – into a discussion on education, in short. Disillusioned by the experiences of life, Plato in the *Laws*, so some interpreters maintain, recants the idealistic schemes which he projected in the *Republic*; in the later work he does not, however, really abandon his earlier principles, but rather seeks to illustrate their application in practice; he describes, if not the ideal city, the pattern of which is laid up in heaven, at least 'the second best', which might be realisable 'in present circumstances.'[122]

The treatment of education in the *Laws* supplements that in the *Republic*, emphasising the practical aspects, and thus approximating to Aristotle's treatment of education in the *Politics*. The aim of education nevertheless remains the same, for as Plato says in the *Laws*:[123] 'At present when we speak in terms of praise or blame about the bringing-up of each person, we call one man educated and another uneducated, although the uneducated man may be sometimes very well educated for the calling of a retail trader, or of a captain of a ship, and the like. For we are not speaking of education in this narrower sense, but of that other education in virtue from youth upwards, which makes a man eagerly pursue the ideal perfection of citizenship, and teaches him how rightly to rule and how to obey. This is the only education which, upon our view, deserves the name; that other sort of training, which aims at the acquisition of wealth or bodily strength, or mere cleverness apart from intelligence and justice, is mean and illiberal, and is not worthy to be called education at all. But let us not quarrel with one another about a word, provided that the proposition which has just been granted holds good: to wit, that those who are rightly educated generally become good men. Neither must we cast a slight upon education, which is the first and fairest thing that the best of men can ever have, and which, though liable to take a wrong direction, is capable of reformation, and this business of reformation is the great business of every man while he lives.'

Education in the *Laws* is to be universal, not restricted as in the *Republic* to the guardian class, and is to be compulsory; 'the children shall come [to the schools] not only if their parents please, but if they do not please; there shall be compulsory education, as the saying is, of all and sundry, as far as this is possible; and the pupils shall be regarded as belonging to the state rather than to their parents. My law shall apply to females as well as males; they shall both go through the same exercises.'[124] To the coeducational principle and the communistic scheme on which it is based Plato frequently alludes in the *Laws*,[125] thus indicating that the proposal in the *Republic* was regarded by him as a serious one. In support of the idea that women and girls should undergo the same gymnastic and military exercises as men and boys Plato states:[126] 'While they are yet girls they should have practised dancing in arms and the whole art of fighting – when grown-up women, they should apply themselves to evolutions and tactics, and the mode of grounding and taking up arms; if for no other reason, yet in case the whole military force should have to leave the city and carry on operations of war outside, that those who will have to guard the young and the rest of the city may be equal to the task; and, on the other hand, when enemies, whether barbarian or Hellenic, come from without with mighty force and make a violent assault upon them, and thus compel them to fight for the possession of the city, which is far from being an impossibility, great would be the disgrace to the state, if the women had been so miserably trained that they could not fight for their young, as birds will, against any creature however strong, or die or undergo any danger, but must instantly rush to the temples and crowd at the altars and shrines, and bring upon human nature the reproach, that of all animals man is the most cowardly!'

The main subjects in the curriculum proposed in the *Laws* are the same as those given in the *Republic* – for the early education music and gymnastic, and for the higher education mathematics; dialectic, the study to which the mathematical subjects were merely preparatory in the *Republic*, is alluded to only indirectly in the more practical *Laws*.

Gymnastic occupies a more prominent place than it does in the *Republic*, where it was treated merely in outline. It is now divided into two branches, dancing and wrestling, and these are, in turn, further subdivided. 'One sort of dancing imitates musical recitation, and aims at preserving dignity and freedom; the other aims at producing health, agility and beauty in the limbs and parts of the body, giving the proper flexion and extension to each of them, a harmonious motion being diffused everywhere, and forming a suitable accompaniment to the dance.'[127] In regard to wrestling, that form 'of wrestling erect and keeping free the neck and hands and sides, working with energy and constancy, with a composed strength, and for the sake of health' is useful and is to be enjoined alike on masters and scholars.[128] The general intent is that of all movements wrestling is most akin to the military art, and is to be pursued for the sake of this, and not for the sake of wrestling.[129]

Plato's treatment of music in the *Laws* follows the lines of that in the *Republic*, the old quarrel between poetry and philosophy being frequently renewed.[130] The same conclusion is reached, namely, that the compositions must impress on the minds of the young the principle 'that the life which is by the gods deemed to be the happiest is also the best'.[131]

The omission in the *Republic* of any reference to the education of the industrial or artisan class is partially rectified in the *Laws*. 'According to my view', Plato now says,[132] 'anyone who would be good at anything must practise that thing from his youth upwards, both in sport and earnest, in its several branches: for example, he who is to be a good builder should play at building children's houses; he who is to be a good husbandman, at tilling the ground;

and those who have the care of their education should provide them when young with mimic tools. They should learn beforehand the knowledge which they will afterwards require for their art. For example, the future carpenter should learn to measure or apply the-line in play; and the future warrior should learn riding, or some other exercise, for amusement, and the teacher should endeavour to direct the children's inclinations and pleasures, by the help of amusements, to their final aim in life. The most important part of education is right training in the nursery. The soul of the child in his play should be guided by the love of that sort of excellence in which when he grows up to manhood he will have to be perfected.'

As in the *Republic* so in the *Laws*, education cannot begin too early;[133] 'Am I not right in maintaining that a good education is that which tends most to the improvement of mind and body? And nothing can be plainer than that the fairest bodies are those which grow up from infancy in the best and straightest manner?' The care of the child even before birth is dealt with by Plato.[134] The early discipline is to be, as with Aristotle, habituation to the good and the beautiful. 'Now I mean by education that training which is given by suitable habits to the first instincts of virtue in children; – when pleasure, and friendship, and pain, and hatred are rightly implanted in souls not yet capable of understanding the nature of them, and who find them, after they have attained reason, to be in harmony with her. This harmony of the soul, taken as a whole, is virtue; but the particular training in respect to pleasure and pain, which leads you always to hate what you ought to hate, and love what you ought to love from the beginning of life to the end, may be separated off; and, in my view, will be rightly called education.'[135]

The early training in the *Republic* comprising music and gymnastic was designed to occupy the first seventeen years of life. The ages at which the various parts of these subjects were to be taken up were not further particularised. In the *Laws*, however, Plato is most precise as to the occupations of the early years and the time to be allotted to each. 'Up to the age of three years, whether of boy or girl, if a person strictly carries out our previous regulations and makes them a principal aim, he will do much for the advantage of the young creatures. But at three, four, five or even six years the childish nature will require sports. . . . Children at that age have certain natural modes of amusement which they find out for themselves when they meet.'[136]

The sports which the children at these early ages engage in, it may be interpolated, are, in Plato's opinion, of supreme significance in maintaining the stability of the state. In the *Republic*[137] Plato repeatedly expresses his fear of innovations in music and gymnastic lest these should imperil the whole order of society. This was natural, for any change in an ideal state could only be regarded as a change for the worse. It was also in accordance with the Greek attitude of mind, to which the modern ideal of an infinite progress brought about by constant innovations was abhorrent, and which conceived of perfection after the manner of the plastic arts as limited and permanent. In the *Laws*, even when the constitution is but 'second-best', the dread of innovations still haunts Plato, and leads him to observe[138] 'that the plays of children have a great deal to do with the permanence or want of permanence in legislation. For when plays are ordered with a view to children having the same plays, and amusing themselves after the same manner, and finding delight in the same playthings, the more solemn institutions of the state are allowed to remain undisturbed. Whereas if sports are disturbed, and innovations are made in them, and they constantly change, and the young never speak of their having the same likings, or the same established notions of good and bad taste, either in the bearing of their bodies or in their dress, but he who devises something new and out of the way in figures and colours and the like is held in special honour, we may say that no greater evil can happen in the state; for he who changes these sports is secretly changing the manners of the young, and making the old to be dishonoured among them and the new to be honoured. And I affirm that there is nothing which is a greater injury to all states than saying this.'

Up to the age of six the children of both sexes may play together. After the age of six, however, they were to be separated – 'let boys live with boys, and girls in like manner with girls. Now they must begin to learn – the boys going to the teachers of horsemanship and the use of the bow, the javelin and sling, and the girls too, if they do not object, at any rate until they know how to manage these weapons, and especially how to handle heavy arms.'[139]

The musical is to alternate with the gymnastic training. 'A fair time for a boy of ten years old to spend in letters is three years; the age of thirteen is the proper time for him to begin to handle the lyre, and he may continue at this for another three years, neither more nor less, and whether his father or himself like or dislike the study, he is not to be allowed to spend more or less time in learning music than the law allows.'[140]

'There still remain three studies suitable for freemen. Arithmetic is one of them; the measurement of length, surface and depth is the second; and the third has to do with the revolutions of the stars in relation to one another. Not everyone has need to toil through all these things in a strictly scientific manner, but only a few.'[141] All that is required for the many is such a knowledge as 'every child in Egypt is taught when he learns the alphabet', and which frees them 'from that natural ignorance of all these things which is so ludicrous and disgraceful'.[142] He who is to be a good ruler of the state, must, however, make a complete study of these subjects and of their interconnections; he must know these two principles – 'that the soul is the eldest of all things which are born, and is immortal and rules over all bodies; moreover, he who has not contemplated the mind of nature which is said to exist in the stars, and gone through the previous training, and seen the connection of music with these things, and harmonized them all with laws and institutions, is not able to give a reason of such things as have a reason. And he who is unable to acquire this in addition to the ordinary virtues of a citizen, can hardly be a good ruler of a whole state.'[143]

While in the *Republic* education was to be in the immediate charge of the guardians of the state, in the *Laws* it is to be delegated to a Director of Education.[144] The end of education nevertheless remains the same. Education is for the good of the individual and for the safety of the state. Thus Plato reaffirms in the *Laws*:[145] 'If you ask what is the good of education in general, the answer is easy – that education makes good men, and that good men act nobly, and conquer their enemies in battle, because they are good. Education certainly gives victory, although victory sometimes produces forgetfulness of education; for many have grown insolent from victory in war, and this insolence has engendered in them innumerable evils; and many a victory has been and will be suicidal to the victors; but education is never suicidal.'

It is virtually impossible to overstate Plato's influence. In

Whitehead's much-quoted opinion, 'the safest general character-isation of the European philosophical tradition is that it consists of a series of footnotes to Plato'. Emerson was making the same point when he remarked, 'I am struck, in reading him, with the extreme modernness of his style and spirit'. The problems with which Plato grappled have continued to be central problems throughout Western history. This is not to say, however, that all succeeding thinkers agreed with him; nor that those who did invariably read him accurately. His idealism, for instance, plays a large part in Christian dogma – what Nietzsche called con-temptuously 'Platonism for the masses' – but Christian thinkers had to adjust his philosophy to fit theirs, replacing reason with faith at the heart of things.[146]

He established the humanistic tradition in Western education. His influence on later educational thought can be traced in Quintilian, in the mediaeval curriculum, the studies constituting the *trivium* (grammar, rhetoric, logic or dialectic) and the *quadrivium* (music, arithmetic, geometry, astronomy), if different in order, being practically identical with those prescribed by Plato for the philosopher, in More's *Utopia*, Elyot's *Governour* and other Renaissance writers, in the educational scheme of *The Book of Discipline* ascribed to John Knox, in Rousseau's *Article on Political Economy* and in Fichte's *Addresses to the German Nation*. Whether this influence has been for good or evil has been vigorously debated. That different interpretations can be derived from the writings of a thinker so original and fertile as Plato is only to be expected.

Thus his comparatively static view of the state, divided into clearly demarcated classes without easy transfer, has been condemned as undemocratic. Karl Popper, who escaped in the 1930s from a brutally authoritarian regime, regarded him as the apologist of totalitarianism, identifying 'justice' with the preserva-tion of a ruling class.[147] Some criticism of this kind has been over-emphatic, even unjustified: there is no evidence in the *Republic* of selection on grounds other than ability. But individual freedom, the prime good of the liberal, requires an open society, and Plato believed unhappiness and injustice to be inevitable in such a society. In his view the greatest happiness of the greatest number could be achieved only by the efforts of those best capable of securing it: 'the price of tolerance is impotence'.[148] On the other hand those who believe in the almost mystical benefits of democracy can adduce the evidence of history that men have never been willing to endure for long a dictated felicity; even the most benevolent autocracy comes in time to be regarded as tyranny. The debate continues: it has seldom, perhaps never, been as lively as it is today in the world of the 'permissive society', of equalisation of opportunity and what a modern Platonist has described as 'the peculiar view that education is only education if what goes on in its name is decided entirely by reference to what the child at the time wants to do or happens to value'.[149] In such a climate people may quarrel with Plato's ideas, but they cannot deny his continuing relevance.

Another unhappy side of Platonic culture, according to Whitehead,[150] was its total neglect of technical education as an ingredient in the complete development of ideal human beings. On the other hand, Whitehead recognises[151] that the Platonic ideal has rendered imperishable service to European civilisation by encouraging art, by fostering that spirit of disinterested curiosity which is the origin of science and by maintaining the dignity of mind in the face of material force. Dewey[152] likewise acclaims Plato's procedure of untrammelled inquiry, remarking: 'Nothing could be more helpful to present philosophising than a "Back to Plato" movement; but it would have to be back to the dramatic, restless, co-operatively inquiring Plato of the *Dialogues*, trying one mode of attack after another to see what it might yield; back to the Plato whose highest flight of metaphysics always terminated with a social and practical turn, and not to the artificial Plato constructed by unimaginative commentators who treat him as the original university professor.' The mistake is to regard the *Republic* as a blueprint, and conclude that its proposed system is therefore impracticable. It is what Plato intended it to be, a device for presenting vividly and convincingly a number of philosophical problems and possible solutions. As such its influence has endured over 2300 years. It may be 'a savage attack upon liberal ideas' and its warm reception 'perhaps the most astonishing example of literary snobbery in all history', but it is also 'perhaps the most consistent and logical work ever written'.[153]

3
Quintilian

WE have Quintilian's own word[1] that the first Roman work on education was Marcus Cato's *De Liberis Educandis*. That book however has not survived, and it is to Quintilian himself that we must turn as the most celebrated Roman educator. Plato details for us the education of the philosopher, Quintilian that of the orator; the former the education for speculative, the latter for practical life. The difference is typical of the national genius of the two peoples, Greek and Roman.[2]

Marcus Fabius Quintilianus was a provincial, born about the year 35 A.D. at Calagurris (the modern Calahorra) on the Ebro in northern Spain. Little is known of his upbringing, but, as the son of a rhetorician, he was probably, though not necessarily, educated in Rome. His own later memories suggest that he had a lively and inventive teacher. His early career was spent pleading in the Roman courts. In the early sixties he returned to his native Spain, where he seems to have become attached to the entourage of the governor of Tarraconensis, Galba, who, when he became Emperor, brought Quintilian back with him to Rome. That was in 68, and Quintilian then became the first man to establish a public school of oratory in the city, receiving a salary of a hundred thousand sesterces from the Imperial Treasury. He continued to plead in the courts, and became not only 'the most significant professor of rhetoric in the period of the Empire',[3] but, as Martial called him, 'the glory of the Roman bar'.

He ran his school for almost twenty years, retiring in 88. About four years later he settled down to write his *magnum opus, The Institutes of the Orator*, but his labours were interrupted when he was charged by Domitian to tutor two of that emperor's great-nephews, the sons of Flavius Clemens, designated Imperial heirs. The *Institutes* was published in 96, shortly before the assassination of Domitian and Quintilian's own death. It was a magisterial work, influenced by the ideas of his own masters, notably Domitius Afer of Nîmes, but substantially Quintilian's own.[4] His principal debt was to Cicero, whom he took as an inspiration and 'touchstone of taste',[5] and through him to the great Athenian tradition of Isocrates. Quintilian's work was a return to the classical style of rhetoric, rejecting the quirks and quiddities of Cicero's critics.

Where it broke new ground was in its scope. Others had written about the training of an orator, but they had usually dealt with the teaching of eloquence to those whose education was otherwise complete. Quintilian however says,[6] 'for my part, being of opinion that nothing is foreign to the art of oratory . . . should the training of an orator be committed to me, I would begin to form his studies from his infancy'. By reason of this, Quintilian's *Institutes of the Orator* is something more than a treatise on rhetoric; it has become an educational classic.

Quintilian would have rejected the antithesis of the speculative and the practical in a comparison of his work with Plato's. The philosopher, he would admit, had become unpractical – and by philosopher, he evidently intends the sophist,[7] but the ideal orator,[8] for whose education he prescribes, cannot be regarded as unspeculative or unphilosophical. Plato's philosopher was also ruler or king; Quintilian's orator is sage as well as statesman, for, since speech is the most characteristic human activity, perfect oratory is the paramount educational aim.[9] Both Plato and Quintilian therefore described the perfect man, and the training which was to produce him.

Quintilian characterises his ideal as follows:[10] 'The perfect orator must be a man of integrity, the good man, otherwise he cannot pretend to that character; and we therefore not only require in him a consummate talent for speaking, but all the virtuous endowments of the mind. For an upright and an honest life cannot be restricted to philosophers alone; because the man who acts in a real civic capacity, who has talents for the administration of public and private concerns, who can govern cities by his counsels, maintain them by his laws, and meliorate them by his judgments, cannot, indeed, be anything but the orator. . . . Let therefore the orator be as the real sage, not only perfect in morals, but also in science, and in all the requisites and powers of elocution.' For brevity Quintilian would adopt the definition of the orator given by Cato, 'a good man skilled in the art of speaking';[11] with emphasis on the goodness, however, for he adds, 'not only that the orator ought to be a good man; but that he cannot be an orator unless such'. Only in the hands of a good man will rhetoric be exercised as it ought to be, to secure morally admirable ends.

No training can produce the perfect orator unless a certain standard of natural endowment is presupposed; nature and nurture must co-operate. Thus Quintilian remarks:[12] 'It must be acknowledged that precepts and arts are of no efficacy unless assisted by nature. The person therefore that lacks a faculty will reap as little benefit from these writings as barren soils from precepts of agriculture. There are other natural qualifications, such as a clear, articulate and audible voice; strong lungs, good health, sound constitution and a graceful aspect; which, though indifferent, may be improved by observation and industry, but in some cases these gifts are lacking to such an extent as to vitiate all the accomplishments of wit and study.'

The training of the orator falls into three stages: the early home education up to seven years of age; the general 'grammar' school education; and the specific training in rhetoric.[13]

With the early home education Quintilian would take as much care and exercise as much supervision as Plato devoted to the early education of the citizens and rulers of his ideal state. Recognising, like Plato, the great part which suggestion and imitation play in the early education of the child, Quintilian demands for his future orator that his parents – not his father only – should be cultured,[14] that his nurse should have a proper accent, that the boys in whose company he is to be educated should also serve as good patterns and that his tutors should be skilful or know their own limitations; the person who imagines himself learned when he is not really so is not to be tolerated. When such conditions do not prevail, Quintilian suggests that an experienced master of language should be secured to give constant attention and instantly correct any word which is improperly pronounced in the pupil's hearing in order that the boy may not contract a habit of it. And he adds:[15] 'If I seem to require too much, let it be considered how hard a matter it is to form an orator.'

Quintilian discusses[16] whether children under seven years of age should be put to learn, and, although he admits that little will be effected before that age, he nevertheless concludes that we should not neglect these early years, the chief reason – now regarded as invalid – being that the elements of learning depend upon memory, which most commonly is not only very ripe, but also very retentive in children.[17] He warns us, however, that great care must be taken lest the child who cannot yet love study, should come to hate it, and, after the manner of Plato, he declares that study ought to be made a diversion. The instruction at this early age is to include reading, and exercises in speech training which consist of repetition of rhymes containing difficult combinations of sounds; writing is also to be taught, the letters being graven on a plate so that the stylus may follow along the grooves therein, a procedure depending on practice in motor-adjustment and later revived in principle by Montessori.

Before proceeding to consider the second stage of education, Quintilian discusses the question whether public or private tuition is the better for children. Aristotle had maintained[18] that education should be public and not private; but the early Roman education had been domestic, and it was only under Greek influences that schools came to be founded in Rome. Aristotle's standpoint was political, that of Quintilian is practical and educational.[19]

Two objections were currently urged against public education, the first being the risk to a child's morals from his intercourse with other pupils of the same age, and the second the difficulty experienced by a tutor in giving the same attention to many as to one. Were the first objection valid, that schools are serviceable to learning but prejudicial to morals, Quintilian would rather recommend the training of a child in uprightness than in eloquent speaking. But he maintains that, though schools are sometimes a nursery of vice, a parent's house may likewise be so – there are many instances of innocence lost and preserved in both places – and children may bring the infection into schools rather than acquire it from them. In answer to the second objection Quintilian relies on the inspiration of numbers stimulating a master to give of his best: 'A master who has but one pupil to instruct, can never give to his words that energy, spirit and fire which he would if animated by a number of pupils.' 'I would not, however,' he adds, 'advise the sending of a child to a school where he is likely to be neglected; neither ought a good master to burden himself with more pupils than he is well able to teach. . . . But if crowded schools are to be avoided, it does not follow that all schools are to be equally avoided, as there is a wide difference between avoiding entirely and making a proper choice.'

Having disposed of the objections to public education, Quintilian enumerates the advantages. At home the pupil can learn only what he is himself taught, but in school he can learn what is taught to others. At school he has others to emulate and to serve as patterns for imitation; he also has the opportunities of contracting friendships. How, Quintilian asks, shall the pupil learn what we call 'common sense' when he sequesters himself from society? And for the orator who must appear in the most solemn assemblies and have the eyes of a whole state fixed upon him, public education has the special advantage of enabling the pupil early to accustom himself to face an audience.

The grammar-school training is considered by Quintilian in its two aspects, the moral and the intellectual.

He recognises that children differ in respect of moral disposition, and that training must be adapted to such differences. But he desires for his future ideal orator the lad who is stimulated by praise, who is sensible of glory and who weeps when worsted. 'Let these noble sentiments work in him; a reproach will sting him to the quick; a sense of honour will rouse his spirit; in him sloth need never be apprehended.'

Children must be allowed relaxation, but, as in other particulars, a mean has to be preserved; deny them play, they hate study; allow them too much recreation, they acquire a habit of idleness. Play also reveals their bent and moral character, and Quintilian observes that the boy who is gloomy, downcast and languid, and dead to the ardour of play, affords no great expectations of a sprightly disposition for study.

The remarkable modernity of Quintilian's opinions is evident in his remarks on corporal punishment. 'There is a thing', he says, 'I quite dislike, though authorised by custom – the whipping of children.[20] This mode of chastisement seems to me mean, servile and a gross affront to more advanced years. If a child is of so abject a disposition as not to correct himself when reprimanded, he will be as hardened against stripes as the vilest slave. In short, if a master constantly exacts from his pupil an account of his study, there will be no occasion to have recourse to this extremity. It is his neglect that most commonly causes the scholar's punishment.' Concluding, he asks, 'If there be no other way of correcting a child but whipping, what shall be done, when as a grown-up youth he is under no apprehension of such punishment and must learn greater and more difficult things?' The important point, in short, is not to cram the child by force into a rigid framework of studies, but to adapt the framework to the stage of his development – a very early example of the psychological approach.

Having stated the disciplinary measures to be observed in moral training, Quintilian proceeds to consider the intellectual training which should be provided by the 'grammar school'.[21] To our surprise the first question which Quintilian raises is whether the Roman youth should begin his grammar-school training with Greek or with Latin. Heine's remark that had it been necessary for the Romans to learn Latin, they would not have conquered the world, derives its force from our ignorance of Roman education, for even though the Roman youths had not to learn Latin they had to learn Greek. It must nevertheless be remarked that Greek was then still a living language, that a knowledge of Greek was almost universal among the upper classes in Rome and that it was indeed the mother tongue of many of the slaves in the Roman households.[22] Quintilian consequently remarks[23] that it is a matter of no great moment whether the pupil begins with Latin or Greek, but in the early education he recommended the learning of Greek first, because Latin being in common use would be acquired unwittingly.

He would not have the boy even at the earliest stages speak only Greek, as in Renaissance schools boys were required to speak only Latin, for this he feared would affect his enunciation; consequently 'the Latin must soon follow and both in a short time go together; so it will come to pass that, when we equally improve both languages, the one will not be hurtful to the other.'

As music with Plato, so grammar with Quintilian comprises literature, especially poetry.[24] Grammar he divides into two parts: the knowledge of correct speaking and writing, and the interpretation of poetry. For good speaking, which must be correct, clear and elegant, reason, antiquity, authority and use are to be the guiding principles. As a practical preparation for the later training in rhetoric Quintilian proposes that the pupils should learn to relate Aesop's fables in plain form, then to paraphrase them into more elegant style.[25] With regard to correct writing or orthography 'unless custom otherwise directs', says Quintilian, 'I would have every word written as pronounced; for the use and business of letters is to preserve sounds, and to present them faithfully to the eye of the reader, as a pledge committed to their charge. They ought therefore to express what we have to say.' This is a plea for 'simplified spelling'.

Like Plato, Quintilian recognises that children should be taught not only what is beautiful and eloquent, but in a greater degree what is good and honest. Homer and Virgil should consequently be read first, even although 'to be sensible of their beauties is the business of riper judgment'. Tragedy and lyric poetry may likewise be employed, but Greek lyrics being written with somewhat too great freedom and elegies that treat of love should not be put into children's hands. When morals run no risk, comedy may be a principal study. The general aim of reading at this stage is to get youths to read such books as enlarge their minds and strengthen their genius; for erudition will come of itself in more advanced years. The study of grammar and love of reading should not, however, be confined to school-days, but rather extended to the last period of life.

Quintilian, after discussing grammar, proceeds to consider the other arts and sciences, a knowledge of which the future orator ought to acquire at the grammar school; and in justification of his selection he reiterates that he has in mind 'the image of that perfect orator to whom nothing is wanting'.[26]

Music must be included in the training of the orator,[27] and Quintilian maintains that he might content himself with citing the authority of the ancients, and in this connection instances Plato, by whom even grammar was considered to fall under music. According to Quintilian, music has two rhythms: the one in the voice, the other in the body. The former treats of the proper selection and pronunciation of words, the tone of voice, those being suited to the nature of the cause pleaded:[28] the latter deals with the gestures and actions which should accompany and harmonise with the voice. But this falls to be dealt with in the school of rhetoric, and is considered at some length by Quintilian towards the conclusion of his work.[29]

Geometry, which includes all mathematics, as in Plato's scheme, is included by Quintilian,[30] but, unlike Plato in the *Republic*, Quintilian does not despise its practical advantages to the orator, who in a court might make an error in calculation or 'make a motion with his fingers which disagrees with the number he calculates,' and thus induce people to harbour an ill opinion of his ability; plane geometry is not less necessary as many lawsuits concern estates and boundaries. Plato made geometry a preparation for philosophy, and Quintilian recommends it as a training for rhetoric. As order is necessary to geometry, so also, says Quintilian, is it essential to eloquence. Geometry lays down principles, draws conclusions from them and proves uncertainties by certainties; does not oratory do the same? he asks. It is thus on the disciplinary value of geometry that Quintilian, following Plato, insists.

Quintilian would also have the pupil resort to a school of physical culture, there to acquire a graceful carriage. Dancing, too, might be allowed while the pupil is still young, but should not be long continued; for it is an orator, not a dancer, that is to be formed. 'This benefit, however, will accrue from it that without thinking, and imperceptibly, a secret grace will mingle with all our behaviour and continue with us through life.'

Having determined the selection of subjects, Quintilian inquires whether they can be taught and learned concurrently, even supposing that they are necessary.[31] The argument against this procedure is that many subjects of different tendency, if taught together, would bring confusion into the mind and distract the attention. It is also contended that neither the intellect, the physique nor the length of day would suffice; and though more robust years might undergo the toil, it should not be presumed that the delicate constitutions of children are equal to the same burden. But Quintilian replies that they who reason thus are not sufficiently acquainted with the nature of the human mind, which is so active, quick and keeps such a multiplicity of points of view before it that it cannot restrict itself to one particular thing, but extends its powers to a great many, not only during the same day, but likewise at the same moment. What, then, he asks, should hinder us applying our minds to many subjects, having several hours for reflection, especially when variety refreshes and renovates the mind? It is the opposite course, namely, to persevere in one and the same study that is painful. To be restricted for a whole day to one master fatigues greatly, but changes may be recuperative. In support of his argument Quintilian adduces the analogy of farming, asking, 'Why do we not advise our farmers not to cultivate at the same time their fields, vineyards, olive-grounds and shrubs?' Any of these occupations continued without interruption would prove very tiresome; in Quintilian's view, it is much easier to do many things than confine ourselves long to one. The principle of the co-ordination of studies is also supported by him on the ground that no age is less liable to fatigue than childhood; but it would have been more scientific had he maintained that no age is more readily fatigued, hence the need for change.

After concluding the survey of grammar-school education, Quintilian turns to consider that of the school of rhetoric, and at the outset complains of a certain overlapping in the work of the two types of schools, maintaining that it would be better if each confined itself to its own proper task.[32] In selecting a school of rhetoric for the youth, the parents' first concern must be the character of the master, for on that, not material circumstances, depends the quality of the school. Quintilian describes his ideal teacher thus: 'Let him have towards his pupils the benevolent disposition of a parent, and assume the place of those by whom he has been entrusted with this charge. Let him be free from moral faults and not countenance such faults. Let him be severe but not harsh, affable but not lax, lest the former generate hatred and the second contempt. Let him speak frequently of what is honourable and good, for the oftener he admonishes the seldomer will he be obliged to punish. Not readily given to anger but not ignoring faults requiring correction. Unaffected in his manner of teaching, persevering and firm rather than excessive in his demands. Let him reply readily to his pupils' questions and stimulate those not inclined to put questions. In praising the recitations of his pupils he must neither be niggardly nor fulsome; the former will cause the work to be irksome, the latter will make the pupils negligent. In correcting faults he must not be sarcastic, still less abusive, for the reproof which creates dislike will result in avoidance of work.'[33] The same high standard as in moral attainment is deemed requisite for the intellectual qualifications of the master of the school of rhetoric. For these reasons the *Institutio*, though it is never explicit on the subject, may be regarded as including the first serious discussion of the training of teachers.[34]

Quintilian characterises as silly the opinion of those who, when their boys are fit for the school of rhetoric, do not consider it necessary to place them immediately under the care of the most eminent, but allow them to remain at schools of less repute; for the succeeding master will have the double burden of unteaching what is wrong as well as teaching what is right. Distinguished masters, it might be maintained, may think it beneath them or may not be able to descend to such small matters as the elements, but he who cannot, Quintilian retorts, should not be ranked in the catalogue of teachers, for it is not possible that he who excels in great should be ignorant of little things. The plainest method, he adds, is always the best, and this the most learned possess in a greater degree than others.

Having discussed the type of school to which the pupil of rhetoric should be sent, Quintilian considers the subjects to be taught and the methods to be employed. The treatment of rhetoric extending from book III to book XII of the *Institutes* is of a highly technical nature and of little value or interest to the student of education, although it may be a profitable study for the writer who seeks to improve his style[35] or for the teacher of classics, as it includes, in addition to choice and arrangement of material and the principles of style, a review of Latin literature from the point of view of the orator.[36]

As the education which Quintilian prescribes is that of an orator, he does not deal with the education of women. From his remark that both parents of the orator should be cultured, it might be inferred, however, that he expected women to receive some form of education. There is no direct evidence of the existence of coeducational establishments in Rome, but it appears that girls were taught the same subjects as boys, although the early age of marriage would doubtless exclude them from the higher education in rhetoric in which, for Quintilian, the early and the grammar-school education culminate.

Though Quintilian's *Institutes* is the most comprehensive, if not the most systematic, treatise on rhetoric in existence,[37] it doubtless appeared too late to influence Roman education greatly: Quintilian is referred to with great respect by Pliny, Juvenal and Suetonius, but it is doubtful whether his book was widely read.

There was a revival of interest at the close of the Roman era in writers like Jerome, but only a mutilated manuscript of the *Institutes* survived into the Middle Ages.[38] Rediscovered in 1416 by Poggio at St Gall, the book became the authoritative work on education. So true is this that Erasmus (in 1512) apologises for touching upon methods or aims in teaching, 'seeing', he says, 'that Quintilian has said in effect the last word on the matter'. Quintilian's ideal personality had been the orator, that of the Renaissance was the 'courtier', the English equivalent of which was the governor – governors including all officers paid or unpaid, involved in executive or legislative activity, royal secretaries, ambassadors, judges, etc.[39] The training in both cases, Roman and Renaissance, was practically identical, namely, a training for public life; and Elyot in his *Governour* merely recapitulates the doctrines of Quintilian. From this high point his reputation declined into lip-service, but through the Renaissance educators Quintilian's *Institutes* has played a part in fashioning educational training throughout Europe up to quite modern times.[40]

4
Loyola

FROM the composition of Quintilian's *Institutes* in A.D. 92–5 to the rediscovery of the complete text in 1416 during the later phase of the Renaissance it was the Church that kept learning alive. There was a minor renaissance in the twelfth century, and thereafter the universities – the offspring of the Church – assumed the main burden of preserving and advancing culture. It is appropriate, therefore, that one of the most influential of the new educators during the Renaissance[1] was inspired by religious fervour and zeal for the defence of the faith.

Ignatius of Loyola[2] was born in 1491 at the castle of Loyola in Spain, the son of Don Beltran Yanez de Oñaz. He received the customary education of a Spanish aristocrat of his day, that is hardly any formal schooling but painstaking instruction in the affairs of the army and the court. After service as a page with Ferdinand and Isabella he went on campaign with the Duke of Nájera, but his military career came to an abrupt end at the French siege of Pamplona in Navarre, when he was severely wounded in both legs. He was thirty. During his long convalescence he read Ludolf of Saxony's *Vita Christi*, had a mystic vision of the Blessed Virgin and Her Son, and resolved to become a 'soldier of Christ'. He gave away his worldly goods, underwent a lengthy period of fasting, flagellation and prayer, and went on pilgrimage to Jerusalem. In 1524, conscious that without proper education his labours would be of no avail, he returned to Spain and joined the children of an ordinary school in Barcelona to acquire some facility in Latin. In 1526 he entered the University of Alcalá, and after an unsuccessful period there and in Salamanca, took his degree in 1534 in Paris. Four years later he was ordained a priest, and in 1539, with a band of like-minded zealots, notably Peter

Faber of Savoy and Francis Xavier of Navarre, he founded the Society of Jesus, a band of 'soldiers of Christ'. The following year the foundation was approved by a bull of Pope Paul III. Ignatius became the first Father-General of the order.

The main purpose of the Society was missionary – to carry the gospel to 'the Turkish lands' and later the New World – and much of its brilliant history was to be made in that field. From a very early date however it found itself a teaching order. Of the *Constitutions of the Society*, completed in the founder's lifetime, half are concerned with arrangements for education. The first external students were admitted in 1546 to the college at Gandia in Spain, and the first classical college was founded at Messina in Sicily two years later. When Ignatius died in 1556 there were already thirty-five colleges in the Mediterranean and central European lands, most admitting 'externs'. From this beginning was to grow 'the most comprehensive single school system in Europe'.[3]

In the Jesuit system the aristocratic tendency which characterises the educational system with which we have already dealt to some extent survives. Ignatius, a knight of noble birth, recognised that, for the crusade which the Company of Jesus was enrolled to wage, all available gifts of intellect and birth would be required; consequently it gave him peculiar satisfaction when the tests imposed on candidates for admission to the Society were passed by youths of noble birth.[4] The Society devotes itself mainly, although not exclusively, to higher education, but for this restriction there is historical justification. Its aim was to arrest the disintegrating forces in the religious life of Europe,[5] and to effect this it was necessary to attack the evils at their source, namely, in the universities, hence the Society's concern for higher education.[6]

While the Jesuits are expressly adjured to address themselves to higher education, they do not hesitate, when necessity compels, to devote themselves to primary instruction.[7] As the Jesuit system is sometimes charged with intentionally and unnecessarily restricting education to its higher forms, it is advisable to state the Society's attitude in its own terms. According to the *Constitutions*[8] of the Society instructing others in reading and writing would be a work of charity if the Society had enough members to be able to attend to everything; but because of the lack of members, these elementary branches are not ordinarily taught. Aquaviva, the fifth

General of the Society, writing[9] on 22 February 1592, regarding the admission of young pupils to the schools of the Society, states that only those are to be admitted who are sufficiently versed in the rudiments of grammar and know how to read and write; nor is any dispensation to be granted to anyone, whatever be his condition of life; but those who press the petitions upon us are to be answered, 'that we are not permitted'. In the *Ratio Studiorum* the twenty-first rule for the Provincial or Superior of a Province provides that for the lower studies there are to be not more than five classes: one for rhetoric, one for humanities and three for grammar. Where there are fewer classes, the Provincial is to see that the higher classes are to be retained, the lower ones being dispensed with.[10] The charge that the Society selected, as a special field for its endeavours, the sphere of education in which it believed its efforts were most required and likely to be most effective, has only to be formulated to be rendered meaningless.

It is evident that there was no intention to further a social exclusiveness, as originally the instruction which the Jesuits did afford was free,[11] even including the university stage, and when tempted to impose fees by the advantages accruing to their competitors who did not scruple to charge for education, no text was more frequently quoted[12] than 'Freely ye have received, freely give'. In this respect the Jesuit system realised a principle which many modern democracies have not yet fully attained, the Jesuit practice in this regard recalling the disinterested Greek attitude to knowledge.

If aristocrats, the Jesuits are not individualists, and for much the same reasons as Quintilian, they extol public education. 'For this moral strengthening of character, no less than for the invigorating of mental energies, the system of Ignatius Loyola prescribes an education which is public – public, as being that of many students together, public as opposed to private tutorism, public, in fine, as requiring a sufficiency of the open, fearless exercise both of practical morality and of religion.'[13]

The aim of the Society of Jesus is avowedly religious. Its characteristic features were its missionary enterprise and its educational activities. Thus Francis Thompson, distinguishing the duties of its members, writes:[14] 'Nor was any order bound to foreign missions. But, above all, their educational obligations were a new thing. The teaching of children and the poor had no body of men vowed to its performance, and its neglect was among the abuses which drew down the censure of the Council of Trent; while in gratuitously undertaking the higher education of youth the Jesuits were absolutely original. In his missionary assault, by preaching and ultimately by writing, upon the people of power and intellect, who were the brain and marrow of the anti-Catholic movement, he confronted the present; in his masterly seizure of the school, he confronted the future. He not only confronted, but anticipated it: he tore from the revolt the coming generation, and levied immediate posterity under the Catholic banner. If the coming years prospered a counter-reformation, a sudden return-tide of Catholicism which swept back and swamped the renaissance, that counter-movement was prepared in the Jesuit schools.'

In the original draft of what might be termed the articles of association of the new society, mention is made of teaching. On 3 May 1539 a series of resolutions was adopted by the few companions to whom Ignatius had communicated his ideas of founding a society, agreeing (1) to take an explicit vow of obedience to the Pope; (2) to teach the commandments to children or anyone else; (3) to take a fixed time – an hour more or less – to teach the commandments and catechism in an orderly way; (4) to give up forty days in the year to this work.[15] In the First Papal Approbation it is affirmed that the members of the Society 'shall have expressly recommended to them the instruction of boys and ignorant people in the Christian doctrine of the ten commandments, and other the like rudiments, as shall seem expedient to them according to the circumstances of persons, places and times'. In the last vows which the Jesuit takes[16] he promises 'peculiar care in the education of boys'.

In the *Constitutions* of the Society, a work begun at the request of the Pope in 1541, Ignatius set forth the fundamental principles of the Society. This work consists of ten parts,[17] the fourth and largest of which presents in outline the plan of studies which was later more fully elaborated in the *Ratio Studiorum*. Part I of the *Constitutions* prescribes the conditions of Admission of Applicants, and part II the causes justifying the Dismissal of Those Found Unsuitable. The qualifications which, according to Ignatius the Society should demand of its entrants recall in several particulars the qualities which Plato in the *Republic* required of his philosophers. 'It is needful', Ignatius states,[18] 'that those who are admitted to aid the Society in spiritual concerns be furnished with these following gifts of God. As regards their intellect: of sound doctrine, or apt to learn it; of discretion in the management of business, or, at least, of capacity and judgment to attain to it. As to memory: of aptitude to perceive, and also to retain their perceptions. As to intentions: that they be studious of all virtue and spiritual perfection; calm, steadfast, strenuous in what they undertake for God's service; burning with zeal for the salvation of souls, and therefore attached to our Institute; which directly tends to aid and dispose the souls of men to the attainment of that ultimate end, from the hand of God, our Creator and Lord. In externals: facility of language, so needful in our intercourse with our neighbour, is most desirable. A comely presence, for the edification of those with whom we have to deal. Good health, and strength to undergo the labours of our Institute. Age to correspond with what has been said; which in those admitted to probation should exceed the fourteenth year and in those admitted to profession the twenty-fifth. As the external gifts of nobility, wealth, reputation and the like are not sufficient, if others are wanting; so, if there be a sufficiency of others, these are not essential; so far, however, as they tend to edification, they make those more fit for admission, who, even without them, would be eligible on account of the qualities before mentioned; in which, the more he excels who desires to be admitted, so much the more fit will he be for this Society, to the glory of God our Lord, and the less he excels, so much the less serviceable will he be. But the sacred unction of the divine Wisdom will instruct those who undertake this duty to His service and more abundant praise, what standard should be maintained in all these things.'

Part III of the *Constitutions* is devoted to the Preservation and Improvement of Those who Remain for Probation in the Novitiate, and, what more especially concerns the educationist, a chapter is included 'Of the Superintendence of the Body'. Loyola, speaking from his own experience, frequently warned his companions against the subversive influence of an enfeebled bodily condition. Thus we find him writing to Borgia:[19] 'As to fasting and abstinence, I think it more to the glory of God to preserve and strengthen the digestion and natural powers than to weaken them. . . . I desire then that you will consider that, as soul and body are given you by God, your Creator and Maker, you will have to give an account of both, and for His sake you should not weaken your bodily nature, because the spiritual could not act with the same energy.' The same sentiment inspires the treatment in the *Constitutions*:[20] 'As over-much solicitude in those things which pertain to the body is reprehensible; so a moderate regard for the preservation of health and strength of body to the service of God is commendable, and to be observed by all. . . . Let a time for eating, sleeping and rising be appointed for general observation. In all those things which relate to food, clothing, habitation and other things needful for the body, let care be taken with the divine aid, that in every probation of virtue and act of self-denial, nature be nevertheless sustained and preserved for the honour of God and his service, due regard being paid to persons in the Lord. As it is not expedient that anyone be burdened with so much bodily labour that the intellect be overwhelmed, and the body suffer detriment, so any bodily exercise, which aids either, is generally necessary for all, those not excepted who ought to be occupied in mental pursuits which should be interrupted by external employments, and not continued nor taken up without some measure of discretion. The castigation of the body should neither be immoderate nor indiscreet in vigils, fastings, and other external penances and labours, which usually do harm and hinder better things. . . . Let there be some one in every house to preside over everything that relates to the good health of the body.' The charge frequently made against the Jesuit system of education, that it does not regard the physical care of the pupil, is accordingly not warranted by the *Constitutions* of the Society.

While the vows to be taken, the conduct of missions and the administration of the Society are the subjects treated in the later sections of the *Constitutions*, the fourth part is devoted to the regulations governing the instruction in literature and other studies of those who remain in the Society after their two years' period of probation. The first ten chapters of this part are concerned with the organisation and management of the colleges, the remaining seven with the universities of the Society.

The aim and scope of the work of colleges is thus defined:[21] 'the end of the learning acquired in this Society is, with the help of God, to aid the souls of its own members and those of their neighbours. This, therefore, is the criterion to be used in deciding, both in general and in the case of individual persons, what subjects members of the society ought to learn, and how far they ought to progress in them. To speak in general, the humane letters of the various languages, and logic, natural philosophy, moral philosophy, metaphysics, scholastic theology, positive theology, and Sacred Scripture are helpful. These are the branches to which those who are sent to the colleges should apply themselves. They will devote themselves with greater diligence to the parts which are more helpful for the end mentioned above. Furthermore, account is to be taken of circumstances of time, place, persons, and other such factors, according to what seems best in our Lord to him who holds the chief responsibility.'

The order of studies to be followed is first the Latin language, then the liberal arts, thereafter scholastic, then positive theology. Scripture can be studied either concomitantly or later on.[22]

The students should be faithful in attendance at the lectures, diligent in preparing for them beforehand, and afterwards in reviewing them. They must ask about points they do not understand, and note down what may be useful later on to assist the memory.[23] Latin was commonly to be spoken by all, but especially by the students of the humanities;[24] and since the practice of debating is useful, especially to the students in arts and scholastic theology, instructions are given[25] as to when and how these debates or disputations are to be arranged and conducted. There should be in each college a general library, of which the key is to be given to those who in the rector's judgment ought to have it. Furthermore, each one should have the necessary books.[26]

Those scholars who intend to devote their lives to the work of the Society are further instructed in the performance of the ordinances of the Church;[27] and to discharge this duty they should endeavour to learn the vernacular language well.[28]

The universities which the Society establishes or maintains will be divided into the three faculties: languages, arts and theology;[29] 'the study of medicine and laws, being rather remote from our Institute, will not be taught in the universities of the Society, or at least the Society will not undertake this activity through its own members'.[30] The curriculum in arts shall extend over three and a half years, and that in theology over four years. In the arts curriculum reference is made to the natural sciences which prepare the intellectual powers for theology, and are highly serviceable for the perfect understanding and use of it, and also of themselves help to attain the same ends,[31] and it is further enjoined, and is an interesting comment on the criticism that the Society neglects the natural sciences, that they 'should be treated with fitting diligence and by learned teachers. In all this, the honour and glory of our Lord should be sincerely sought.'

Provision was made by Ignatius in the *Constitutions*[32] for modification of his outline plan of studies. 'According to circumstances of place and persons there must be great variety in particular details.' That this concession should not be abused and the uniformity of the system destroyed, it was considered expedient that an authoritative, yet more detailed, plan of studies than that outlined in the *Constitutions* should be issued for the guidance of the schools and colleges of the Society.

The *Ratio atque Institutio Studiorum Societatis Jesu*, usually referred to as the *Ratio Studiorum*, was accordingly prepared, becoming the main source of the educational doctrines of the Society; and Jouvancy's *Ratio Discendi et Docendi*[33] is regarded as the official complement to, and commentary on, the *Ratio Studiorum*. It has been described as 'the most precisely detailed and thoroughgoing programme of school instruction ever seen'.[34]

The first draft of the *Ratio Studiorum* was the result of the labours of six Jesuits summoned to Rome in 1584 by Claudius Aquaviva, the fifth Father-General of the order, and it took them over a year to prepare. By then, almost thirty years after Ignatius's death, the Society had over 160 colleges, almost all open to external students. Availing themselves of all the material regarding methods and administration of education which they could assemble and of the experience which the practice of the Society itself afforded, the authors were able to present in August 1585 to the General of the Society the results of their efforts. In 1586 the report was sent by the General to the Provinces for examination and comment. A new report was issued in 1591 as *Ratio atque Institutio Studiorum*, and after further revision the final plan of studies was published at Naples in 1599 under the title *Ratio atque Institutio Studiorum Societatis Jesu.*[35]

The *Ratio Studiorum*, unlike the *Constitutions*, deals exclusively with education. It sets forth the regulations which are to direct the Superior of a Province in dealing with education in his Province, then the regulations which the rector of a college is to apply in governing a college, thereafter rules for the guidance of the prefect of studies. General regulations for the professors of the higher faculties – theology and philosophy – are followed by special rules for the professors of each subject in these faculties, namely, sacred writings, Hebrew, scholastic theology, ecclesiastical history, canonical law and moral or practical theology, moral philosophy, physics and mathematics. Regulations for the prefects of the lower studies, together with regulations for the conduct of written examinations and for the awarding of prizes, are also prescribed, and these are succeeded by the general regulations for the professors of the lower classes and by detailed regulations for the professors of rhetoric, humanity, and higher, intermediate and lower grammar. Rules for the pupils for the management of academies,[36] etc., are added. So comprehensive, systematic and exhaustive are the regulations that the modern reader is inclined to forget that the *Ratio Studiorum* is one of the first attempts on record at educational organisation, management and method, at a time when it was unusual even to grade pupils in classes, and one is tempted to compare it, not always to the disadvantage of the *Ratio*, with the regulations of a modern school system which have only after some generations been evolved and perfected. The *Ratio Studiorum* comprehends all subjects from the principles governing the educational administration of a Province to the fixing of school holidays, the textbooks to be used in teaching Latin grammar, and the method of correcting exercises.

The general organisation of the educational work of the Society may be gathered from the regulations issued for the direction of the Provincial.[37] The theological course of four years is the highest, and this is preceded by a course of philosophy extending over three years. Although the course for the study of humanity and rhetoric cannot be exactly defined, it is enacted that the Provincial shall not send pupils to philosophy before they have studied rhetoric for two years. All students in the philosophical course must, according to the *Ratio* of 1599, attend lectures in mathematics; and provision is made that students who show special proficiency in any subject should have the opportunity of extending their study of that subject. The classes for the lower studies are not to exceed five: one for rhetoric, another for humanity and three for grammar. These classes are not to be confused with one another, a warning which recalls the complaint of

Quintilian. Where the number of pupils warrants it, parallel classes for the various grades are to be instituted.

In the regulations for the rector of a college[38] the need of trained teachers even for the lowest classes is recognised. That the teachers of the lower classes should not take up the work of teaching without training, it is there enacted[39] that the rector of the college from which the teachers of humanity and grammar are wont to be taken should select someone specially skilled in teaching, and that towards the end of their studies the future teachers should come to him three times a week for an hour to be trained for their calling in methods of exposition, dictation, writing, correcting and all the duties of a good teacher.

In colleges the rector appoints a prefect of studies as his assistant,[40] the position of the latter being somewhat analogous to that of the dean of a faculty. He is responsible to the rector for the proper organisation of studies and the regulating of classes so that those who attend may make as much advancement as possible in uprightness of life, the arts and doctrine.[41] The prefect of lower studies, analogous to a head master, aids the rector in ruling and governing schools in such a way that those who attend may progress no less in uprightness of life than in the liberal arts. In day schools the prefect of studies is ordinarily responsible for both studies and discipline, and in boarding schools he exercises both functions within class hours.[42] But the rules for the rector[43] provide, where necessary, for a prefect of studies having as assistant a prefect of discipline whose duties in a boarding school would be somewhat analogous to those of a bursar in an English public school or in a university college.

In the general regulations for all the professors of the higher faculties[44] the educational aim of the Society is recalled, namely, to lead the pupil to the service and love of God and to the practice of virtue. To keep this before him each professor is required to offer up a suitable prayer before beginning his lecture. Directions are given as to the extent to which authorities are to be followed and used by the professors in lecturing, and how they are to lecture that the students may be able to take proper notes.[45] After each lecture the professor is to remain a quarter of an hour that the students may interrogate him about the substance of the lecture.[46] A month is to be devoted at the end of each session to the repetition of the course.[47] And the last of the general rules for all the professors declares that the professor is not to show himself more familiar with one student than with another; he is to disregard no one, and to further the studies of the poor equally with the rich; he is to promote the advancement of each individual student.[48]

Detailed directions for the professors of each of the subjects in the faculties of theology and philosophy follow; and of these it need only be mentioned here that in the 1832 revision of the *Ratio* special provision was made for the teaching of physics, which had previously been treated under the general title philosophy, and the regulations for the teaching of mathematics were modernised. That the Society did not neglect the natural sciences is confirmed by these statements, and the charge that the Society ignores changing conditions is refuted by a glance at the parallel columns on these subjects in Pachtler's edition of the *Ratio Studiorum*.[49]

Amongst the rules for the prefect of the lower studies[50] the following may be noted. He is to help the masters and direct them, and be especially cautious that the esteem and authority due to them be not in the least impaired.[51] Once a fortnight he is to hear each one teach.[52] He is to see that the teacher covers the textbook in the first half-year, and repeats it from the beginning in the second term.[53] The reasons for the repetition are two:[54] what is often repeated is more deeply impressed on the mind; it enables the boys of exceptional talents to pass through their course more rapidly than the others, as they can be promoted after a single term. Promotion is generally to take place after the long vacation; but where it would appear that a pupil would make better progress in a higher class he is not to be detained in the lower, but after examination to be promoted at any time of the year.[55] When there is a doubt whether a pupil should ordinarily be promoted, his class record is to be examined, and his age, diligence and the time spent in the class are to be taken into consideration.[56] In intimating promotions the names of pupils gaining special distinction are to be announced first; the others are to be arranged in alphabetic order.[57] A censor is to be appointed, one who is held in esteem by his fellow-pupils and who shall have the power to impose small penalties.[58] For the sake of those who are wanting in diligence and in good manners and on whom advice and exhortation have no effect, a corrector, who is not to be a member of the Society, is to be appointed. When this is not possible some other suitable plan is to be devised.[59] When reformation is despaired of, and the pupil is likely to become a danger to his fellows, he is to be expelled.[60]

Among the general regulations for the professors of the lower studies[61] are those dealing with the *praelectio*, or method of exposition of a subject or lesson, and those concerning emulation. In the exposition of a lesson or passage four stages are to be distinguished:[62] (1) The whole passage, when not too long, is to be read through. (2) The argument is to be explained, also, when necessary, the connection with what went before. (3) Each sentence is to be read, the obscure points elucidated; the sentences are to be connected together, and the thought made evident. (4) The whole is to be repeated from the beginning.

In this section the subject of emulation is also introduced.[63] Throughout the *Constitutions* and the *Ratio* anything likely to excite contention or produce invidious distinctions is deprecated. Graduates are not to occupy special seats in the university classes, and except in cases in which pupils have specially distinguished themselves, the class lists are to be in alphabetic order. That emulation is not a dominant or integral part of the Jesuit system may be judged from the fact that only four regulations are here devoted to it.[64] It was merely one among other devices to enliven instruction and develop in the pupils a ready command of the knowledge which they had acquired.

To the Jesuits must be given the credit of providing education with a uniform and universal method. 'So far as the evidence of history extends,' it has been said,[65] 'an organised caste of priests, combining the necessary leisure with the equally necessary continuity of tradition, was at all times indispensable to the beginnings of scientific research'; it appears also to have been necessary, as it was undoubtedly advantageous, for the beginnings of teaching method. The need of a uniform and universal method in teaching was thus declared in the proem to the 1586 *Ratio*:[66] 'Unless a ready and true method be adopted much labour is spent in gathering but little fruit. . . . We cannot imagine that we do justice to our functions, or come up to the expectations formed of us, if we do not feed the multitude of youths in the same way as nurses do, with food dressed up in the best way, for fear they grow up in our schools without growing up much in learning.'

The Jesuit system does not, however, exalt the method at the expense of the teacher, as Comenius did later. In the selection of teachers something of the same discrimination as Ignatius exercised in his choice of the first members of the Society is still demanded; and the selected candidates are subjected to a training which in length and thoroughness no other educational system, with the possible exception of that sketched by Plato in the *Republic*, has attempted to approach.[67] Even yet the educational authorities in many modern countries have failed to realise the importance of thorough professional training for all engaged in higher education, including university teaching. The value of training was recognised in the draft *Ratio* of 1586 in the statement:[68] 'It would be most profitable for the schools, if those who are about to be preceptors were privately taken in hand by some one of great experience, and for two months or more were practised by him in the method of reading, teaching, correcting, writing, and managing a class. If teachers have not learned these things beforehand, they are forced to learn them afterwards at the expense of their scholars; and then they will acquire proficiency only when they have already lost in reputation; and perchance they will never unlearn a bad habit. Sometimes such a habit is neither very serious nor incorrigible, if taken at the beginning; but if the habit is not corrected at the outset, it comes to pass that a man, who otherwise would have been most useful, becomes well-nigh useless. There is no describing how much amiss preceptors take it, if they are corrected, when they have already adopted a fixed method of teaching, and what continual disagreement ensues on that score with the prefect of studies. To obviate this evil, in the case of our professors, let the prefect in the chief college, whence our professors of humanities and grammar are usually taken, remind the rector and Provincial, about three months before the next scholastic year begins, that, if the Province needs new professors for the following term, they should select someone eminently versed in the art of managing classes, whether he be at the time actually a professor or a student of theology or philosophy, and to him the future masters are to go daily for an hour, to be prepared by him for their new ministry, giving prelections in turn, writing, dictating, correcting, and discharging the other duties of a good teacher.'

The predominant place assigned to classics in the Jesuit curriculum has historical justification. The Society has not, however, as is frequently laid to its charge, bound itself slavishly to a seventeenth-century curriculum. From the outset provision was made for extension and modification of the curriculum, and of this liberty the Society has availed itself. While it has not rashly incorporated in its educational system every innovation, it has adopted such changes as seem to it permanent and valuable. The widening of the conception of culture to connote not only the classical languages but also a precise use of the mother tongue, an appreciation of modern literature, the principles of mathematics and the methods of natural science, has been recognised by the Jesuits; and the new subjects, when admitted to the curriculum, have been taught with the same thoroughness as the old. Indeed the changes which time has brought have been more fully recognised and more effectively met by the Jesuits than by some of the schools whose pupils have condemned in quite unmeasured terms the conservatism of the Jesuits.

In retaining the drama as an educational instrument[69] the Jesuits anticipated the modern movement represented by what is termed the dramatic method of teaching.[70] In insisting on the speaking of Latin they likewise anticipated the direct method of teaching the classics. In repeating the work of the class twice in the year, and thus enabling the abler pupils to spend only half a session in a grade and be promoted more rapidly, they introduced a procedure now adopted by some modern school systems.

The Jesuits' contribution to school discipline was as notable as the advance made by the *Ratio* in the teaching practice it displaced. To the early Jesuits we owe the substitution of supervision for compulsion, and while later writers have generally condemned the Jesuit policy,[71] it has only to be contrasted with the barbarities of the disciplinary measures current in their day to realise the revolution they effected. The principle implied is that prevention is better than cure. They did not, however, dispense with punishment altogether, for the *Ratio* of 1599[72] recommended the introduction of a corrector. The office of corrector was later dispensed with, but the principle of dissociating punishment from teaching has been retained. It must not be inferred that there is undue severity in their methods. Gentleness is especially enjoined towards the pupils, Ignatius prescribing as the maxim of the Society that it 'must always govern by love'.[73] That obedience is one of the vows taken by the members of the Society must lighten the work of teaching, and in the confession and the communion the Society possesses powerful instruments for the moral and religious education of the pupil. Whatever others may think of the confessional, the Jesuit Society recognises that it is of inestimable value in the moral training of the pupil,[74] and through the communion the Society secures practice in worship, an exercise which distinguishes the religious from the moral attitude to life, and a training in which is essential to a complete and generous education.[75]

In the eighteenth century the Society of Jesus lost some of the pristine purity of its missionary and educational zeal, and involved itself in political manoeuvre. The dire consequence was that Pope Clement XIV, at the instigation of France and Spain, issued a bull suppressing the Order. In educational matters there had always been the danger that the precise provisions of the *Ratio* would harden into rigidity. But in the event the Jesuit system adapted itself with a certain measure of success to conditions that changed massively over the years.[76] Its fathers, for example, were to become leaders not only of theological, but of scientific research. In 1814 Pope Pius VII restored the Society, and its history since then has been one of steady growth.

The limitations of the system are mainly self-imposed, and its defects are doubtless best known to, and can be best stated by, those who are applying it, the criticisms of others tending to be beside the mark. As its exponents are not merely educators but also missionaries of a religious faith, it has been applied in almost every country in the world. For these reasons its founder is as worthy of a place amongst the great educators as amongst the saints.

Although with a chivalrous self-effacement the modern exponents of this system attribute its success to the original methods of the *Ratio Studiorum*, it is doubtless to be attributed in part also to the thoroughness of the training and the devotion to their vocation of the exponents themselves. Francis Thompson, writing of Loyola – and the statement may be taken to apply to his present-day representatives – says: 'When he spoke, it was not what he said, it was the suppressed heat of personal feeling, personal conviction which enkindled men. This has ever been the secret of great teachers, were they only schoolmasters; it is the communication of themselves that avails.'[77] Their reward, it may be added, is the respect and affection of their pupils, the only reward of the true teacher; and probably no class of teachers has constrained such affection in their pupils as the Jesuits have done, and still do. The Jesuit educational system, then, has taught the world the value of a uniform and universal method in education, and the economy of a cultured and highly-trained teaching profession.

5
Comenius

JOHN Amos Komensky ('Comenius')[1] had the misfortune to live
during one of the most vexed eras of European history, and in one
of the most troubled regions. It is not surprising that he regarded
history as a succession of challenges and man's chief end as the
acquisition of wisdom to cope with these.

He was born in 1592 in a small Moravian village near Uhersky
Brod. His father was a man of standing in the small religious sect
called 'the Unity of Brethren' but more generally known as the
Moravian Brethren. He died when his son was twelve, along with
the boy's mother and two of his three sisters. When John was
sixteen he became a candidate for the ministry, and his church sent
him to the grammar school at Prerov, where he proved to be not
only a diligent and successful scholar but so attractive in his
character that the rector of the school, Bishop Lanecky, gave him
the extra name of Amos ('loving'). After higher education at the
Calvinist Academy of Herborn, a year at Heidelberg and a short
spell as a teacher in Prerov, he was ordained in 1616. He spent the
next two years as assistant to Bishop Lanecky, then married and
went to a charge in Northern Moravia.

But it was now 1618, the year in which the Thirty Years' War
broke out. Almost at once Comenius became a fugitive from the
Imperial Army. For seven years he was on the run, while his wife
and children died of the pestilence. In 1624 he married again, and
four years later found some protection for his sect and his new
family over the mountains at Leszno in Poland. He also became
Secretary to the Brethren, and in time their Senior Bishop, but
their numbers were steadily falling. From 1641 to 1656 he travelled
widely on missionary work – a year in England until the Civil War

drove him out, visits to Sweden, West Prussia and Hungary. When his second wife died, he married for a third time. In 1656, when the Polish Army brutally destroyed Leszno, he buried his books and manuscripts, fled with his family to Silesia, and set himself to rewrite his principal works. His *Opera Didactica Omnia* was published in 1657.

He was now sixty-five, a great age in the seventeenth century. One by one all his friends and his third wife died. His last years he spent in Holland, where he died in 1670. His grave in Naarden was soon lost and has never been discovered.[2]

The early educators had confined their attention to the training of the governing classes of the community, and until the time of Comenius it was only idealists like More who could hazard the suggestion that 'all in their childhood be instruct in learning . . . in their own native tongue'.[3] Comenius not only proposed to teach 'all things to all men' – 'that everybody shall learn everything of substance by all means with versatility, exhaustiveness and thoroughness'[4] – but also set about in a practical fashion planning a universal system of education, devising methods of teaching which would hasten the attainment of his ideal, and even preparing school books to illustrate how his principles should be applied in practice. It was not that, foreseeing the triumph of democracy, he would take time by the forelock and 'educate our masters', nor was it on the grounds of an abstract political principle like the equality of man that he based his belief, but rather by reason of the infinite possibilities in human nature and of the uncertainty as to the position to which providence might call this or that man that he advocated that education should be accessible to all. It was only on religious grounds that such a faith in the universal education of the people could at that time be based, for the idea of universalising education has proved more difficult of realisation than could have been foreseen by Comenius.[5]

For Comenius a universal system of education was inescapable, for the final goal of human life was preparation for a blessed existence after death, and all human beings must be given their chance of bliss.[6] Apart from his exertions to succour his exiled and persecuted people and his endeavours to assuage the bitter dissensions among the factions of the Reformed Church, his most influential gift to the religious life of his nation was *The Labyrinth of the World and the Paradise of the Heart*, the supplementary title of which reads: 'a book that clearly shows that this world and all matters concerning it are nothing but confusion and giddiness, pain and toil, deceit and falsehood, misery and anxiety, and lastly, disgust of all things and despair; but he who remains in his own dwelling within his heart, opening it to the Lord God alone, will obtain true and full peace of mind and joy'.[7]

The Labyrinth is in many respects analogous to Bunyan's *Pilgrim's Progress*, and in Czech literature has become a classic and one of the great books of mystical devotion.[8] The sections in *The Labyrinth* having educational significance are those in which he describes the current pedagogical practice and what Comenius considers ought to be the practice. 'I speak not of their pouches,' he says,[9] 'but of their skins which had to suffer, for fists, canes, sticks, birch rods struck them on their cheeks, heads, backs and posteriors till blood streamed forth, and they were almost entirely covered with stripes, scars, spots and weals.' In the ideal state, the paradise of the heart, however, Comenius describes[10] how he found 'no few learned men, who, contrary to the customs of the world, surpassed the others in humility as greatly as they did in learning, and they were sheer gentleness and kindness. Therefore, not he, they said, who can speak many languages, but he who can speak of useful things, is learned. Now they call useful things all God's works, and they said that arts are of some use for the purpose of understanding Him; but they also say that the true fountain of knowledge is Holy Writ, and the Holy Ghost our teacher, and that the purpose of all true knowledge is Christ, He who was crucified.'

Although Comenius's efforts for educational reform were undoubtedly inspired by religious motives, the great interest of his life, apart from religion, lay in a scheme of universal knowledge or pansophism, and this influenced, and on occasion diverted him from, his educational activities. Pansophism is not to be identified with mere encyclopaedism, as Kenneth Richmond in *The Permanent Values in Education*[11] was at pains to point out: 'Encyclopaedic teaching is neither practicable nor desirable; pansophic teaching is both. The one aims at making the learner an inexhaustible mine of information upon every subject, the other would make him capable of wisdom in his regard for any subject and able to see any subject in relation to others and to general principles.' Nor is it merely 'the correlation of sciences in a unity' as Laurie in his *Comenius*[12] proposes, for correlation is, after all, a somewhat artificial and external process. Pansophism is best understood when expressed in modern terms as a recognition of the organic conception of knowledge – the 'flower in the crannied wall'. In a sketch of his pansophic work Comenius himself explains that it was to be 'an accurate anatomy of the universe, dissecting the veins and limbs of all things in such a way that there shall be nothing that is not seen, and that each part shall appear in its place and without confusion'. The purpose, as he explains at length in *The Way of Light*,[13] is not so much to make men learned as to make them wise, to give them understanding of their own ends and of the end of all things. This pansophic conception reflects the influence of Bacon and recalls the *New Atlantis* rather than the scientific method of the *Advancement of Learning* or the *Novum Organum*. In the *New Atlantis* the central feature is Salomon's House, 'which house or college is the very eye of the kingdom'. This foundation is the embodiment of the scientific spirit which Bacon hoped might bring happiness to humanity. Salomon's House is a great laboratory equipped with all manner of scientific instruments, and associated with it is an organised army of scientific investigators. All the processes of nature are there artificially reproduced, and the results made to serve mankind.[14] While Comenius failed to appreciate the value of experiment in science on which Bacon insisted, he believed that the progress of humanity could be materially advanced by the collection of all available knowledge of God, nature and art, and by its reduction, on what he considered scientific principles, to a system which he denoted by the term Pansophia or Universal Wisdom.

Although *The Great Didactic*[15] belongs to the earlier period of Comenius's life – to the religious rather than to the pansophic – the title 'The Great Didactic setting forth the whole Art of Teaching all Things to all Men' nevertheless reveals 'the desire for omniscience' which, according to Adamson,[16] is very rarely absent from the seventeenth-century writers. The sub-title likewise formulates Comenius's democratic attitude; it runs: 'a certain Inducement to found such schools in all the Parishes, Towns and Villages of every Christian Kingdom that the entire youth of both sexes, none being excepted, shall quickly, pleasantly and thoroughly become learned in the Sciences, pure in Morals, trained to Piety, and in this manner instructed in all things necessary for the present and for the future life.'

That a reorganisation of educational institutions and a revolution in educational methods were urgent is evident from the complaint as to the condition of the schools of their day common to all the pedagogical writers of the period; of these schools Comenius wrote: [17] 'they are the terror of boys and the slaughter houses of minds – places where a hatred of literature and books is contracted, where ten or more years are spent in learning what might be acquired in one, where what ought to be poured in gently is violently forced in and beaten in, where what ought to be put clearly and perspicaciously is presented in a confused and intricate way, as if it were a collection of puzzles – places where minds are fed on words'. In *The Great Didactic* he dismisses existing schools more succinctly as 'terrors for boys and shambles for their intellects'.

In accordance with the ideal of the universal school expressed in the sub-title of *The Great Didactic* Comenius would establish such a system of education that all the young, 'not the children of the rich or of the powerful only but all alike, boys and girls, both noble and ignoble, rich and poor, in all cities and towns, villages and hamlets, should be sent to school. Let none therefore be excluded unless God has denied him sense and intelligence.'[18] His plea for the inclusion of girls runs: 'They are endowed with equal sharpness of mind and capacity for knowledge, and they are able to attain the highest positions since they have often been called by God Himself to rule over nations. Why, therefore, should we admit them to the alphabet, and afterwards drive them away from books?'

Like Quintilian, Comenius contends that school education is preferable to home education, schools being necessary since it is seldom that parents have adequate ability or the necessary leisure to instruct their children. 'And although there might be parents with leisure to educate their own children, it is nevertheless better that the young should be taught together and in large classes, since better results and more pleasure are to be obtained when one pupil serves as an example and a stimulus for another. For to do what we see others do, to go where others go, to follow those who are ahead of us, and to keep in front of those who are behind us is the course of action to which we are all most naturally inclined. Young children especially are always more easily led and ruled by example than by precept. If you give them a precept, it makes little impression; if you point out that others are doing something, they imitate without being told to do so.'[19] Comenius is likewise an advocate of the common school. 'We wish all men to be trained in all the virtues, especially in modesty, sociability and politeness, and it is therefore undesirable to create class distinctions at such an early age, or to give some children the opportunity of considering their own lot with satisfaction and that of others with scorn.'[20]

Comenius would organise schools on the following plan: a mother or nursery school[21] for children up to the age of six, a vernacular or primary school in every village for pupils of six to twelve,[22] a Latin or secondary school in every city for pupils of twelve to eighteen, and a university in every kingdom or province for youths from eighteen to twenty-four preparing for the professions. Promotion was throughout to be by ability: 'When boys are only six years old, it is too early to determine their vocation in life, or whether they are more suited for learning or for manual labour. At this age neither the mind nor the inclinations are sufficiently developed. Nor should admission to the Latin school be reserved for the sons of rich men, nobles and magistrates, as if these were the only boys who would ever be able to fill similar positions. The wind blows where it will, and does not always begin to blow at a fixed time.'[23] University entrance is to be more stringently restricted:[24] 'The studies will progress with ease and success if only select intellects, the flower of mankind, attempt them. The rest had better turn their attention to more suitable occupations, such as agriculture, mechanics or trade', a recommendation that recalls the advice of Montaigne, who, for a pupil having no aptitude for learning, suggests as the best remedy 'to put him prentice to some base occupation, in some good town or other, yea, were he the son of a Duke'.[25]

The lack of internal organisation of the existing schools sorely distressed Comenius. Among the defects which he diagnosed were that each school, also each teacher, used a different method, that one procedure was followed in one language and another in a second, and even in the same subject the method was so varied that the pupil scarcely understood in what way he was expected to learn. No method was known by which instruction was given to all the pupils in a class at the same time; the individual only was taught.[26] To remedy these defects he proposed[27] that there should only be one teacher in each school or at any rate in each class; only one author should be used for each subject studied; the same exercises should be given to the whole class; all subjects and languages should be taught by the same method; everything should be taught thoroughly, briefly and pithily; all things that are naturally connected ought to be taught in combination; every subject should be taught in definitely graded steps, that the work of one day may thus expand that of the previous day, and lead up to that of the morrow; and finally, everything that is useless should be invariably discarded.

Not only would Comenius make instruction more methodical but he would also make it more agreeable to the pupil. He suggests[28] that the school should be situated in a quiet spot, far from noise and distraction, and explains further:[29] 'The school itself should be a pleasant place, and attractive to the eye both within and without. Within, the room should be bright and clean, and its walls should be ornamented by pictures. These should be either portraits of celebrated men, geographical maps, historical plans, or other ornaments.[30] Without, there should be an open place to walk and to play in (for this is absolutely necessary for children), and there should also be a garden attached, into which scholars may be allowed to go from time to time and where they may feast their eyes on trees, flowers and plants. If this be done, boys will in all probability go to school with as much pleasure as to fairs, where they always hope to see and hear something new.'

With greater insistence than any of his predecessors Comenius reiterates the principle that the child should be first instructed in things before being taught to express them in language,[31] that everything should be first learned through the medium of the senses.[32] 'Men must,' he explains,[33] 'as far as possible be taught to become wise by studying the heavens, the earth, oaks, and beeches, but not by studying books; that is to say, they must learn to know and investigate the things themselves, and not the observations that other people have made about the things. We shall thus tread in the footsteps of the wise men of old, if each of us obtain his knowledge from the originals, from things themselves, and from no other sources.' And echoing Bacon, he adds: 'That no information should be imparted on the grounds of bookish authority, but should be authorised by actual demonstration for the senses and to the intellect.'

The common school for all pupils from six to twelve years of age necessitates not only that the teaching of other languages should be carried on through the mother tongue,[34] but also that direct instruction in the mother tongue itself should be given. 'To attempt to teach a foreign language before the mother tongue has been learned is', says Comenius,[35] 'as irrational as to teach a boy to ride before he can walk. Cicero declared that he could not teach elocution to those who were unable to speak, and, in the same way, my method confesses its inability to teach Latin to those who are ignorant of their mother tongue, since the one paves the way for the other. Finally, what I have in view is an education in the objects that surround us, and a brief survey of this education can be obtained from books written in the mother tongue which embody a list of the things that exist in the external world. This preliminary survey will render the acquisition of Latin far easier, for it will only be necessary to adapt a new nomenclature to objects.' Montaigne had earlier recommended[36] learning first the mother tongue, but, unlike Comenius, he was proposing an education suitable for 'a complete gentleman born of noble parentage'.

Comenius's curriculum would include 'all those subjects which are able to make a man wise, virtuous and pious'.[37] He requires, in fact, that every pupil should, in Milton's phrase, have a universal insight into things, and the qualification which he adds is apparent rather than real:[38] 'But do not, therefore, imagine that we demand for all men a knowledge (that is to say, an exact or deep knowledge) of all the arts and sciences. It is the principles, the causes, and the uses of all the most important things in existence that we wish all men to learn; all, that is to say, who are sent into the world to be actors as well as spectators. For we must take strong and vigorous measures that no man in his journey through life may encounter anything unknown to him that he cannot pass sound judgment upon it and turn it to its proper use without error.'

All the errors of the past could be avoided and all his aims achieved, Comenius assumed, by the adoption of the principles of order. Order, he believed, was education's, as well as heaven's, first law; he accordingly contended that the art of teaching demands nothing more than the skilful arrangement of time, of the subjects taught and of the method. Just as Bacon, however, with his new inductive methods failed to appreciate the part which the mind must play in originating hypotheses, so Comenius belittled the importance in education of the teacher;[39] as Bacon believed that by his method truth could straightway be attained, so Comenius assumed that it could be easily conveyed to all. Thus we find him adding:[40] 'As soon as we succeed in finding the proper method it will be no harder to teach schoolboys in any number desired than with the help of the printing press to cover a thousand sheets daily with the neatest writing.'

The right order, or proper method, Comenius conceives, can be secured if, after the manner of the writers of his time, we 'follow nature'; thus he declares:[41] 'That order which is the dominating principle in the art of teaching all things to all men, should be, and can be, borrowed from no other source but the operations of nature. As soon as this principle is thoroughly secured, the processes of art will proceed as easily and as spontaneously as those of nature.' For Comenius, 'following nature' nevertheless consists merely in adducing analogies from natural processes in support of preconceived and independently acquired principles; the analogies are in many instances quite fanciful and lend no authority to the maxims of method which are supposed to be based on them.

Among the precepts of Comenius are to be found certain of the traditional maxims of teaching method, for example, 'Proceed from what is easy to what is more difficult',[42] and instead of the maxim 'Proceed from the particular to the general' we find 'Proceed from the general to the particular'.[43] The principle of correlation or integration of studies is implied in the admonitions: 'Great stress [should] be laid on the points of resemblance between cognate subjects';[44] and 'all things that are naturally connected ought to be taught in combination'.[45] The inductive method of teaching, or what Adams terms 'anticipatory illustra tion',[46] is expressed thus:[47] 'It is necessary that examples come before rules.' Herbart's doctrine of interest is anticipated in such remarks as: 'The desire to know and to learn should be excited in the boy in every possible manner.'[48] 'Every study should be commenced in such a manner as to awaken a real liking for it on the part of the scholars';[49] and although Comenius's own psychology was of the most primitive type, he anticipated the psychological principle of Pestalozzi when he affirmed[50] that nothing should be taught the young unless it is not only permitted but actually demanded by their age and mental strength. He also perceived, and often emphasised, how much children learn from their fellows: 'although elders can do a great deal for children in all these things, yet those of their own age can do far more'.

Some of the principles and methods recommended by Comenius are common to him and to the Jesuits, the success of whose practices he cites[51] in support of the procedures he advocated. Thus Comenius declares that care should be exercised in the selection of texts put into pupils' hands; he maintains[52] that the books which the scholars use should be such as can rightly be termed sources of wisdom, virtue and piety; and he deplores the fact that more caution has not been exercised in the matter.[53] The *Ratio Studiorum* instructs the Provincial[54] to secure that school books which might do harm to virtue or good morals should be withheld from pupils till the offensive passages are expurgated, and the professors of the lower studies are advised[55] to refrain from introducing works prejudicial to good morals, and not only to abstain from expounding these but also to deter pupils as far as possible from reading them out of school. Comenius also recommends[56] the use of epitomes, the use of which by the Jesuits has been criticised.[57] The following extracts from *The Great Didactic* read almost like a translation of the Jesuit regulations:[58] 'If the scholars are to be interested, care must be taken to make the method palatable, so that everything, no matter how serious, may be placed before them in a familiar and attractive manner; in the form of a dialogue, for instance, by pitting the boys against one another to answer and explain riddling questions, comparisons and fables. . . .' 'The civil authorities and the managers of schools can kindle the zeal of the scholars by being present at public performances (such as declarations, disputations, examinations and promotions), and by praising the industrious ones and giving them small presents (without respect of person).' Even emulation is commended by Comenius as 'by far the best stimulus'[59] with school pupils.

On school discipline Comenius held enlightened views, and his recommendations follow the principles enunciated by Quintilian[60] on this subject. Thus he affirms:[61] 'That no blows be given for lack of readiness to learn (for, if the pupil do not learn readily, this is the fault of no one but the teacher who either does not know how to make his pupil receptive of knowledge or does not take the trouble to do so)'; and in his chapter 'Of School Discipline'[62] the analogy he there employs lends force to his argument. Thus he says: 'A musician does not strike his lyre a blow with his fist or with a stick, nor does he throw it against the wall, because it produces a discordant sound; but, setting to work on scientific principles, he tunes it and gets it into order. Just such a skilful and sympathetic treatment is necessary to instil a love of learning into the minds of our pupils, and any other procedure will only convert their idleness into antipathy and their lack of industry into downright stupidity.'

The need of suitable textbooks was early felt by Comenius. 'To him printing was "the marvellous device" by which the ignorance of men everywhere could be overcome.'[63] Like the other educators of his time and in spite of the prominence he assigned to the teaching of the vernacular, Comenius was compelled to devote attention to the teaching of languages, especially of Latin. Here, nevertheless, he met with his greatest practical success, for the manuals he prepared to facilitate the learning of Latin won ready acceptance, his *Janua Linguarum Reserata* being doubtless the most celebrated school book ever published, and his *Orbis Pictus* one of the earliest to introduce visual aids.[64]

A manuscript work in Latin by Comenius – the *Pampaedia*, doubtless his last word on education, was discovered by Professor Dmitrij Tschizewskij in an orphanage library at Halle in Germany in 1934.[65] The Latin text with a German translation was published at Heidelberg in 1960;[66] so far, however, only a few extracts have appeared in English. The *Pampaedia* was one of a series of seven volumes, each of the titles having the prefix *pan* – the Greek for 'all' – and the whole collection the general title: General Considerations concerning Human Improvement. By Pampaedia is to be understood instruction in the true knowledge of the whole, that is, in pansophia.[67]

In an appendix[68] to the German edition of *Pampaedia* H. Geissler claims that pansophia, formerly regarded as irrelevant to Comenius's educational doctrine, is now seen to be the framework of this, and he quotes W. Dilthey to the effect that the connection of pansophia with the *Didactic* is the vantage point from which Comenius's system should be viewed and understood.

Pampaedia itself argues at considerable length, supported freely by texts from the Scriptures, that all should be educated, irrespective of class, creed, sex, or age, in all things, and according to their true nature. All life is to be a school from the cradle, or even prior, to the grave. Seven stages or schools are distinguished:[69] (1) the antenatal, (2) infancy, (3) boyhood, (4) adolescence, (5) youth, (6) adulthood, (7) senescence; death completes the series. The first school has its location in the womb, the second in every home, the third in every village, the fourth in every town, the fifth in every kingdom or province, the sixth in the whole world, and the seventh wherever old men congregate. The first two may be designated 'private schools'; the middle three 'public schools' since they are under the supervision of the Church or the community; and the last two 'personal', since every man thus far advanced in years is, or should be, the architect of his own fortune, and his education is in the hands of himself and of God.[70] Provision for each stage of life in the way of schools, books and teachers must be made, and in the *Pampaedia* a chapter is devoted to each of these.[71] Comenius laid great emphasis on the value of teaching aids: he would certainly have pressed today for the widest possible use of the mass media. But the fact that he devotes a chapter to the characteristics to be possessed by the teacher may help to correct the general impression that he insists unduly on the significance of method in education. The requisites of the true teacher are: he himself should be all that he expects his pupils to become; he should possess the technique of making them so; he should be zealous in his task, that is, he should be able, knowing and willing to make 'pansophes', by showing his pupils the vision towards which they can direct their efforts at self-education.[72] Accordingly the makers of men should be picked people, pious, honourable, serious, keen, industrious and tactful. Teachers must know the aim or purpose of their calling, all the means to attain this, and the whole range of methods.[73] Under twenty-four headings, termed Problems, the issues in teaching are set forth: for example, under Problem vi it is affirmed that examples, principles and practice must be combined, for without examples nothing can be taught easily, without rules or principles nothing orderly, and without practice nothing permanent. Also for correct insight into the natural world analysis, synthesis and syncresis are necessary, the last being the comparison of part with part or whole with whole.[74]

In the succeeding chapters Comenius applies his general maxims to the different age-groups, indicating how the various schools, from the ante-natal to senescence, are to be conducted.[75] In the chapter[76] on the first so-called school, that is, before birth, Comenius offers us what reads like an early attempt to formulate the regulations of a marriage-guidance council and an ante-natal clinic conducted by the mother – and father. Like Locke, he placed great emphasis on preserving children's health. He gave, for example, detailed instructions to mothers on healthy pregnancy and breast-feeding. His concern was to dispel the superstitions which had grown up around the process of birth. Likewise, his advice for rearing very young children was based on such 'laws of health' as natural therapy and the avoidance of habit-forming drugs. He regarded security and happiness as essential in the earliest years. His doctrines have been echoed in much recent research, notably that of John Bowlby.[77]

The infant school,[78] from birth to six years of age, is comparable with the mother school of *The Great Didactic*[79] to which Comenius refers us. To the objection that this age is too early to instruct the child, Comenius retorts that it is the age at which the child learns to speak, and he speaks only what he learns. He stresses the importance of right beginnings, averring that a mistake made in infant education cannot be rectified in later life. A novel feature, not occurring in any of Comenius's other writings, is the proposal of a nursery school from the age of four to the age of six, an idea attributed to one Sophonias Hasenmüller. This anticipates Froebel's kindergarten, but some of the exercises – building up words from sounds – display a formalism analogous to what we shall later encounter in Pestalozzi. The school, Comenius nevertheless keeps reminding us, is to be a place of happiness for the child, who should be encouraged when very young to look forward to entering it.[80]

The aim of the boyhood stage[81] is to make the body, the senses and the innate mental powers more responsive. Not only do pupils more quickly imbibe what is taught them as boys, but they do so more precisely. The teachers of the younger classes, however, need to be more highly skilled than other teachers, and, according to Comenius, ought to receive higher salaries. The principles in accordance with which the appropriate textbooks should be prepared are elaborated, for example, for the third class of this school moral maxims are deduced from natural phenomena, thus, the rose smells sweetly but has thorns, so erudition and virtue are worthy but work and discipline are necessary for their attainment, and these represent the thorns. Religious exercises are planned for this and later years. In addition, handwriting is prescribed throughout, calligraphy for the first two years, rapid writing for the next two, and orthography for the final two. Comenius advises beginning handwriting with large roman capitals, then proceeding to small letters. He advocates a form of simplified spelling in which sound and symbol should correspond. In arithmetic, exercises in number, mass and weight are necessary for all. Music is included, and for pupils of ten and eleven the beginnings of a modern language.[82]

At the adolescent state we must survey the world, the mind and Holy Writ to get an insight into the grounds of all things; as means thereto we must enlist philosophy, politics and theology respectively; the corresponding methods are dialogue, disputation, dramatic presentation and letters. The three divisions of the curriculum are: (1) languages, (2) sciences and arts, (3) morals. Languages comprise one or two modern languages of neighbouring peoples, together with Latin, Greek and Hebrew. All can be mastered in six years – Latin in three, Greek in two and Hebrew in one. The sciences and arts include a study of nature, of the technical achievements of man, and of the Scriptures for faith, hope and action. On the analogy of the care of the body Comenius prescribes for the training of character. The three factors which must be considered are (1) environmental influences, (2) bodily humours, (3) natural tendencies of the mind or otherwise acquired imaginings; these, properly directed, lean to virtue's side, neglected, they precipitate us into evil.

The aim of the school of youth[83] is fuller wisdom. Through the senses, intellectual deliberation and the witnesses of Holy Writ together, will an integrated knowledge of the whole be attained, since the perfecting of understanding depends on pure insight into the natural world, the perfecting of the will on the choice of the right things, and the perfecting of skill on the deft handling of all things. This school or stage of young manhood has three divisions: (1) academy, (2) travel, (3) vocational preparation. An academy is a permanent body of students and scholars, a library and a laboratory, where theoretical exercises and mechanical demonstrations can be undertaken. This is also the appropriate stage for travel, the benefits of which are enumerated, and warnings issued against the temptations incidental to it.

The aim of the stage of manhood is expressed in the text: Seek ye first the kingdom of heaven. This is the one thing needful. We must, however, take care that nothing acquired in the earlier stages in the way of erudition, morals or piety is forfeited; it is foolish to forgo the advantages of previous training. Thus books are not to be abandoned as most people do at this time of life, but are to be used wisely. The books that should be read are the books of the mind, of the world, of Holy Writ; in addition, history, philosophy and theology; further, to improve one's style, oratory and poetry; lastly, moral and technical authors to enable one to perform his work properly and wisely. As the school demands examples, precepts and practice, so at the school of manhood men must concern themselves with history for examples, seek abstract wisdom in books, and engage in regular practice. This is the stage of self-education. A man's calling is a school in which he himself is master, and sets examples, precepts and exercises to himself. A definite vocation is to be chosen which will serve both God and humanity; the choice lies between agriculture, trade and commerce, and Comenius shows an undoubted preference for the first. The career should be one suitable to a man's natural inclinations and powers, and he ought to be able to say: 'it is the job for me' – the ideal of vocational guidance. Since emulation is a characteristic of school life, man should engage in righteous rivalry to attain the good – a justification of emulation borrowed from the Jesuits. Finally, man must so live at this stage that he will be able to enjoy what remains of life.

Comenius's reflections on the school of old age or the stage of senescence read like a lecture on geriatrics. This stage of life is not to be regarded as a grave with the cessation of all labour, as Ecclesiastes bemoans: 'there is no work, nor desire, nor knowledge, nor wisdom in the grave where thou goest.' It is part of life, in which Job counsels: 'O that they were wise, that they understood this, that they consider the latter end.' Its aim should be to bring to a successful conclusion what has already been begun; nothing in the foregoing stages must be made to appear useless or in vain. Comenius modifies a saying of Seneca to the effect that the young shall prepare, the adult use, and the old bring everything to fruition. The aged are not to seek satisfaction in idleness, but are to continue in well doing, and even to undertake, when the opportunity presents itself, work they had not previously thought of, but they should avoid what is beyond their strength, and must not attempt through rashness or presumption – faults at any stage – any new project which can only lead to disaster if they lack the necessary foresight. Old age has its peculiar faults, and its habits reveal special defects; these should be guarded against. Throughout this still active period of life the aged should reflect on the past, rejoicing in what was good, and considering how what was done could have been improved, and what was defective could be amended; they should review the present, look upon it as the Sunday of their week; should consider what remains to be done and plan how it can be carried out; take care to avoid such mishaps as the aged are prone to; and guard against infirmities and illnesses by taking more care than hitherto.

As an afterthought Comenius added a brief chapter on Death, the final school; it balances the first school, birth, and correlates with the eight planes or worlds: (1) possible, (2) ideal, (3) angelic, (4) material, (5) technical, (6) moral, (7) spiritual, (8) eternal.

Such an education as set forth in the *Pampaedia*, he claims, is salutary for the world. Its aim is to make all men 'truly rational, truly moral and truly pious', so that they may be 'completely happy both here and in eternity'.[84] It can be attained through the means described which make it easy and pleasant, and as a consequence such a culture will afford for the human race an open paradise of joy. A prayer for eternal wisdom concludes this work.

There is much repetition and some contradiction among the principles of Comenius; but throughout his writing is evinced a sincere sympathy with childhood, issuing in an earnest aspiration to make education available to all, to lighten the drudgery of learning for the child, and to introduce into schools a humane treatment of the pupil. It has been claimed[85] that the establishment of the United Nations Educational, Scientific and Cultural Organisation marks the culmination of a movement for the creation of an international agency for education which began with Comenius, and in support Comenius is quoted: 'Universal harmony and peace must be secured for the whole human race. By peace and harmony, however, I mean not that external peace between rulers and peoples among themselves, but an internal peace of mind inspired by a system of ideas and feelings.' To guarantee the stability of the world there must be 'some universal rededication of minds', and on this Kandel comments: 'The "universal rededication of minds", the guidance of "will and purpose and the desires of the peoples and nations of the world" must begin in the schools of each nation.' And Ulich sums up: 'For Comenius education was the instrument to lead a suffering and divided world out of war and divisions toward peace and international understanding.'[86]

Comenius achieved international renown in his lifetime, but it was as the author of a textbook. His *Janua Rerum (The Gateway of Tongues Unlocked)* ranks with the works of Donatus and Despauter among the most celebrated and widely used textbooks ever written. For the rest he was most commonly regarded as a dreamer, far removed from the real world. An attempt in 1694 by A. H. Francke to put his system into practice at Halle achieved no great success, and although his church employed some of his ideas in the following century, there is little evidence that other educators drew on them.

His renaissance came in the second quarter of the nineteenth century, when the ground had become fertile for experiments in popular education. His reputation revived first in his own country: in 1829 Frantisek Palacky wrote of his greatness. But it was after 1841, when the Czech manuscript of his *Didaktika Velika (The Great Didactic)* was discovered, that his international status grew. In the following year Von Raumer described him in his *History of Pedagogy* as 'the real founder of the science of education'. Herbart, though he died in 1841, may have known something of Comenius's work; Froebel certainly knew and drew on *The School of Infancy*. Thereafter his pedagogical (though not his philosophical) ideas were widely studied and acclaimed. The familiar pattern appeared of societies named after him – in Leipzig, for instance, in 1871 and Berlin (1892). The Scotsman Simon Laurie first drew him to the attention of British educationists, though the first published commentary in English was a chapter by R. H. Quick in his *Educational Reformers* (1868). The best English translation of *The Great Didactic* is still M. Keatinge's, published in 1896.

Like several other great educators, he suffered something of an eclipse in the early years of the twentieth century, when the concept of 'child-centring' altered some of the old balances in education, but two important factors have since brought him back into general notice. Several of his manuscripts, lost for centuries, have been rediscovered, notably that of his most ambitious account of his philosophy, the *General Consultation Concerning the Improvement of Human Affairs*, which Dimitrij Tschizewskij found in 1934 at Halle. Second, as a philosopher who believed that human nature could be affected, even altered by education, he was popular with the new masters of his homeland, and the quartercentenary of his birth in 1970 was widely celebrated in the Communist bloc.

Certainly he stands as one of the first educators to propose education for more than a narrow circle of pupils, however these might be selected; his system should be compared, for example, with that of Locke. And there are many echoes in modern writers of his individual ideas. His stages of learning are closely similar to those of Piaget, and the Plowden Report of 1967 'envisages an almost exact Comenian pattern'.[87] But as a power in the main development of European education, Comenius, because of the long spell during which some of his principal works remained undiscovered, is in a unique situation, much less influential than those works deserved.

6
Locke

As we are now learning to our cost, educational ideas and systems reflect the condition of their society: when the latter is in flux, so are they. John Locke[1] lived from 1632 to 1704, when civilised Europe was disturbed by new political, religious and intellectual theories. The systems of thought and education he advocated were more influential than any others in their contribution to the comparatively settled life of the leisured classes in the eighteenth century.

He was not, however, as were Rousseau and Pestalozzi, a rebel. He achieved personal success and fame within the rules of the world in which he grew up. The son of a Somerset attorney and nephew of a Bristol man who made a considerable fortune in brewing, he kept warm respect and affection all his life for his father, commending the upbringing which held him at a distance in childhood but ripened into close friendship as he grew up. In 1647 he was sent to Westminster, the best public school of his day, and although he condemned the severity of the discipline there, he retained a high opinion of his headmaster, Richard Busby. The education he received was narrowly classical: he took his entrance examination for Oxford in Latin, Greek, Hebrew and Arabic. But he had no sooner entered Christ Church in 1652 than he began a lifelong study of medicine through books and experiments.

Six years later he entered on a career in university teaching at Oxford; his appointments were in Greek rhetoric and moral philosophy, but he showed increasing proficiency in science and medicine. He became a Fellow of the Royal Society in 1668, only eight years after its foundation, and amassed an excellent scientific library. In 1675 he took the degree of Bachelor of Medicine, and was appointed to a senior medical studentship in the university. In the meantime however he had become a friend of Anthony Ashley Cooper, later the famous Earl of Shaftesbury. Through his influence Locke became tutor to several children of the nobility and gentry, and achieved renown as an expert on education. His *Thoughts* on the subject began in 1684 as a series of letters to his friend Edward Clarke of Chipleigh House, Somerset, on the best form of training for the latter's children, especially his eldest son, Edward; when the *Thoughts* were published, nine years later, Locke dedicated the book to Clarke.

During the last four decades of his life he travelled widely in the households of various patrons, notably Shaftesbury. He spent several years in Shaftesbury's home, Exeter House. In 1675 he made the Grand Tour as tutor to a young gentleman, the son of Sir John Banks. In 1683, when the Tories came to power, he followed Shaftesbury into exile in Holland, where he worked on his masterpieces, *An Essay Concerning Human Understanding*[2] and *Two Treatises of Government*.[3] For the last thirteen years of his life, from 1691 to 1704, he lived under the patronage of Sir Francis and Lady Masham at their country house in Essex. Most of his scholarly effort was expended on works of philosophy and politics.

In short, Locke was not a professional educator. *Some Thoughts Concerning Education*[4] is not a seminal work, as are his own *Essay* and *Treatises* in their fields. We have a list of the educational works in his library, of which nine were published before his own. Five of these are in French, published between 1660 and 1687 and concerned mainly with advice to parents of gentlemen; the only author of distinction is Fénelon, who writes on the education of girls. The four English books, by Burghly (1636), Osborne (1656), Walker (1673) and Sir Walter Ralegh (1636), are similarly concerned almost exclusively with 'young gentlemen'. Frankly, we continue to read the *Thoughts* because it was written by the author of the *Essay* and the *Treatises*.[5] In the circumstances of Locke's own life and upbringing we recognise the source of many of his ideas, notably his preference for a home tutor over public schooling and the central importance he gives to the education of the body, the 'clay tenement'. He himself claimed to have scant experience of pedagogy, but the facts scarcely bear this out; perhaps his modest disclaimer arose from his desire to be regarded first and foremost as a philosopher.[6]

In the early chapters of the *Second Treatise of Government*

Locke declares that in a state of nature all men are born free and equal.[7] The law of nature is, for Locke,[8] also the law of reason, and both have a divine origin. In the state of nature all men are naturally in 'a state of perfect freedom to order their actions and dispose of their possessions', 'a state also of equality . . . no one having more than another . . . and the use of the same faculties should also be equal one amongst another . . . without subordination or subjection'.[9] Although all men are equal politically, in actual life differences must be recognised:[10] 'Though I have said above that all men by nature are equal, I cannot be supposed to understand all sorts of equality; age or virtue may give men a just precedency; excellence of parts and merit may place others above the common level; both may subject some and alliance or benefits others, to pay an observance to those to whom nature, gratitude or other respects may have made it due; and yet all this consists with the equality which all men are in.' The inequality of parts, or talents, here mentioned is also recognised in Locke's *Conduct of the Understanding:*[11] 'There is, it is visible, great variety in men's understandings, and their natural constitutions put so wide a difference between some men in this respect that art and industry would never be able to master, and their very natures seem to want a foundation to raise on it that which other men easily attain unto. Amongst men of equal education there is great inequality of parts.' The concept of equality must also be qualified in the case of children.[12] 'Children, I confess, are not born in their full state of equality though they are born to it. Their parents have a sort of rule and jurisdiction over them when they come into the world and for some time after, but 'tis but a temporary one.'

With regard to freedom Locke likewise recognises certain limitations in the case of children.[13] Only in a community with an established system of law can man be regarded as politically free, according to Locke. 'Where there is no law, there is no liberty.' Freedom is not a liberty for every man to do as he likes, but a liberty to dispose of his person and property within the allowance of the laws and not to be subject to the arbitrary will of another. To appreciate the law on which liberty is dependent a man must have reason. To turn a child loose before he has reason to guide him is not to grant him freedom 'but to thrust him out amongst brutes and abandon him to a state as wretched and as much beneath that of man as theirs'. Thus[14] 'we are born free as we are born rational, not that we have actually the exercise of either; age that brings one brings with it the other too, and thus we see how freedom and subjection to parents may consist together and are both founded on the same principle'.

Having thus disposed of equality and freedom we can now consider the duties and rights of parents. In the chapter headed 'Paternal Power'[15] Locke prefaces his treatment by remarking that the title should rather be 'Parental Power', as such power is vested in both parents and not in the father only.[16] The rights of parents he defines thus:[17] 'Paternal or parental power is nothing but that which parents have over their children, to govern them for the children's good till they come to the use of reason or a state of knowledge wherein they may be supposed capable to understand that rule whether it be the law of nature or the municipal law of their country they are to govern themselves by, capable, I say, to know it as well as several others who live as free men under the law. The affection and tenderness which God hath planted in the breasts of parents towards their children makes it evident that this is not intended to be a severe arbitrary government but only for the help, instruction and preservation of their offspring.' The child's rights are summed up in the statement:[18] 'All that a child has right to claim from his father is nourishment and education, and the things nature furnishes for the support of life.' In return, the child is expected to honour his parents.

An approach to Locke's educational position from another angle, the psychological, is through the famous *Essay Concerning Human Understanding*.[19] Although an educational system cannot be based on psychological considerations, it cannot afford to neglect such data; these qualify any pronouncements made on philosophical or social grounds. It is for this reason that Locke's *Essay* has significance for the educationist.[20]

Locke's intention in the *Essay* is to make an analysis and reconstruction of mental content, or, in his own words,[21] 'to examine our own abilities and see what objects our understandings were or were not fitted to deal with'. His method is the method of introspection: 'I could look into nobody's understanding but my own to see how it wrought'.[22] Before proceeding to his main task, however, Locke finds it necessary, as he puts it,[23] 'to clear my way to those foundations which I conceive are the only true ones' by disposing of two general misconceptions, namely, the presence in the mind of innate ideas, and of mental faculties. The term 'idea' Locke uses in a wide sense: 'It being that term which I think serves best to stand for whatsoever is the object of the understanding when a man thinks, I have used it to express whatever is meant by phantasm, notion, species, or whatever it is which the mind can be employed about in thinking.'[24] It thus comprises all the contents of the mind including what later psychologists designate by sensations, percepts, images and concepts.

There are two types of innate ideas – speculative, and practical or moral – and Locke contends that both types are acquired and are not innate. He refutes the arguments advanced on behalf of such ideas, maintaining that nothing should be regarded as innate the presence of which in the mind can be accounted for otherwise; the analogy he uses in support is:[25] 'It would be impertinent to suppose the ideas of colour innate in a creature to whom God had given sight.' The conviction that truths which are generally or universally accepted must be innate is challenged by citing the example of mathematical propositions. Moral principles he also maintains[26] require reasoning and discourse and some exercise of the mind to discover the certainty of their truth, and he adds:[27] 'Were there any such innate principles, there would be no need to teach them.' He nevertheless recognises 'a law knowable by the light of nature', such a one being 'a desire of happiness and an aversion to misery'.[28] And in the *Second Treatise of Government* he instances[29] 'that Cain was so convinced that everyone had a right to destroy such a criminal that after the murder of his brother he cries out: "Everyone that findeth me shall slay me." So plain was it writ in the hearts of all mankind.' Laslett comments that the final phrase is the most conspicuous instance in the whole book of Locke's willingness to take advantage of the belief in innate ideas and innate practical principles.

In dealing with 'Power'[30] Locke refers to the powers of the mind – perceiving and preferring – and remarks that the ordinary way of speaking 'is that the understanding and the will are two faculties of the mind, a word proper enough if it be used . . . so as not to breed any confusion in man's thoughts by being supposed to stand for some real beings in the soul that performed those actions of understanding and volition'. He adds:[31] 'For if it be reasonable to suppose and talk of faculties as distinct beings that can act as we do when we say "The will orders" and "The will is free" it is fit that we shall make a speaking faculty, and a walking faculty, and a dancing faculty, by which these actions are produced, which are but several modes of motion.' He further explains:[32] 'But the fault has been that faculties have been spoken of and represented as so many distinct agents. For it being asked, what it was that digested the meat in our stomachs, it was a ready and very satisfactory answer to say that it was the digestive faculty . . . and so on in the mind, the intellectual faculty, or the understanding, understood; and the elective faculty, or the will, willed or commanded; which is, in short, to say that the ability to digest, digested; and the ability to move, moved; and the ability to understand, understood. For "faculty, ability, and power", I think, "are but different names for the same thing".'

Having thus disposed of innate ideas and of mental faculties Locke first classifies the contents of mind under two main heads – understanding[33] and volition. Modern psychologists might add a third, namely 'feeling', but Locke regards feeling as a derived condition resulting from the integration of various experiences, including sensations:[34] 'The term operations I use in a large sense as comprehending not barely the actions of the mind about its ideas, but some sort of passions arising sometimes from them, such as is the satisfaction or uneasiness arising from any thought'.[35] Feeling is nevertheless an experience having a character of its own and definitely distinguishable from every other; it may even become dissociated from the original occasion and be incorporated in what is known as a complex.

Locke's rejection of mental faculties enables him to deal somewhat drastically with the vexed problem of the freedom of the will. To the question, What is it that determines the will? Locke replies:[36] 'The true and proper answer is the mind'. Or[37] more precisely: 'Every man is put under a necessity by his constitution as an intelligent being to be determined in willing by his own thought and judgment, what is best for him to do.' Locke thus preserves man's freedom by sacrificing the will. Man's actions are regulated by the understanding through desire. One condition nevertheless must be observed; the idea or the desire that motivates the will or leads man to act must be regarded as attainable: 'desire is stopped or abated by the opinion of the impossibility or unattainableness of the good proposed'.[38]

Understanding, for Locke, comprises all the cognitive processes – sensation, perception, imagination and thinking, the bases of all being 'simple ideas' – and what he calls 'ideas of reflection', the latter merely being the mental processes themselves regarded as objects or ideas. Locke usually refers to simple ideas and to ideas of reflection as if they were of equivalent standing, but ideas of reflection must come later in the child's development, since, as Locke says,[39] they 'require attention', or, as we should now say, they involve introspection. When we ask how we acquire simple ideas or sensations, all that Locke can offer in reply is – by experience.[40] His doctrine thereby came to be designated empiricism. As Locke's classification of ideas is not restricted to sensory percepts, he is not strictly speaking an empiricist.[41] Empiricism assumes that the mind is constituted of independent impressions passively imprinted on it from without. Rationalism, to which it is opposed, assumes that knowledge is derived by deduction from certain first principles intuitively apprehended. Locke does not carry his analysis further, and inquire, as did Kant in effect later, how experience is possible. Kant's answer in *The Critique of Pure Reason*, given here in a line, is that the structure of the mind determines the type of experience we have; the experience of minds otherwise constituted than ours would be in another dimension. Experience is thus mentally conditioned, and idealism rather than empiricism would accordingly appear to be the ultimate answer.

Locke's assumption that simple ideas or simple sensations were unrelated and essentially disconnected necessitates an agency or agencies in the mind to arrange and combine these, whereas the mind that registers the impressions is conceived by Locke merely as a blank sheet or plain surface – a *tabula rasa*, the ideas being related only by the laws of association. To enable Locke's psychology to be profitable the notion of the simple idea would require to be abandoned; 'the pure sensation we may regard as a psychological myth', says James Ward;[42] it is a product of psychological abstraction and never encountered in actual experience. Some synthetic activity must also be attributed to mind, as Kant later affirmed, if science, or even experience itself, is to be possible. In metaphysics the view of mind as constituted of simple unrelated ideas led to Hume's scepticism, for such a hypothesis, as he confessed, rendered it impossible to account for the necessary connection implied in causality which science demanded. Some recent philosophers who have appropriated the title 'realists' base their system on sense-data which are merely hypothetical elements of psychological abstraction, and analogous to Locke's simple ideas. Had Locke adopted the genetic, instead of the introspective, standpoint he would have come to realise that the original state of mind is an undifferentiated continuum out of which single objects gradually emerge, and that the child's earliest mental experience is, in William James's words, 'a great big blooming buzzing confusion'.

No systematic account of education was ever contemplated by Locke. He repeatedly protests: 'I would not have it thought that I looked on it as a just treatise on this subject'; 'But to enter into particulars would be beyond the design of this short treatise'; 'I am far from imagining that it contains all those particulars which his growing years or peculiar temper may require'.[43] Publication was justified on the grounds that 'it may give some light to those . . . that dare venture to consult their own reason in the education of their children rather than wholly rely upon old custom', also 'it is every man's indispensable duty to do all the service he can to his country' and 'the well educating of their children is so much the duty and concern of parents, and the welfare and prosperity of the nation so much depends on it that I would have every one lay it seriously to heart'.[44]

Locke's standpoint in producing the *Thoughts* he defines in another connection. In reply to a request for advice on the education of her son Locke wrote in 1697 to Lady Peterborough:[45] 'I have always thought that to direct a young gentleman's studies right, it is absolutely necessary to know what course of life – either by the destination of his quality or fortune or the choice and determination of his parents – he is designed to.' Instead of a uniform classical training for all Locke insisted that education should be tailored to fit the prospective mode of life of the pupil; this is more definitely formulated in the *Thoughts*: 'I think a prince, a nobleman and an ordinary gentleman's son, should have different ways of breeding.'[46] His main concern in the *Thoughts*, however, is with 'the breeding of a young gentleman', who would in the natural course of events fall heir to the family estates. Referring to *Some Thoughts Concerning Reading and Study* and to everything else he published Laslett says:[47] 'They were to be part of the assimilated atmosphere of the English gentleman, the member of Parliament, the administrator and politician, at home and overseas, but above all the landowner, the local notable'; and later, 'The ideal of the English gentleman is with us today, and in part it is Locke's invention.' Locke's conception of the ideal gentleman, interposed in his condemnation of affectation,[48] is: 'he that will examine wherein that gracefulness lies which always pleases, will find it arises from the natural coherence which appears between the things done and such a temper of mind as cannot but be approved of as suitable to the occasion. We cannot but be pleased with an humane, friendly, civil temper wherever we meet with it. A mind free and master of itself and all its actions, not low and narrow, not haughty and insolent, not blemished with any great defect is what everyone is taken with.'

In short, Locke's intention was to produce a properly educated English country gentleman, interested in science and agriculture as well as the affairs of his daily round. Such men would have an important role to play in the running of the country: they would be, in their own comparatively modest way, philosopher-kings. But from the outset commentators on Locke's work recognised his educational principles as having wider application. Thus Pierre Coste, who produced the first edition of the *Thoughts* in French, published in Locke's lifetime, remarked in his preface: 'It is certain that this work was particularly designed for the education of Gentlemen: but this does not prevent its serving also for the education of all sorts of children, of whatever class they are'.[49]

Locke's virtually vocational outlook on education implies a pragmatic attitude in the sense that the outcomes must have practical worth: 'we shall not have reason to complain of the narrowness of our minds, if we but employ them about what may be of use to us.'[50] This is reflected in his emphasis on practical studies; what he recommended was not 'brain-stuffing', but the formation of a healthy learning habit. Newman in *The Idea of a University* accuses Locke, 'that celebrated philosopher',[51] of having anticipated the Edinburgh reviewers in advocating 'that no good could come of a system which was not based upon the principle of utility'.

Unlike Comenius, Locke does not assume that man should be omniscient: 'How short soever their knowledge may come of an universal or perfect comprehension of whatever is, yet secures their great concernments that they have light enough to lead them to a knowledge of their Maker and the sight of their own duties',[52] and in the introduction to the *Essay* he says: 'Our business here is not to know all things, but those which concern our conduct.' In the *Thoughts*[53] it is not the tutor's business 'to teach them all that is knowable'. In his essay 'Of Study' he elaborates:[54] 'The extent of knowledge of things knowable is so vast . . . that the whole time of our life is not enough to acquaint us with all those things, I will not say which we are capable of knowing, but which it would not be only convenient but very advantageous to know.' In accordance with this view Locke formulates the principle which has come to be known as 'frequency of use', a principle extensively exploited by modern curriculum makers: 'And since it cannot be hoped he [the pupil] should have time and strength to learn all things, most pains should be taken about that which is most necessary, and that principally looked after which will be of most frequent use to him in the world.'[55]

Whether the young gentleman should be educated at home under a tutor or sent to a public school is a problem that perplexes Locke. 'I confess both sides have their inconveniences.'[56] But whether as a result of his own experience or not under the famous Dr Busby at Westminster School he, in opposition to Quintilian and Comenius, decided: 'I cannot but prefer breeding of a young gentleman at home in his father's sight under a good governor as much the best and safest way to this great and main end of education when it can be had and is ordered as it should be.' Locke's prescription for the upbringing of the lad as set forth in the *Thoughts* does not seem to have worked so efficaciously as he had intended, for we find from one of his letters[57] that he recommended a change of tutor, and then, as he suspected want of application, he even suggested[58] to his father that the boy might be sent to 'Westminster, or some other severe school, where if he were whipped soundly while you are looking out another fit tutor for him, he would perhaps be more pliant and willing to learn at home afterwards'.

'A sound mind in a sound body is a short but full description of a happy state in this world. He that hath these two, has little more to wish for; and he that wants either of them, will be but little the better for anything else.'[59] Such are the opening sentences of the *Thoughts*. Locke, who had some pretensions to medical skill,[60] disposes first of health education, advocating a hardening régime which is the natural lot of the children of the poor but necessary to give Locke's pupil, who might otherwise become pampered and spoiled, some of the advantages of what has been termed 'the education of the gutter'.[61] Thus Locke recommends[62] that the youth is 'to have his shoes made so as to leak water', and he sums up his advice on the physical upbringing of the boy thus:[63] 'Plenty of open air, exercise and sleep, plain diet, no wine or strong drink, and very little or no physic, not too warm and strict clothing, especially the head and feet kept cold, and the feet often used to cold water and exposed to wet.' In his chapter on 'Physical Education' in *Education: Intellectual, Moral and Physical*, Herbert Spencer comments on Locke's rigorous régime in the following terms:[64] 'The common notion about "hardening" is a grievous delusion. Not a few children are "hardened" out of the world; and those who survive, permanently suffer either in growth or constitution. . . . The reasoning on which this hardening theory rests is extremely superficial. Wealthy parents, seeing little peasant boys and girls playing about in the open-air only half-clothed, and joining with this fact the general healthiness of labouring people, draw the unwarrantable conclusion that the healthiness is the result of the exposure and resolve to keep their own offspring scantily covered! It is forgotten that these urchins who gambol upon village-greens are in many respects favourably circumstanced – that their lives are spent in almost perpetual play; that they are all day breathing fresh air; and that their systems are not disturbed by over-taxed brains. For aught that appears to the contrary, their good health may be maintained not in consequence of, but in spite of, their deficient clothing. This alternative conclusion we believe to be the true one; and that an inevitable detriment results from the loss of animal heat to which they are subject. For when, the constitution being sound enough to bear it, the exposure does produce hardness, it does so at the expense of growth.'

In fashioning his ideal type of personality four things, according to Locke, are necessary:[65] virtue, wisdom, breeding and learning. Wisdom is beyond the reach of children since it implies natural good temper, application of mind and experience.[66] Breeding is largely a matter of right company: 'such as his company, such will be his manners.'[67] Its aim is to secure 'a carriage suitable to his rank', and the rule to be observed is: 'Not to think meanly of ourselves, and not to think meanly of others.'[68]

Of virtue Locke says:[69] "'Tis virtue, then, direct virtue, which is the hard and valuable part to be aimed at in education. . . . All other considerations and accomplishments should give way and be postponed to this. This is the solid and substantial good [on] which tutors should not only read lectures, and talk of, but the labour and art of education should furnish the mind with, and fasten there, and never cease till the young man had a true relish of it, and placed his strength, his glory, and his pleasure in it.' The foundations of virtue are to be laid in religion: 'There ought to be imprinted on his mind a true notion of God as of an independent supreme being, author and maker of all things, from Whom we receive all our good, Who loves us, and gives us all things', a confession of faith similar to that which Rousseau in *Émile* later formulates for Sophie.

Learning Locke puts last, and regards it as the least part of education. 'This may seem strange in the mouth of a bookish man; and this making usually the chief, if not only hustle and stir about children, this being almost that alone which is thought on when people talk of education, makes it the greater paradox.'[70] The explanation that he offers in *Thoughts Concerning Reading and Study for a Gentleman* is that 'a gentleman's proper calling is the service of his country, and so is most properly concerned in moral and political knowledge; and thus the studies which more immediately belong to his calling are those which treat of virtue and vices, of civil society and the arts of government, and will take in also law and history'.[71]

Rousseau's criticism of Locke in the *New Héloïse*, that he speaks much more of what should be required of children than of the means that have to be employed in getting it, is hardly justified, for Locke does recognise the importance of method in education. 'Order and constancy are said to make the great difference between one man and another: This I am sure, nothing so much clears a learner's way, helps him so much on in it, and makes him go so easy and so far in any inquiry, as a good method. His governor should take pains to make him sensible of this, accustom him to order, and teach him method in all the applications of his thoughts; shew him wherein it lies, and the advantages of it; acquaint him with the several sorts of it either from general to particulars, or from particulars to what is more general, exercise him in both of them, and make him see in what cases each different method is most proper, and to what ends it best serves.'[72] His own general principle of method he states thus:[73] 'He that hath found a way how to keep up a child's spirit easy, active and free, and yet at the same time to restrain him from many things he has a mind to, and to draw him to things that are uneasy to him; he, I say, that knows how to reconcile these seeming contradictions, has, in my opinion, got the true secret of education.'

Locke anticipated the play-way in education. 'Children should not have anything like work, or serious, laid on them; neither their minds nor their bodies will bear it.'[74] And 'were matters ordered right, learning anything they should be taught might be made as much a recreation to their play as their play is to their learning'. A condition of realising this fortunate state of affairs is that the task should be begun at the psychological moment, when the pupil is in the right mood for it – 'the favourable seasons of aptitude and inclinations be heedfully laid hold of'.[75] It should not be prolonged till exhaustion or aversion sets in: 'Care should be taken that what is of advantage to them they should always do with delight; and before they are wearied with one they should be timely diverted to some other useful employment'.[76] In the course of the task 'masters and teachers should raise no difficulties to their scholars but on the contrary should smooth their way and readily help them forwards where they find them stop'.[77] As constant attention is one of the hardest tasks that can be required of children, 'he that requires their application should endeavour to make what he proposes as grateful and agreeable as possible, at least he ought to take care not to join any displeasing or frightful idea with it'. 'The great skill of a teacher is to get and keep the attention of his scholar; whilst he has that, he is sure to advance as fast as the learner's abilities will carry him, and without that, all his hustle and pother will be to little or no purpose. To attain this he should make the child comprehend (as much as may be) the usefulness of what he teaches him, and let him see by what he has learnt that he can do something which he could not do before, something which gives him some power and real advantage above others who are ignorant of it. To this he should add sweetness in all his instructions, and by a certain tenderness in his whole carriage make the child sensible that he loves him and designs nothing but his good, the only way to beget love in the child which will make him hearken to his lessons and relish what he teaches him.'[78]

The aim should be to create in the pupils 'a liking and inclination to what you propose to them to be learned and that will engage their industry and application'.[79] This, Locke adds, should be no hard matter if children are handled as they should be. Children, too, are to be treated as rational creatures.[80] Locke explains what he means by reasoning with children:[81] 'I do not intend any other but such as is suited to the child's capacity and apprehension.'

A believer in teaching without tears, Locke held advanced views on child discipline. 'I am very apt to think that great severity of punishment does but very little good, nay, great harm in education; and I believe it will be found that *alteris paribus* those children who have been most chastised, seldom make the best men.'[82] He was strongly opposed to the use of the rod. 'The usual lazy and short way by chastisement and the rod which is the only instrument of government that tutors generally know, or ever think of, is the most unfit of any to be used in education.'[83] This sort of correction, he adds,[84] 'naturally breeds an aversion to that which 'tis the tutor's business to create a liking to'. If need be that offences come, then Locke offers advice[85] suggesting the employment of a Corrector after the manner of the Jesuits, but repeating: 'Beating is the worst and therefore the last means to be used in the correction of children and that only in cases of extremity after all gentle ways have been tried and proved unsuccessful.'

That Locke, rather than Rousseau, should be designated the father of the child-study movement can be justified by the exhortation:[86] 'He that is about children should well study their natures and aptitudes and see by often trials what turn they easily take and what becomes them; observe what their native stock is, how it may be improved, and what it is fit for; he should consider what they want, whether they be capable of having it wrought into them by industry and incorporated there by practice, and whether it be worth while to endeavour it. For in many cases all that we can do, or should aim at, is to make the best of what nature has given, to prevent the vices and faults to which such a constitution is most inclined, and give it all the advantages it is capable of. Everyone's natural genius should be carried as far as it could, but to attempt the putting another upon him, will be but labour in vain, and what is so plastered on will at best sit untowardly and have always hanging to it the ungracefulness of constraint and affectation.'[87]

But if the young gentleman is not to remain 'more ignorant than the clerk of our parish' he must learn to read and write. Various contrivances for learning his letters are described by Locke; after mastering these he is to commence reading, the general procedure advocated by Locke being: 'Let him never be driven to nor chid for; cheat him into it if you can, but make it not a business. 'Tis better it be a year later before he can read than that he should get an aversion to learning.'[88] After reading comes writing. In dealing with the acquisition of this skill Locke enunciates the principles that if one would do anything well he should not attempt to do two parts of an action at the same time if they can be separated; learning to hold the pen must accordingly be taught independently of learning to form the letters.[89] Representational drawing is added not for any aesthetic but merely for its practical value, and at a later stage shorthand is mentioned as an optional subject.[90]

Although it is not mentioned in his treatise on education, Locke advocated spelling reform. The following appears in shorthand in his Journal (dated 15 August 1676): '*Spelling* . . . How little a lover so ever I am of fresh fashions . . . considering that letters are but the lasting marks of sounds, I think we would avoid much confusion and great many needless difficulties if we would always apply as near as we could the same characters to the same pronunciation. [It would] perhaps look a little strange and awkward at first to make a change all at once, as in this paragraph, so much is custom able to confirm us in love and admiration even of inconveniences, although it cannot but be acknowledged that it would be much better if it were reformed, and nobody can deny that it may be done by degrees and must have a beginning. It would prevent a great many mistakes and make languages of which we have so great a need and so constant use much *easier* to be learnt, read and written by all strangers, by the women and illiterate of the same country.'[91]

Locke is a convinced believer in 'English for the English'. Care is to be taken when the boy is learning French and Latin, that his English is not neglected[92] . . . 'since 'tis English that an English gentleman will have constant use of, that is the language he should chiefly cultivate. . . . I am not here speaking against Greek and Latin; I think they ought to be studied, and the Latin at least understood well by every gentleman. But whatever foreign languages a young gentleman meddles with (and the more he knows the better) that which he should critically study and labour to get a facility, clearness and elegancy to express himself in, should be his own; and to this purpose he should be daily exercised in it.'[93]

In spite of his general pragmatic standpoint Locke cannot evade the issue of the place of languages in the education of his pupil. After English, French is proposed, the reason for its priority over Latin being that it is a living language and can be acquired by the direct method.[94] Latin, too, Locke regards as absolutely necessary to a gentleman, but it should, like French, be taught by the direct method and not after the traditional grammatical manner which Locke roundly condemns. No man can pass for a scholar that is ignorant of the Greek tongue, Locke admits,[95] but protests that he is not considering the education of a professed scholar, but of a gentleman to whom Latin and French are by everyone acknowledged to be necessary. While Latin is looked upon as necessary to a gentleman, it is ridiculous for a boy designed for a trade to spend time on a language for which he will never have any use.

To complete his curriculum Locke, unmindful perhaps of his previous warning regarding the extent of human knowledge and the limitation of the pupil's mind, adds arithmetic, astronomy, geometry, geography, chronology, history, ethics, law, natural philosophy. Other accomplishments include dancing and music, and wrestling is preferred to fencing. One more addition, which Locke recognises will evoke astonishment, is his recommendation of a trade. 'And yet I cannot forbear to say I would have him learn a trade, a manual trade, nay two or three, but one more particular. . . . I should propose one, or rather both these, namely gardening or husbandry in general, and working in wood as a carpenter, joiner or turner, these being fit and healthy recreations for a man of study or business.'[96] After that Locke did not expect to meet the same opposition in advocating that a young gentleman should learn to keep accounts, 'though a science not likely to help a gentleman to get an estate, yet possibly there is not any thing of more use and efficacy to make him preserve the estate he has'.[97]

The young Englishman's education was rounded off with the Grand Tour, but Locke regards the usual age, namely, from sixteen to twenty-one, as of all times the least suitable, preferring seven to fourteen as the best age to acquire the correct accent in foreign languages; at this age, too, a tutor's presence is not resented as it would be by an older pupil.

Two controversial issues emerge from Locke's reflections on education – the nature – nurture dilemma, and the validity of formal training. In justification of his intervention in embarking on the *Thoughts* he stresses the importance of education to the extent of declaring that education can accomplish everything, whereas in more philosophic mood in the *Second Treatise of Government* and in the *Conduct of the Understanding*, as we have seen, he acknowledges that nature sets limits to the efficacy of education. Thus in the opening sections of the *Thoughts*[98] he says that 'of all men we meet with, nine parts of ten are what they are, good or evil, useful or not, by their education. 'Tis that which makes the great difference in mankind.' And he repeats: 'That the difference to be found in the manners and abilities of men is owing more to their education than to anything else.' Later in the *Thoughts* he qualifies his statement,[99] averring 'God has stamped certain characters upon men's minds which, like their shapes, may be a little mended, but can hardly be totally altered and transformed into the contrary'.

Most dispute has, however, arisen in the history of education on the issue whether Locke can be regarded as an upholder of the doctrine of formal training. As we have already seen, Plato cannot be acquitted of the charge of introducing the disciplinary conception of education or formal training. In Milton's tractate *Of Education* the term is definitely used:[100] 'These are the studies wherein our noble and our gentle youth ought to bestow their time in a disciplinary way.' Locke cannot consequently be saddled with the responsibility for initiating the doctrine or for introducing the term. The question then resolves itself into whether he upholds the doctrine. His advocacy of certain Spartan practices in the physical upbringing of his young gentleman, and such a remark in regard to his moral training:[101] 'it seems plain to me that the principle of all virtue and excellency lies in the power of denying ourselves the satisfaction of our own desires', might seem to justify us in ascribing to him the disciplinary conception of education, but it is in the intellectual sphere that a decision must be taken. The warrant for attributing the disciplinary view to Locke is to be found in the *Thoughts*.[102] 'The studies which he [the tutor] sets him upon, are but as it were the exercise of his faculties and employment of his time, to keep him from sauntering and idleness, to teach him application and accustom him to take pains, and to give him some little taste of what his own industry must perfect.'

The formal training of school subjects rests on the assumption that in the mind there are powers or faculties which can be improved by the teaching of such subjects. Locke's devastating criticism in *An Essay Concerning Human Understanding*, as we have seen, has effectively disposed of mental faculties, although even today the lesson has not been learnt by many educationists. In the *Thoughts*, written in a more popular strain, he says: 'I hear it is said that children should be employed in getting things by heart, to exercise and improve their memories. I could wish this were said with as much authority of reason as it is with forwardness of assurance, and that this practice were established upon good observation more than old custom; for it is evident that strength of memory is owing to an happy constitution, and not to any habitual improvement got by exercise. 'Tis true, what the mind is intent upon, and, for fear of letting it slip, often imprints afresh on itself by frequent reflection, that it is apt to retain, but still according to its own natural strength of retention. But the learning pages of Latin by heart no more fits the memory for retention of anything else than the graving of one sentence in lead makes it the more capable of retaining firmly any other characters.'

With regard to reasoning Locke likewise rejects what has come to be known as transfer of training; in the *Conduct of the Understanding*[103] he says: 'We see men frequently dexterous and sharp enough in making a bargain who, if you reason with them about matters of religion, appear perfectly stupid.' And later he explains:[104] 'The mistake is that he that is found reasonable in one thing is concluded to be so in all, and to think or say otherwise is thought so unjust an affront, and so senseless a censure, that nobody ventures to do it.' Locke also suggests[105] that there is no transfer between ability in Latin and in English; in Latin 'the manner of expressing of one's self is so very different from ours that to be perfect in that would very little improve the purity and facility of his English style'.

Locke's treatment of grammar may be regarded as a 'crucial instance' in deciding the question whether his educational doctrine in the *Thoughts* is disciplinarian or utilitarian, for no subject lends itself more readily to justification on disciplinarian grounds. Grammar is throughout regarded purely as an instrumental subject and ancillary to language; its formal training value is ignored. Logic and rhetoric, frequently justified for their value as means of training the mind, are dismissed by Locke with but slight reference, the criterion applied being again the utilitarian – 'because of the little advantage young people receive from them'.[106] The weight of evidence is accordingly against the charge that Locke supports formal training and that he is a representative of the disciplinary view of education; the lapses which we have indicated are such as are likely to be encountered in a writer who does not specifically set himself to avoid the implications of the doctrine.

Although the *Thoughts* was directed to the upbringing of an ordinary gentleman's son, Locke was prepared, if called upon, to advise on the education of the young man's sister, as we should expect from the many expressions in his letters of tender solicitude for Elizabeth Clarke to whom, when little more than a year old, he speaks in playful terms as his 'little mistress' and a little later as 'his wife'. In a covering letter attached to a fair copy of the early draft of the *Thoughts* sent in 1684 to Edward Clarke, he evidently contemplated dealing with the education of girls, the last sentence running: 'Be therefore both you and your lady as severe as may be in examining these rules, doubt as much as you can of every one of them, and when upon a scrupulous review we have settled this part and supplied what possibly you may find wanting, I shall be ready to talk my mind as fully to Madame concerning her daughters, if she continue to be of the mind that may be worth her patience to hear it.'[107] And in the *Thoughts*[108] he explains: 'I have said *he* here because the principal aim of my discourse is how a young gentleman should be brought up from his infancy, which in all things will not so perfectly suit the education of daughters though where the difference of sex requires different treatment, 'twill be no hard matter to distinguish.'

Locke's contribution to education has been variously assessed. The publication in 1690 of the *An Essay Concerning Human Understanding* has been said to mark the opening of an epoch in the history of education.[109] While it undoubtedly initiated a new era in philosophic thought, its influence on education was mainly indirect. Adamson in his Introduction to the *Educational Writings of John Locke* later admitted[110] that these have proved much less influential than his philosophy. Adams, on the other hand, claims:[111] 'Locke's influence far exceeds his fame. Most of his followers do not know their master. His point of view coincides so completely with that of the ordinary intelligent man in the street that his following in all English-speaking countries is infinitely greater than any other philosophical writer can command.' His influence on education on the Continent, where theories of education are taken more seriously than in this country, has also been considerable.

Nevertheless, as we have seen, *Some Thoughts Concerning Education* will not bear comparison with *Émile* or *The Republic* as one of the key works in the history of educational ideas. Its impact was mainly in the century and a half after Locke's death, when the ideas on which it was constructed found acceptance in the minds of the more liberal members of the English gentry. When he died, in 1704, the book had already achieved its fifth edition, and, like all his works, it was translated remarkably widely. But there was no real place for it in the vexed world which resulted a century later from the social, political and intellectual upheavals of the Revolutionary Era, and, as Axtell says,[112] its influence 'largely worked itself out in the nineteenth century'.

This is not to say that there is nothing of interest to us in Locke's educational ideas. Firmly grounded in practical common sense,[113] they often strike sympathetic chords in the mind of a modern reader. His emphasis, a century before Rousseau and Pestalozzi, on the psychological approach, continues to be accepted as an educational axiom, and his prescription for a happy state in this world – a sound mind in a sound body – has always appealed, through its moderation and balance, to men of liberal mind.

7
Rousseau

IN an age of superpowers it might reasonably be asserted that there are two – and only two – Great Educators, Plato and Rousseau. In a way Western education today is a battlefield between two groups of philosophical ideas derived from these men. For all his shiftless youthful wanderings, Rousseau was a powerful and original thinker; *Émile* is a seminal book.

It is dangerous, of course, to found theories on events of his early years,[1] for most of the evidence is in his own *Confessions*, much of which is more a romance than an autobiography. The story of the heartless wretch who packed off his five illegitimate children to a foundlings' hospital immediately after their birth is probably a fabrication, intended to cloak his impotence.[2] Furthermore, accounts of him written by others are sometimes biased: criticism of his inconsistency on the educational role of parents, based on the memoirs of Madame d'Épinay, loses its force when the original manuscript is contrasted with the published text.[3]

Nevertheless the picture remains of a man who, during the first forty years of his life, consistently failed by the standards of his time. Born in Geneva in 1712, the son of a watchmaker who also taught dancing, he lost his mother when he was a week old. His father was a highly strung man, given to ungoverned rages, and he enjoyed neither an orthodox education nor a secure home life. In 1728, after two unsuccessful apprenticeships, in law and engraving he ran away from Geneva. His next few years were spent searching for security. He was received into the Roman Catholic Church, but failed to qualify for training as a priest. He formed successive attachments to ladies older than himself, notably Madame de Warens, with whom he had an intermittent but close relationship from 1728 to 1741. Given some training as a musician, he failed to support himself in this way, and was no more successful in 1740 as a private tutor to two boys in Lyons, or in 1743 as secretary to the French ambassador in Venice, who dismissed him for insolence.

In the course of all his misadventures, however, he contrived to widen and deepen his education, and in 1749 began a career as a writer. A *Discourse on the Arts and Sciences* won a prize offered by the Academy of Dijon. Three years later his short opera, *Le Devin du village*, was performed successfully before King Louis XIV at Fontainebleau. In 1755 he published a *Discourse on the Origin of Inequality*, in 1758 one on *Political Economy*. His productivity reached its peak in 1761 and 1762, when he published a classic of political philosophy, *The Social Contract*, and two novels, *La Nouvelle Héloïse* and *Émile*, the latter to become one of the most powerful influences in Western education. Of his later writings the most interesting educationally is his *Considerations on the Government of Poland* (1772). His extraordinary *Confessions* began to appear in 1782, four years after his death.

His books won immediate notoriety in France, but he never succeeded in coming to terms with the contemporary Establishment, nor even with many people who attempted to help him. When the Archbishop of Paris condemned *Émile* on religious grounds, Rousseau fled from the city. The book was also condemned by the authorities in Geneva. He quarrelled with Diderot and the Encyclopaedists, and later with the Scottish philosopher Hume, who had offered him asylum in England. For the last decade of his life he exhibited clear signs of persecution mania.

Rousseau, if he was not conscious when he was writing *The Social Contract* that he was initiating a political revolution, was nevertheless under the impression, when penning *Émile*,[4] that he was effecting a revolution in education. 'My thoughts are not those of others', he declares in the author's preface, and later in regard to method he counsels:[5] 'Reverse the usual practice and you will almost always do right.' In spite of these protests Rousseau owed much to the past and to earlier writers. His view of a rational principle governing the universe he derived from the Stoics, as he did also his anti-social views. His political ideas are developments of Locke's, and his early educational views also owe much to Locke,[6] whose concepts of the infant mind as a *tabula rasa*, of the importance of teaching by practice rather than precept, and the value of a trade, of the central importance of morality, all appear in Rousseau's work. Just as obvious is the effect of Rousseau's own experiences. It is hardly a matter of wonder that a man with his record should develop a philosophy which puts the blame for man's failure on society.

The *Discourse on the Arts and Sciences* expresses Rousseau's anti-social doctrine or rather his protest against the artificial conventional standards which controlled current society.[7] Appearance, he says, has usurped reality. The theatre is an illustration of this process, a 'dark prison', essentially corrupt. Towns, 'the abyss of the human race', represent an artificial way of life.[8] Rousseau's complaint is not modern; the book of Genesis records how it was through eating of the tree of knowledge that evil entered into the world, and Ecclesiastes, the preacher, proclaimed that he that increaseth knowledge increaseth sorrow. The early Stoic philosophers, repelled by the doctrine that happiness was to be attained through the search after pleasure, taught man to seek in his own soul the source of his satisfaction, that he was sufficient unto himself would be but to estimate at their true worth the externalities of life. This view finds expression in Seneca's *Ad Lucilium Epistulae Morales*, especially in that 'On the Part Played by Philosophy in the Progress of Man' from which Rousseau doubtless derived his *Discourse on the Arts and Sciences*.[9] Therein Seneca declares: 'Nature suffices for what she demands. Luxury has turned her back upon nature. A thatched roof once covered free men; under marble and gold dwells slavery.' In the *Discourse* Rousseau writes 'in praise of ignorance'. He assembles instances to prove that the decline and fall of ancient peoples coincided with the growth of knowledge among them. He argues that the days of their poverty, simplicity and ignorance were also the days of their strength, their happiness and their innocence, that, as Hegel later said, 'the owl of Minerva – the bird of wisdom, does not begin its flight till the evening shadows fall'. This argument is a defence of the supremacy of the moral life, for making virtue ruler. With Milton would he plead: 'Love virtue, she alone is free'.

The extravagances against which Rousseau inveighed in his *Discourse on the Arts and Sciences* he seeks to account for in his *Discourse on the Origin of Inequality*.[10] They are, in fact, the results of man's sense of possession and desire for private property; were he true to his own self there would be but few inequalities in social life. To sustain his contention Rousseau has to define the original nature of man, and it is this part of the *Discourse on Inequality* that has educational interest. Plato, it may be recalled, had postulated the existence of innate inequalities as the condition of even the most rudimentary form of social community: Rousseau emphasises the common nature of mankind.[11] For both Plato and Rousseau the question was mainly political; in Rousseau's view political power always works to the benefit of the strong. In modern times it takes a different form: the anthropologist now studies 'our contemporary ancestors' to deduce from their manners and customs the original nature of man; the psychologist attempts an analysis and classification of man's innate capacities, mainly in the interests of education. Rousseau, ignoring the comparative treatment, attacks directly the question of the nature of man; he frankly warns us that he is likewise not following the historical method – 'Let us begin then by laying facts aside, as they do not affect the question'. The plan he adopts is the hypothetical or conjectural. Wherein then lies the difference between the procedure of Rousseau and that of the modern psychologist? The latter generally accepts the biological standpoint, whereas Rousseau adopts what might be designated the meta-biological. Even some modern geneticists recognise the total inadequacy of any explanation of man's life in terms of animal behaviour. Thus, H. S. Jennings declared:[12] 'There is no organism that differs so much from other organisms as do human beings. The things that are of most importance about children must be known from a study of children, rather than from a study of other organisms; and the same truth holds for human affairs in general.' This is Rousseau's position. Animal behaviour can be explained by the laws of mechanism, but man, according to Rousseau, is a free agent, and has some share in his own operations. Rousseau would even go to the length of attributing ideas and intelligence to animals, allowing man in this respect to differ only in degree from them, but he adds that it is not so much the understanding that constitutes the specific difference between the man and the brute as the human quality of free agency. It is particularly in the consciousness of this liberty that, according to Rousseau, the spirituality of man's soul is displayed. In his analysis of human endowment Rousseau thus gives priority to the higher spiritual values, the existence of which modern psychologists are apt to ignore. To freedom he links progress, or self-improvement, anticipating Browning when he says that progress is man's distinctive mark alone, not God's, and not the beasts.

In *A Discourse on Political Economy*,[13] the subject being the principles of political obligation, Rousseau formulates the differences between public and domestic administration, also the principles of public education. His plan of public education is communistic, recalling the schemes set forth by Plato in the *Republic* and in the *Laws*, and anticipating the communistic arrangement advanced by Fichte in *Addresses to the German Nation*. Reformers, impatient to have their ideals realised, and depressed by the hopelessness of their task in the face of the forces of heredity, physical and social, would drastically dispose of the family and start afresh; but if they thus dispose of the obstacles that obstruct their paths, they at the same time remove the supports which render progress possible. Plato had hoped, while destroying the family, to retain the family virtues, and Rousseau but reiterates the fallacy of composition whereby Plato's argument derived a certain plausibility, namely, that the love which each parent bore to his own child and the child to his parent would be intensified proportionally as all parents in common came to regard all the children of the state as their care. Aristotle in his *Politics* had indicated the fallacy in Plato's proposals, but it is perhaps more clearly exposed by Kant's apt illustration that there would result a harmony like that which a certain satirical poem depicts as existing between a married couple bent on going to ruin, 'O marvellous harmony, what he wishes, she wishes also', or like what is said of the pledge of Francis I to the Emperor Charles V, 'What my brother Charles wishes, that I wish also (namely, Milan)'. But for the most eloquent refutation of Rousseau's communistic views we do not require to go beyond Rousseau's own writings, for in *Émile*[14] he asks: 'Will the bonds of convention hold firm without some foundation in nature? Can devotion to the state exist apart from the love of those near and dear to us? Can patriotism thrive except in the soil of that miniature fatherland, the home? Is it not the good son, the good husband, the good father, who makes the good citizen?'

If we ignore the communistic aspect of the *Discourse on Political*

Economy, Rousseau's view of national education accords with Greek theory and Spartan practice. He agrees with Aristotle[15] who declares that since service to the state as a whole has a single end, it is plain that the education of all must be one and the same, and that the supervision of this education must be public and not private . . . public training is wanted in all things that are of public interest. Rousseau echoes Aristotle, asserting:[16] 'Public education under regulations presented by the government, and under magistrates established by the Sovereign, is one of the fundamental rules of popular or legitimate government.'

In his *Lettres à M. de Malesherbes*[17] Rousseau designates the first *Discourse*, the *Discourse on Inequality* and the treatise on education (*Émile*) his three principal works, and indicates that they are inseparable and together constitute a complete whole. For his educational views it could equally well be said that three at least of his works should be consulted, namely, *La Nouvelle Héloïse*, *Émile* and the *Considerations on the Government of Poland*.

In his *Considerations on the Government of Poland*[18] Rousseau applied his principles of national education, and although it is a departure from the historical order to consider it before *La Nouvelle Héloïse* and *Émile*, it is a natural and logical order. The precedence thus accorded to it may help to counteract the popular belief that Rousseau was an individualist in education, as a cursory reading of *Émile* might suggest.[19]

In *Émile* Rousseau distinguishes three phases of education – the natural or negative; the social or moral; the civic or political. Only in dealing with Émile's experience of foreign travel does Rousseau refer in *Émile* to the third aspect. In the *Considerations on the Government of Poland* he makes this civic aspect the chief aim; in it he preaches the most aggressive nationalism which, however necessary for the preservation of the national spirit of Poland at that time and for the later emancipation of that country, is now outmoded. Rousseau's pedagogical intention, however, is reputable enough – to concentrate the pupil's attention on those matters in which he may be expected to show interest and knowledge, his own land and his own people. Unfortunately, such a method does nothing to discourage chauvinism.

Rousseau recognises in this treatise the importance and recommends the inclusion of physical exercises, emphasising their moral value and the social training to be derived from participation in common games. He cites with approval an arrangement at Berne by which pupils acquire a training for the public duties which will later fall to their lot. Of intellectual studies there is practically no mention, the whole scheme being planned to develop a national character. Education should be virtually free, and teaching should not be a profession but rather a civic duty undertaken at the outset of a career of public service. The administration of education was to be under the control of a council of magistrates, as advocated by Plato in the *Laws* and as earlier practised in Sparta. Throughout the *Considerations on the Government of Poland* Rousseau, as he repeatedly does in *Émile*, reverts to the tradition of the ancients when he is required to give practical form to his proposals, for, as he maintains in *Émile*, 'the ancients are nearer to nature and their genius is more distinct.'

Some time between the publication of *Émile* and his flight from England, that is, between 1762 and 1767, Rousseau had prepared a *Comparison between Public and Private Education*.[20] Had this been preserved, it would have been appropriately treated here and would have facilitated the transition from the national or civic conception of education presented in *Considerations on the Government of Poland* to the private or domestic view of education expounded in *La Nouvelle Héloïse* and in *Émile*. Rousseau himself had recognised that such a comparison was requisite in any complete system of education and had intended to incorporate it in a revised edition of *Émile*.

The private or domestic education presented in *La Nouvelle Héloïse*[21] is what we should call home education. Locke in his *Thoughts* had suggested, as stated above, that the principles determining physical upbringing 'might all be dispatched in this one short rule, namely, that gentlemen should use their children as the honest farmers and substantial yeomen do theirs'. This maxim Rousseau adopted and elaborated in *La Nouvelle Héloïse*, admitting as much when he says: 'Accustomed like the children of peasants to expose themselves to the heat and cold they grow as hardy; are equally capable of bearing the inclemencies of the weather; and become more robust as living more at their ease. This is the way to provide against the age of maturity, and the accidents of humanity.' The idyllic picture which in *La Nouvelle Héloïse* Rousseau delineates of the early education of her own two boys and her cousin's daughter at the hands of Madame de

Wolmar served as the model for Pestalozzi's *Leonard and Gertrude*, Pestalozzi merely making of necessity a virtue and transposing Rousseau's conception into the terms of an underprivileged class.

In *Émile* Rousseau distinguishes various stages in the pupil's development: (1) infancy characterised by habit and the training of the emotions; (2) childhood characterised by 'necessity' and the training of the senses; (3) boyhood characterised by 'utility' and the training of the intellect; (4) adolescence, the stage of 'morality' and of moral, aesthetic and social education. In *La Nouvelle Héloïse* he treats at greater length and in more detail of the childhood stage – 'till his understanding ripens', when the child will be placed under a tutor, as was Émile; but up to the age of understanding, which he puts much earlier than in *Émile*, namely, at six instead of at twelve years of age, Rousseau would in *La Nouvelle Héloïse* have the children educated at home by the mother, introducing even a girl cousin and approving of co-education, till the boys are of age to come under the care of a tutor, when the girl would become the special care of her instructress and be thereafter educated on quite other lines.

The fundamental principles of education set forth in *La Nouvelle Héloïse* are identical with those of *Émile*, *La Nouvelle Héloïse* for this reason being the natural and best introduction to *Émile*. Rousseau regards the original nature of the child as good, and he assumes an initial equality among pupils, inequalities being the result of intercourse with a perverted society. Education, he contends, is necessary – 'the best disposition must be cultivated' – and, like Plato, Rousseau believes that it cannot begin too early – 'the first and most important part of education, precisely that which all the world neglects, is that of preparing a child to receive education'. The aim of education is the liberty and happiness of the child, but Rousseau recognises that liberty and constraint are compatible, and does not attempt to minimise the influence of the 'heavy yoke of necessity' which nature lays upon the pupil at this stage. The education is an education through things, and it is a matter of indifference whether at twelve years of age or even at fifteen the pupil is totally ignorant of book knowledge. Throughout the whole work we have an eloquent plea for the predominance of environmental over hereditary influences.

Rousseau in *Émile* counsels us to live according to nature,[22] and in education to follow the order of nature.[23] But the views of education according to nature usually attributed to Rousseau have, we suggest, been derived not from his writings but rather from a sentimentalism which finds expression in the poetic effusions of Wordsworth. The fault is largely Rousseau's own: despite his conspicuously lucid style, he never gives a clear and explicit statement of what he means by 'nature'. For him it has several connotations. When he says that 'education comes to us from nature, from men, or from things',[24] he is regarding nature as equivalent to 'endowment' – the inherited disposition and capacities of the individual. Before our innate tendencies are warped by our prejudices, they are what Rousseau terms 'nature'.[25] Nature in this sense, the sense in which the same term is used by Aristotle, is beyond our control: 'Now some hold that we become good by nature, some we become so by habit, and others that it is by teaching. As to nature, that is clearly not in our power; it is something vouchsafed to the truly fortunate by some divine cause.'[26]

Education according to nature is frequently interpreted to mean nothing more than the spontaneous development of the innate dispositions of the child, nothing more than what modern psychologists term 'maturation'. Education according to nature, nature in the sense of endowment, leads to the non-interventionist policy in education, a hands-off procedure for which, however, there is no warrant in *Émile*. Education Rousseau may regard as an evil, but it is a necessary evil. In fact, he specifically warns us against such a misconception: 'Things would be worse without this education. . . . Under existing conditions a man left to himself from birth would be more a monster than the rest.'[27] Later he says:[28] 'When I want to train a natural man, I do not want to make him a savage and to send him back to the woods, but that living in the whirl of social life it is enough that he should not let himself be carried away by the passions and prejudices of men; let him see with his eyes and feel with his heart, let him own no sway but that of reason.' He repeats:[29] 'Émile is no savage to be banished to the desert, he is a savage who has to live in the town.' Rousseau's ideal is thus no Tarzan of the Apes.[30]

The second meaning attached to the term 'nature' in *Émile* is a negative one, a consequence of Rousseau's adoption of the anti-social attitude. Society, for Rousseau, is not a natural, but an artificial, product, the outcome of a contract. And for Rousseau what is natural is good, and what is conventional or artificial is evil. Nature and society thus become opposed to each other; nature is accordingly defined negatively to society. A natural or a negative education does not mean no education; it signifies simply a non-social education. Rousseau's natural or negative education thus becomes what we should call a preventive education; it is not a preparation for life but rather a preparation against the social conditions in which, Rousseau fully realises, Émile must later play his part. Gradually and sadly does he seek to disillusion Émile as to the wicked world into which he is born.

> Full soon the soul shall have its earthly freight
> And custom lie upon thee with a weight
> Heavy as frost and deep almost as life.

Rousseau does not aim at producing an unsocial creature; he hopes to establish in Émile an ethical constancy before his inevitable entrance into society. The ultimate aim is nevertheless to reconcile the natural and the social training: 'If their teaching conflicts, the scholar is ill-educated and will never be at peace with himself; if their teaching agrees, he goes straight to his goal, he lives at peace with himself, he is well-educated.'[31]

The third meaning attached by Rousseau to the term 'nature' is a positive one, inherited from the Stoics who in turn derived it from Plato.[32] Nature or the universe is governed by a divine providence. To live 'according to nature' is to live in accordance with the rational principle of the universe, to live according to reason; 'he who obeys his conscience is following nature.'[33] A divine will sets the universe in motion and gives life to nature; a divine intelligence exists 'not merely in the revolving heavens, not in the sun which gives us light, not in myself alone but in the sheep that grazes, the bird that flies, the stone that falls, and the leaf blown by the wind'.[34]

Not only is the ultimate principle of the universe spiritual, as idealism contends, but human nature is likewise spiritual and is not to be accounted for on mechanical or biological lines. 'For physics may explain', as Rousseau maintains in *The Origin of Inequality*,[35] 'in some measure the mechanism of the senses and the formation of ideas; but in the power of willing or rather of choosing, and in the feelings of this power, nothing is to be found but acts which are purely spiritual and wholly inexplicable by the laws of mechanism.' And whereas instinct may govern man in a state of nature, that is, before morality has emerged and men are bound by social ties, thereafter the voice of duty takes the place of physical impulses, and reason must be consulted before he listens to his inclinations.[36] Or, as Rousseau says in *Émile,*[37] 'Distrust instinct as soon as you cease to rely altogether upon it. Instinct was good while he acted under its guidance only; now that he is in the midst of human institutions, instinct is not to be trusted; it must not be destroyed, it must be controlled which is perhaps a more difficult matter.'

Rousseau is almost universally regarded as a naturalist in philosophy, the result of a superficial rendering of 'living according to nature', whereas from the interpretation given above and from the articles of faith formulated in the 'Creed of a Savoyard Priest' he is manifestly an idealist. He serves as the bridge between the Stoics and Kant.[38] *Émile* is likewise not a work on individual education, as might at first sight be inferred, but actually propounds a universal system. At the outset of *Émile* he states that education comes from nature, from men or from things, that is, the problem of education is the relationship of man to his physical and social environment. Emphasis may be laid either on the individual or on the social aspect of education. 'Two conflicting types of educational systems spring from these conflicting aims. One is public and common to many, the other private and domestic.'[39] If Rousseau refers the reader of *Émile* to Plato's *Republic* for an account of public education, it is because he himself had evidently studied the *Republic* not without profit. In *Émile*, however, he professes to restrict himself to 'the education of the home',[40] but the scheme he there presents is a scheme suited not to one individual only but to all; it is a universal scheme, and for this reason has become the fount of democratic education.[41] Many of the features nevertheless contribute to obscure this fact. The introduction of the individual pupil suggests the contrary interpretation, but it was merely the exigencies of exposition that compelled him to particularise and personify his principles in Émile; as Rousseau himself warns us: 'Lest my book should be unduly bulky I have been content to state those principles the truth of which is self-evident. But as to the rules which call for proof I have applied them to Émile or to others, and I have shown in very great detail how my theories may be put into practice. Such at least is my plan.'[42] And elaborating this literary technique he adds: 'At first I have said little about Émile, for my earliest maxims of education, though very different from those generally accepted, are so plain that it is hard for a man of sense to refuse to accept them, but, as I advance, my scholar . . . appears upon the scene more frequently, and towards the end I never lose sight of him for a moment.' Rousseau maintains too that we must look at the general rather than the particular, and consider our scholar as man in the abstract;[43] he further explains: 'I have discarded as artificial what belongs to one nation and not to another, to one rank and not to another; and I have regarded as proper to mankind what was common to all, in any age, in any station, and in any nation whatsoever'.[44] He also believes in fitting a man's education to his real self, not to what is no part of him. That Rousseau is propounding a universal and not an individualist system is confirmed by his choice of a pupil: 'If I had my choice', he says,[45] 'I would take a child of ordinary mind. . . . It is ordinary people who have to be educated, and their education alone can serve as a pattern for the education of their fellows'; he repeats: 'I assumed that my pupil had neither surpassing genius nor a defective understanding. I chose him of an ordinary mind to show what education can do for man.' Another assumption postulated in regard to the pupil for whom Rousseau proposes to prescribe an education, is that he should be 'a strong, well-made, healthy child'. Rousseau would not undertake the care of a feeble sickly pupil, for a healthy body is not only a condition of a healthy mind, but also the basis of moral character. The ideal of the superman of Plato, Quintilian and others gives place with Rousseau to the ideal of the common or natural man; the great souls, he believes, can find their way alone.[46]

Further difficulties are created by Rousseau's selection of Émile from among the rich and by his introduction of a tutor for Émile. Rousseau's apology for choosing his scholar from among the rich is: 'we shall have made another man; the poor may come to manhood without our help'. And if Émile comes of a good family so much the better: 'he will be another victim snatched from prejudice'. He proposes to give the sons of the rich a natural education that whatever might befall them in later life they would be independent of fate or fortune. A more penetrating interpretation is that the education which Rousseau proposed would be accepted as suitable for the poor, whereas by demonstrating that it was quite appropriate for the children of the rich Rousseau established that it was an education for all. It is necessary to emphasise this fact, that Rousseau is expounding a universal system of education, for frequently *Émile* is regarded as an account of an individualistic scheme of education, and difficulty is thereby encountered in explaining how the democratic systems of Pestalozzi and others originated in *Émile*.

Although the intervention of the tutor recalls Locke's procedure in the *Thoughts Concerning Education*, Rousseau disclaims any similarity in standpoint: 'I have not the honour of educating a young gentleman.'[47] The introduction of the tutor is indeed something more than a mere literary expedient; it is, in fact, a stroke of genius on the part of Rousseau. There must be only one voice if the scheme proposed is to be an integrated whole. It may be mistaken but it will at least be consistent, whereas when the child is subject to two parents his education may be both mistaken and inconsistent; in fact, as is now recognised, it is the dissensions and estrangements of parents that constitute one of the most serious obstacles in the upbringing of some children, and Rousseau obviates this by placing Émile under the sole charge of a tutor, for whom he has the highest possible regard: 'A tutor! Oh how sublime a being!'

The anti-social bias of Rousseau, first enunciated in the *Discourse on the Arts and Sciences*, is reflected in *Émile* and divides the work into two contrasting sections – the natural or negative education up to adolescence, and thereafter the moral or social. Aristotle had declared in the *Politics*[48] that man is by nature a social or political animal and that the state is a creation of nature. In the perfect state, too, the good man would also be the good citizen.[49] For Rousseau, however, nature and society are eternally at strife – 'Forced to combat either nature or society, you must make your choice between the man and the citizen, you cannot train both'.[50] Rousseau should nevertheless have added 'at the same time', for *Émile* is an attempt first to train the man, then to train the citizen. The boy must be brought up to live well in his society, and not be corrupted by it, to be, in Kant's term, 'morally autonomous'.[51] 'Man's proper study', Rousseau explains,[52] 'is that of his relation to his environment. So long as he only knows that environment through his physical nature, he should study himself in relation to things; this is the business of childhood; when he begins to be aware of his moral nature, he should study himself in relation to his fellow men; this is the business of his whole life.' Again:[53] 'We are working in agreement with nature, and while she is shaping the physical man, we are striving to shape his moral being.' Thus the aim of education for Rousseau, as for Herbart later, was virtue or morality, the natural or physical education being but the preparatory stage.

The definite break, even direct opposition, between the natural or negative stage of education and the social or positive stage is the extreme instance of Rousseau's doctrine of the serial emergence of the faculties.[54] That it cannot be completely effected Rousseau is forced to confess:[55] 'I think it impossible to train a child up to the age of twelve in the midst of society without giving him some idea of the relations between one man and another, and of the morality of human actions. It is enough to delay the development of these ideas as long as possible, and when they can no longer be avoided to limit them to present needs, so that he may neither think himself master of everything nor do harm to others without knowing or caring.'[56] The impossibility of isolating Émile entirely from the moral and social order should have led Rousseau to revise his view of human development as demarcated into well-pronounced stages, but its retention is not without its compensations.

It necessitated the adoption of what has come to be known as the psychological standpoint in education. This is one of Rousseau's fundamental principles. 'My method', he says,[57] 'does not depend on my examples; it depends on the amount of a man's powers at different ages and the choice of occupations adapted to these powers.' 'There is a time for every kind of teaching and we ought to recognise it, and each has its own dangers to be avoided.'[58] 'Every stage, every station in life, has a perfection of its own.'[59] 'Childhood has its own ways of seeing, thinking and feeling.'[60]

The principle is also expressed negatively. 'We know nothing of childhood; and with our mistaken notions the further we advance the further we go astray. The wisest writers devote themselves to what a man ought to know, without asking what a child is capable of learning. They are always looking for the man in the child, without considering what he is before he becomes a man.'[61] 'Nothing is useful and good for him which is unbefitting his age.'[62] 'Beware of anticipating teaching which demands more maturity of mind.'[63] 'Man's lessons are mostly premature.'[64] Émile 'should remain in complete ignorance of those ideas which are beyond his grasp. My whole book is one continued argument in support of this fundamental principle of education.'[65] 'To make an imitation man of a boy is to corrupt him.' It will foster hypocrisy, and this, to Rousseau (though he was not free of it himself), was a deadly sin. One of the most remarkable properties of Rousseau is the shrewdness of his psychological insight.[66]

A consequence of the psychological standpoint was the acceptance of the 'participation' as opposed to the 'preparation' view of education.[67] Rousseau argued that the possibilities of each stage of life should be fully exploited before proceeding to the next stage, a principle assumed later by Froebel and Montessori, although generally associated with the name of Dewey. Thus Rousseau says:[68] 'What is to be thought of that cruel education which sacrifices the present to an uncertain future, that burdens a child with all sorts of restrictions and begins by making him miserable in order to prepare him for some far-off happiness which he may never enjoy?' Again:[69] 'What a poor sort of foresight to make a child wretched in the present with the more or less doubtful hope of making him happy at some future day.'[70]

The perfect adaptation to his capabilities of the tasks undertaken by the pupil creates interest, and Rousseau by providing for this anticipates Herbart's doctrine of interest[71] and its present-day equivalents, the Play Way and the Project Method. Thus Rousseau claims to be justified in saying of Émile:[72] 'Work or play are all one to him; his games are his work; he knows no difference.'

Education becomes for Rousseau a matter of guidance. In detailing the qualifications of the tutor he introduces the very term:[73] 'I prefer to call the man who has this knowledge master rather than teacher, since it is a question of guidance rather than instruction.' For the same reason Montessori later substitutes 'directress'. 'The art of teaching,' Rousseau further explains,[74] 'consists in making the pupil wish to learn.' Or negatively expressed:[75] 'We learn nothing from a lesson we detest.' He summarises his guidance programme for Émile in the statement:[76]

'Surround him with all the lessons you would have him learn without awaking his suspicions.'

'Mankind has its place in the sequence of things; childhood has its place in the sequence of human life; the man must be treated as a man and the child as a child. Give each his place.'[77] It was because Rousseau was the first to give the child his rightful place that *Émile* was characterised by Lord Morley as the charter of youthful deliverance,[78] and that led Frederika Macdonald to write:[79] 'Throughout Europe Rousseau's voice went proclaiming with even more resistless eloquence than it had proclaimed the *Rights of Man*, the *Rights of Childhood*. Harsh systems, founded on the old medieval doctrine of innate depravity, were overthrown. Before Pestalozzi, before Froebel, the author of *Émile* laid the foundation of our new theory of education, and taught the civilised world remorse and shame for the needless suffering and the quenched joy that throughout long ages had darkened the dawn of childhood.' Rousseau's own panegyric on childhood reads thus:[80] 'Love childhood, indulge its sports, its pleasures, its delightful instincts. Who has not sometimes regretted that age when laughter was ever on the lips, and when the heart was ever at peace? Why rob these innocents of the joys which pass so quickly, of that precious gift which they cannot abuse? Why fill with bitterness the fleeting days of early childhood, days which will no more return for them than for you? Fathers, can you tell when death will call your children to him? Do not lay up sorrow for yourselves by robbing them of the short span which nature has allotted to them. As soon as they are aware of the joy of life, let them rejoice in it, so that whenever God calls them they may not die without having tasted the joy of life.'

What 'the delights of liberty' signify Rousseau explains in the statement: 'That man is truly free who desires what he is able to perform, and does what he desires. This is my fundamental maxim. Apply it to childhood, and all the rules of education spring from it.'[81] Rousseau's aim is 'a well-regulated liberty',[82] the same as that adopted later by Montessori. Rousseau is well aware of the distinction between liberty and licence, for he retorts to those who object to this aim: 'If such blundering thinkers fail to distinguish between liberty and licence, between a merry child and a spoilt darling, let them learn to discriminate'.[83] He would train his pupil to be 'as self-reliant as possible', whereas he contends that the ordinary educator 'teaches him everything except self-knowledge and self-control, the arts of life and happiness'.[84]

What simplifies the problem for Rousseau is his assumption of the innate goodness of the child. 'Man is by nature good', he says.[85] 'God makes all things good,'[86] and 'what is, is good.'[87] 'Our first impulses are always good.'[88] Locke had claimed that the mind instead of being by nature evil and desperately wicked was a clean slate. Rousseau goes further and maintains[89] 'that the first impulses of nature are always right; there is no original sin in the human heart, the how and the why of the entrance of every vice can be traced.' Dealing with the education of Sophie in book v, he repeats[90] that all our natural inclinations are right. This doctrine of the innate goodness of the child is inherited by Fichte, Hegel and Froebel,[91] and contrasts oddly with the modern psycho-analytic view of human nature. Without the reforming influences of education the individual, according to the psycho-analysts,[92] 'would remain a selfish, jealous, impulsive, aggressive, dirty, immodest, cruel, egocentric and conceited animal, inconsiderate of the needs of others, and unmindful of the complicated social and ethical standards that go to make a civilised society'.

If nevertheless we accept Rousseau's position and assume that our endowment is good and all our natural inclinations are right, the task of education should be simple; we have merely to fix the inborn propensities by habit, for, as Rousseau declares,[93] 'if the voice of instinct is not strengthened by habit, it soon dies'. Habit is all that is needed, as we have nature on our side, he says, speaking of Sophie's education.[94] Education, then, being but habit,[95] care must be taken to see that only right habits are established, and Rousseau issues his warning in the form of a paradox: 'The only habit', he says, 'the child should be allowed to contract is that of having no habits.'[96] Later he says of Émile:[97] 'No doubt he must submit to rules; but the chief rule is this – be able to break the rule if necessary.'

Commentators, heedless of Rousseau's warning[98] – 'I must admit that my words are often contradictory, but I do not think there is any contradiction in my ideas'[99] – have seized on Rousseau's apparently incompatible statements to score easy triumphs, but Rousseau's antinomy is resolved when we recognise that he distinguishes two types of habit, the natural and the social, and that while he advocates establishing natural habits – 'leave his body its natural habit' – he protests against making his pupil 'a mere slave of public opinion'.[100] Thus he explains:[101] 'Always distinguish between natural and acquired tendencies', and again:[102] 'The only useful habit for children is to be accustomed to submit without difficulty to necessity, and the only useful habit for man is to submit without difficulty to the rule of reason. Every other habit is a vice.'

To attain liberty education must act both negatively and positively. The negative training consists in restricting the child's desires, the positive in supplying the pupil with the strength he lacks so far as it is required for freedom, not for power.[103] Rousseau effects the former by keeping the child dependent on things. 'Keep the child dependent on things only' is his prescription. 'By this course of education you will have followed the order of nature.' 'There are two kinds of dependence; dependence on things which is the work of nature and dependence on men which is the work of society. Dependence on things, being non-moral, does no injury to liberty, and begets no vices, dependence on men, being out of order, gives rise to every kind of vice.'

Keeping the child dependent on things has two aspects – intellectual and moral. The intellectual aspect is the basis of Pestalozzi's *Anschauung* – the direct awareness of objects or the immediate experience of situations. Negatively it implies the postponement of book knowledge. 'Give your scholar no verbal lessons; he should be taught by experience alone.'[104] 'Reading is the curse of childhood. . . . When I thus get rid of children's lessons I get rid of the chief cause of their sorrow.'[105] 'I hate books; they only teach us to talk about things we know nothing about.'[106] 'I am pretty sure Émile will learn to read and write before he is ten, just because I care very little whether he can do so before he is fifteen.'[107] Languages he dismisses as among the useless lumber of education;[108] geography is only learning the map;[109] as a real knowledge of events cannot exist, apart from the knowledge of their causes and effects, history is beyond their grasp. And more generally he says:[110] 'I do not like verbal explanations. Young people pay little heed to them, nor do they remember them. Things! Things! I cannot repeat it too often. We lay too much stress upon words; we teachers babble, and our scholars follow our example.'[111] And he sums up:[112] 'Never substitute the symbol for the thing signified unless it is impossible to show the thing itself.'

The moral aspect of Rousseau's negative education consists not in teaching virtue or truth, but in preserving the heart from vice and from the spirit of error,[113] and takes the form of 'the discipline by natural consequences'. 'Children should never receive punishment as such,' recommends Rousseau,[114] 'it should always come as the natural consequence of their fault.' 'He must never act from obedience, but from necessity.'[115] Having removed Émile from parental care without conferring on the tutor the necessary authority over his pupil's conduct, the only control left to Rousseau that could be exercised, was the discipline by natural consequences. Nature and reason are for Rousseau, as they were for Locke, equivalent, but Rousseau failed to recognise what Locke did, that it was only when he reached the age of reason and could understand the workings of nature and the conventions of society that the child could be allowed to govern himself. Dewey agrees with Locke rather than with Rousseau, maintaining:[116] 'If a person cannot foresee the consequences of his act, and is not capable of understanding what he is told about its outcome by those with more experience it is impossible for him to act intelligently.'

Not only are there to be no direct moral lessons but there are also to be no indirect moral lessons. Thus in contrast to Plato, who advocated beginning with the false first, Rousseau protests against young children learning fables. 'Men may be taught by fables; children require the naked truth.'[117] The reason he adds is that the child is attracted by what is false and misses the truth, and the means adopted to make the teaching pleasant prevent him profiting by it. Rousseau does not, however, propose to proscribe fables altogether; he would merely postpone their introduction till such time as they could be properly understood and applied, that is, till the adolescent stage; 'the time of faults is the time for fables. When we blame the guilty under the cover of a story we instruct without offending him, and he then understands that the story is not untrue by means of the truth he finds in its application.'[118]

The importance of the negative aspect of education may be inferred from the statement that 'the most dangerous period in human life lies between birth and the age of twelve'[119] and from the attention Rousseau devotes to it. It is also a very onerous prescription for the tutor, for whom arranging the environment is much more difficult and time-consuming than making 'teaching statements' – a fact that teachers are still learning with difficulty.

The positive education of the childhood period comprises physical[120] and sensory[121] training. The physical education is modelled on that of Sparta. 'This was the education of the Spartans; they were not taught to stick to their books, they were taught to steal their dinners. Were they any the worse for it in after life? Ever ready for victory, they crushed their foes in every kind of warfare, and the prating Athenians were as much afraid of their words as of their blows.'[122] But for a temporary reinstatement by some of the early humanists this reversion to Greek practice initiated in Europe a new development in physical culture which had suffered from the medieval doctrine of the mortification of the flesh.

The importance of physical condition for the moral and mental training of the child is frequently insisted on by Rousseau. It is, as with Plato, 'the body for the sake of the soul'. Rousseau remarks: [123] 'A feeble body makes a feeble mind.' 'All wickedness comes from weakness.' 'The weaker the body, the more imperious its demands; the stronger it is, the better it obeys.' 'Would you cultivate your pupil's intelligence, cultivate the strength it is meant to control? Give his body constant exercise, make it strong and healthy, in order to make him good and wise; let him work, let him do things, let him run and shout, let him be always on the go; make a man of him in strength, and he will soon be a man of reason.' 'As he grows in health and strength he grows in wisdom and discernment. This is the way to attain to what is generally incompatible, strength of body and strength of mind, the reason of the philosopher and the vigour of the athlete.'[124]

The other aspect of the positive education during the age of childhood is the training of the senses. Man's first reason is, in Rousseau's opinion, a reason of sense experience. Our first teachers are our feet, hands and eyes. 'To substitute books for them does not teach us to reason, it teaches us to use the reason of others rather than our own; it teaches us to believe much and know little.'[125] Training the senses does not, however, for Rousseau consist in practising formal exercises; it implies judgment by their means in concrete situations encountered in life, and is accordingly not open to the objections which have been urged on psychological grounds against some doctrines of sensory training. Thus he proposes such tasks as determining whether a ladder is big enough to reach the cherries on a tree, whether a plank is long enough to bridge a stream, the length of line required for fishing or how much rope to construct a swing. In running races the distances are made unequal, and Émile has to estimate their length so that he may choose the shortest.

The main concern of earlier educators was to assist pupils to acquire the contents of a prescribed course of study. The outstanding feature of *Émile* is the complete abandonment of a predetermined curriculum. Émile was to be educated entirely through activities and by first-hand experience. Kant[126] claimed that he was effecting a Copernican revolution in metaphysics by assuming not that knowledge should conform to objects, but that objects should conform to our method of knowing. Rousseau's attempt to shift the centre of gravity from the curriculum to the child may be regarded as a parallel revolution in education. This new standpoint has been adopted by later writers, notably Pestalozzi and later Nunn:[127] 'The school must be thought of primarily not as a place where certain knowledge is learnt, but as a place where the young are disciplined in certain forms of activity, namely, those that are of greatest and most permanent significance in the wider world.' The Consultative Committee's Report on *The Primary School*[128] repeats: 'the curriculum is to be thought of in terms of activity and experience rather than of knowledge to be acquired and facts to be stored'.

Another surprising feature of *Émile* is the prolongation of childhood up to twelve years of age. The long preparatory period recalls Greek education, and could hardly be justified in a more complex age. Rousseau keeps protesting that he is not educating Émile but merely preparing him for education.[129] The art of teaching, at this stage, 'is to lose time and save it'.[130] 'Give nature time to work', he advises,[131] 'before you take over her business, lest you interfere with her dealings. You assert that you know the value of time and are afraid to waste it. You fail to perceive that it is a greater waste of time to use it ill than to do nothing, and that a child ill-taught is further from virtue than a child who has learnt nothing at all. . . . Do not be afraid, therefore, of this so-called idleness. What would you think of a man who refused to sleep lest he should waste part of his life? You would say, "He is mad; he is not enjoying his life, he is robbing himself of part of it; to avoid sleep he is hastening to his death.'' Remember that these two cases are alike, and that childhood is the sleep of reason.' The result that Rousseau expects from this course he formulates thus:[132] 'His ideas are few but precise, he knows nothing by rote but much by experience. If he reads our books worse than other children, he reads far better in the book of nature; his thoughts are not in his tongue but in his brain; he has less memory and more judgment; he can only speak one language, but he understands what he is saying, and if his speech is not so good as that of other children his deeds are better.' 'He has reached the perfection of childhood; he has lived the life of a child; his progress has not been bought at the price of his happiness; he has gained both.'

Now the ability to reason rapidly develops, and now, during the years of transition between childhood and adolescence, the boyhood stage between twelve and fifteen, the lost ground must be recovered and education accordingly speeded up. 'Time was long during early childhood; we only tried to pass our time for fear of using it ill; now it is the other way; we have not time enough for all that would be of use.'[133] Rousseau is accordingly compelled to restrict Émile's training to what is useful. 'What is the use of that? This is the sacred formula.'[134] 'This is the time for work, instruction and inquiry. And note that this is no arbitrary choice of mine, it is the way of nature herself.' The experiences must likewise be preselected and are not quite haphazard: 'Take care that all the experiments are connected together by a chain of reasoning, so that they may follow an orderly sequence in the mind.'[135]

The occupations rejected at the previous stage must now be reviewed in the light of the principle of utility and to those that stand the test Émile is to be introduced. They comprise practical science, geography and manual work. Rousseau accordingly plies Émile with concrete problems and engineers him into situations which challenge explanation. These satisfy the definition of the project – a practical problem in its natural setting. The aim is not 'to teach him the various sciences, but to give him a taste for them and methods of learning them when this taste is more mature'.[136] Against the formalism of abstract science Rousseau protests: 'The scientific atmosphere destroys science,'[137] 'among the many short cuts to science we badly need someone to teach us the art of learning with difficulty.' The apparatus Émile uses in his investigations is to be self-invented: 'We should make all our apparatus ourselves. . . . I would rather our apparatus was somewhat clumsy and imperfect, but our ideas clear as to what the apparatus ought to be, and the results to be obtained by means of it.'

The method which Rousseau recommends is commonly identified with the heuristic method. Rousseau's heurism nevertheless is not strictly a heuristic method; it is a method of discovery, but it does not necessitate following the order of the original discoverers. It is more akin to Dewey's experimental procedure. It is formulated thus:[138] 'Let him know nothing because you have told him, but because he has learnt it for himself.' 'You have not got to teach him truths so much as to show him how to set about discovering them for himself.'

Geography[139] is to be learnt by observation of natural phenomena. 'His geography will begin with the town he lives in and his father's country house, then the places between them, the rivers near them, and then the sun's aspect and how to find one's way by its aid. Let him make his own map, at first containing only two places; others may be added from time to time, as he is able to estimate their distance and position. You see at once what a good start we have given him by making his eye his compass.'

Like Locke, although for quite different reasons, Rousseau would prescribe a trade for his pupil. Locke[140] had proposed gardening or husbandry in general, and working in wood as carpenter, joiner or turner, these being fit and healthy recreations for a man of study or business. Rousseau requires Émile to learn a trade that with any change of fortune he might be independent economically, for its social value in recognising the dignity of labour, in helping him to overcome the prejudices which otherwise he would acquire, and to aid generally in training the mind.[141] 'In society', Rousseau maintains,[142] 'a man either lives at the cost of others or he owes them in labour the cost of his keep; there is no exception to this rule. . . . Man in society is bound to work; rich or poor, weak or strong, every idler is a thief.' 'Remember,' Rousseau counsels,[143] 'I demand no talent, only a trade, a genuine trade, a mere mechanical art, in which the hands work harder than the head, a trade which does not lead to fortune but makes you independent of her.' The trade which most completely satisfies Rousseau's demands is that of the carpenter: 'It is clean and useful; it may be carried on at home; it gives enough exercise; it calls for skill and industry, and while fashioning articles for everyday use, there is scope for elegance and taste.'[144] Not content with this, Rousseau contends that technical training has a transfer value:[145] 'If instead of making a child stick to his books I employ him in a workshop, his hands work for the development of his mind. While he fancies himself a workman, he is becoming a philosopher.' 'He must work like a peasant and think like a philosopher, if he is not to be as idle as a savage. The great secret of education is to use exercise of mind and body as relaxation one to another.'

The general principle governing Émile's education during these transition years is that of learning by doing. 'Teach by doing whenever you can, and only fall back upon words when doing is out of the question.' 'Let all the lessons of young people take the form of doing rather than talking; let them learn nothing from books which they can learn from experience.'[146] Books, as the vehicles of human and therefore artificial authority, are to be forbidden. There is only one exception – a significant one – the one book which to Rousseau's thinking 'supplies the best treatise on an education according to nature'. It is *Robinson Crusoe*. 'This is the first book Émile will read; for a long time it will form his whole library and it will always retain an honoured place. It will be the text to which all talks about natural science are but the commentary.'[147]

Émile's knowledge is still restricted to nature and things: 'The very name of history is unknown to him, along with metaphysics and morals. He knows the essential relations between men and things, but nothing of the moral relations between man and man.'[148] The résumé of his training up to fifteen runs thus: 'Having entered into possession of himself our child is now ready to cease to be a child. He is more than ever conscious of the necessity which makes him dependent on things. After exercising his body and his senses we have exercised his mind and his judgment. Finally we have joined together the use of his limbs and his faculties. We have made him a worker and a thinker; we have now to make him loving and tender-hearted, to perfect reason through feeling.'

To adolescence, 'the crown and coping-stone of education', Rousseau was doubtless the first great educator to devote special attention; he complains:[149] 'Works on education are crammed with wordy and unnecessary accounts of the imaginary duties of children; but there is not a word about the most important and most difficult part of their education, the crisis which forms the bridge between the child and the man'. The period when education is usually finished is, he insists, just the time to begin; it is our second birth, for 'we are born so to speak twice over; born into existence, and born a man.'[150]

Adolescent education is designed to prepare Émile for the moral and social order in which he must play his part. Instead of studying himself in relation to things he must now study himself in relation to his fellow-men:[151] 'As there is a fitting age for the study of the sciences, so there is a fitting age for the study of the ways of the world.'[152] 'We have reached the moral order at last; we have just taken the second step towards manhood.'[153] 'What then is required for the proper study of men? A great wish to know men, great impartiality of judgment, a heart sufficiently sensitive to understand every human passion, and calm enough to be free from passion. If there is any time in our life when this study is likely to be appreciated, it is this that I have chosen for Émile; before this time men would have been strangers to him; later on, he would have been like them.'[154]

Émile's earlier social contacts were restricted to casual encounters with village boys; there was occasionally co-operation with other youths, but no opportunity of companionship with boys of his own social class. There were visits to hospitals which would create disgust in Émile at mankind. The early education was largely a preparation against the hazards of life. It demanded estrangement from society. Émile was in the social order, but not of it. Rousseau had condemned Plato's communistic scheme, contending that the home was the best training ground for governing the state; he should have recognised that companionship with other boys of his own age would have been Émile's best preparation for associating with them in later manhood. Any social training Émile received was like learning to swim without going into the water, with the same result, as Dewey tells, to the youth so taught.[155]

Even the social training to which Rousseau would introduce Émile at the adolescent stage is to be acquired second-hand, through the experiences of others, in contrast to the early education which was to be first-hand. The hazards involved in participation are too great; people cannot be left to learn the laws by breaking them. In the moral sphere there may be no second chance; one mistake may only lead to another, not to its elimination; social training must be given in advance of the situation, for example, in matters of sex. Instruction before experience is the order here.[156] 'We must take the opposite way from that hitherto followed and instruct the youth rather through the experience of others than through our own.'[157] The attitude Rousseau would have Émile adopt, reads: 'I would have you so choose the company of a youth that he should think well of those among whom he lives, and I would have you so teach him to know the world that he should think ill of all that takes place in it. Let him know that man is by nature good, let him feel it, let him judge his neighbour by himself; but let him see how men are depraved and perverted by society; let him find the sources of all their vices in their preconceived opinions; let him be disposed to respect the individual, but to despise the multitude; let him see that all men wear almost the same mask, but let him also know that some faces are fairer than the mask that conceals them.'[158]

The moral training was not only to be at second-hand, but it was also to be indirect, through history, fables, etc. The studies which Rousseau had previously dismissed as premature and inappropriate are now reinstated; for the realistic subjects of the transition years the humanistic subjects are now substituted. There is, in fact, a complete inversion of the earlier education, just as Plato's higher education necessitated the conversion of the soul from the sensible to the intelligible aspects of the world.

This is accordingly the time to introduce the pupil to history: 'With its help he will read the hearts of men without any lessons in philosophy; with its help he will view them as a mere spectator, dispassionate and without prejudice; he will view them as their judge, not as their accomplice or their accuser.'[159]

Of the difficulties in turning history to moral account Rousseau is fully conscious. The first is that history records the evil rather than the good: 'It is revolutions and catastrophes that make history interesting; so long as a nation grows and prospers quietly in the tranquillity of a peaceful government, history says nothing. . . . History only makes them famous when they are on the downward path. . . . We only hear what is bad; the good is scarcely mentioned. Only the wicked become famous, the good are forgotten or laughed to scorn, and thus history, like philosophy, is for ever slandering mankind.'[160] In 'Crabbed Age and Youth' R. L. Stevenson echoes with a quite unfeigned satisfaction the same complaint.

A further difficulty which Rousseau recognises is that 'history shows us actions rather than men, because she only seizes men at certain chosen times in full dress; she only portrays the statesman when he is prepared to be seen; she does not follow him to his home, to his study, among his family and his friends; she only shows him in state; it is his clothes rather than himself that she describes.'[161]

Against the use of the figures of history as moral examples for the instruction of youth Morley has protested in the following terms: 'The subject of history is not the heart of man but the movements of society. Moreover the oracles of history are entirely dumb to one who seeks from them maxims for the shaping of daily conduct, or living instruction as to the motives, aims, caprices, capacities of self-restraint, self-sacrifice of those with whom the occasions of life bring us into contact.' Even this objection was foreseen by Rousseau: 'History in general is lacking because it only takes note of striking and clearly marked facts which may be fixed by names, places and dates; but the slow evolution of these facts, which cannot be noted in this way, still remains unknown. We often find in some battle, lost or won, the ostensible cause of a revolution which was inevitable before this battle took place. War only makes manifest events already determined by moral causes, which few historians can perceive.'[162]

The dilemma with which we are confronted in attempting to exploit history as a means of moral instruction is that the more scientifically history is treated the more is it regarded as a history of great movements and general tendencies, a matter of principles rather than of personalities, and the less adapted consequently does it become to provide moral examples; whereas, even assuming that the historical heroes are worthy moral examples, to secure biographical material for moral lessons we are compelled to distort the presentation of history. The choice is therefore between the incompatible alternatives, history or moral instruction.

These difficulties limit the field of choice, and Rousseau is reduced to commending the ancient writers of historical biographies, especially Plutarch, the modern biographies being too conventional.[163] The spectacles of history portrayed in such biographies are to serve the pupil sometimes as warnings, sometimes as forms of 'catharsis', as the vicarious expression of his own passions; thus 'the play of every human passion offers lessons to anyone who will study history to make himself wise and good at the expense of those who went before.'[164] The examples of history are thus not to be regarded as models for imitation, 'for he who begins to regard himself as a stranger will soon forget himself altogether'.[165]

In spite of all the care exercised on the training of the pupil it must need be that offences come. Their correction, Rousseau suggests, should be secured indirectly, not by corporal punishment, in which the corrective influence ceases with the pain, but by removal of privileges. 'The time of faults is the time for fables';[166] for 'when we blame the guilty under the cover of a story we instruct without offending him'. The moral of the fable should accordingly not be formulated. 'Nothing is so foolish and unwise as the moral at the end of most fables; as if the moral was not, or ought not to be, so clear in the fable itself that the reader cannot fail to perceive it.' But the best corrector is the father, and a close partnership ought to exist between him and his son's teacher.

Till now Émile has scarcely heard the name of God;[167] 'at fifteen he will not even know that he has a soul, at eighteen even he may not be ready to learn about it.'[168] Some instruction is now inevitable, Rousseau recognises, and this he formulates in the 'Creed of a Savoyard Priest'. Rousseau does not explain why a creed is advisable. It may be, as a modern writer puts it:[169] 'Definitions, formulae (some would add, creeds) have their use in any society, in that they restrain the ordinary intellectual man from making himself a public nuisance with his private opinions.'

The 'Creed of a Savoyard Priest' makes no pretext to be the theoretical formulation of the tenets of revealed religion, and the title is unfortunate. After relating the obstacles in the way of accepting any theological dogma Rousseau turns back to the book of nature. Rousseau's aim was to refute the materialistic philosophy of his age,[170] to re-establish the validity of the concepts of God, freedom and immortality, and to reaffirm the principles of right conduct. The materialists regarded matter as inert and lifeless; they postulated motion without accounting for its origin.

Rousseau, rejecting the idea of self-initiated or self-perpetuating motion, contended that voluntary action was the only type of motion of which we had direct experience, hence the first article of his creed: 'There is a will which sets the universe in motion and gives life to nature.'[171] As the universe is an orderly system, he is led to infer the second article of his creed – the proof of God's existence – from the well-known argument from design: 'If matter in motion points me to a will, matter in motion according to fixed law points me to an intelligence.'[172] And he adds:[173] 'This being who wills and can perform his will, this being active through his own powers, this being who moves the universe and orders all things, is what I call God.'

As man's will is determined by his judgment, and his judgment by his intelligence, the determining cause of action is in himself and he is accordingly free. Freedom, for Rousseau, is thus self-determinism. The third article of his creed is: Man is therefore free to act, and as such he is animated by an immaterial substance.[174]

Justice and goodness are inseparable, Rousseau claims,[175] for that love of order which creates order we call goodness, and that love of order which preserves order we call justice. 'Conscience', the voice of the soul, is the supreme expression of self-love, *amour de soi*. To redress the apparent disparity between justice and goodness in this life an infinite time is required; such is Rousseau's argument for the immortality of the soul. 'Had I no other proof of the nature of the soul, the triumph of the wicked and the oppression of the righteous in this world would be enough to convince me.'[176]

In support of his objections to innate ideas Locke cites instances to illustrate the diversity of human behaviour; Rousseau condemns this procedure, assailing those writers who, venturing to reject the clear and universal agreement of all peoples and setting aside this striking unanimity in the judgment of mankind, seek out some obscure exception known to them alone.[177] He challenges Montaigne to tell him if there is any country upon earth where it is a crime to keep one's plighted word, to be merciful, helpful and generous, where the good man is scorned and the traitor held in honour. Contrariwise, Rousseau emphasises the universality of the principles of good conduct and assumes an innate principle of goodness: 'Do you think there is anyone upon earth so depraved that he has never yielded to the temptation of well-doing?'[178]

The ultimate sanction of the moral laws[179] is to be found in religion, but after eloquently recounting the obstacles in the way of accepting any definite religious belief Rousseau turns again to the book of nature:[180] 'In this good and great volume I learn to serve and adore its Author. There is no excuse for not reading this book, for it speaks to all in a language they can understand.' Such is the method to be adopted in reasoning with Émile on religion. 'So long as we yield nothing to human authority nor to the prejudices of our native land, the light of reason alone, in a state of nature, can lead us no further than to natural religion; and this is as far as I should go with Émile. If he must have any other religion, I have no right to be his guide; he must choose for himself.'[181]

The 'Creed of a Savoyard Priest' is frequently regarded as an unwarranted interpolation in *Émile*, but a review of Rousseau's religious doctrines as expressed in this section of his work is necessary to make intelligible, or to justify, the postponement of religious instruction till the adolescent stage. If it is necessary for Émile to have an intelligent appreciation of the proofs of God's existence, of freedom and of immortality, then it is not to be wondered at that at fifteen he need not have heard the name of God nor even known that he had a soul. Rousseau has evidently ignored the fact that he is legislating for the ordinary man who takes his creed on trust and does not usually trouble to justify it on rational grounds.

In addition to instruction in ethics and religion, Rousseau would prescribe for the adolescent the study of aesthetics, the philosophy of the principles of taste. Rousseau's account of these principles is somewhat vague. It must take nature as its model, but can be exercised only in towns, where the products of art are to be found. Rousseau was fascinated by the theatre which he condemned: he even wrote for it successfully.[182] But this is not surprising when we remember the state of the development of the science of the beautiful at the time he wrote. The simplicity of taste which goes straight to the heart is, in Rousseau's opinion, only to be found in the classics,[183] and these Rousseau would employ for purposes of instruction in aesthetics as he previously had recommended them for instruction in morals.

During the critical period of adolescence Émile's physical

training is not neglected. He is required to engage in an occupation which keeps him busy, diligent and hard at work, an occupation which he may become passionately fond of, one to which he will devote himself entirely. For this purpose Rousseau recommends the chase,[184] although he does not even profess to justify the cruel passion of killing; it is enough that it serves to delay a more dangerous passion.

Because love of others is not instinctive, whereas sex is, Rousseau believes it necessary to prescribe for Émile direct moral exhortation on chastity, although he admits that he has had to abandon the task of giving examples of the form which the lessons should take. The general plan of sexual instruction he outlines in the following passage:[185] 'If instead of the empty precepts which are prematurely dinned into the ears of children, only to be scoffed at when the time comes when they might prove useful, if instead of this we bide our time, if we prepare the way for a hearing, if we then show him the laws of nature in all their truth, if we show him the sanction of these laws in the physical and moral evils which overtake those who neglect them, if while we speak to him of this great mystery of generation, we join to the idea of the pleasure which the author of nature has given to this act the idea of the duties of faithfulness and modesty which surround it, and redouble its charm while fulfilling its purpose; if we paint to him marriage, not only as the sweetest form of society, but also as the most sacred and inviolable of contracts, if we tell him plainly all the reasons which lead men to respect this sacred bond, and to pour hatred and curses upon him who dares to dishonour it; if we give him a true and terrible picture of the horrors of debauch, of its stupid brutality, of the downward road by which a first act of misconduct leads from bad to worse, and at last drags the sinner to his ruin; if, I say, we give him proofs that on a desire for chastity depend health, strength, courage, virtue, love itself, and all that is truly good for man – I maintain that this chastity will be so dear and so desirable in his eyes, that his mind will be ready to receive our teaching as to the way to preserve it; for so long as we are chaste we respect chastity; it is only when we have lost this virtue that we scorn it.'[186]

The sexual instinct must be, in the later terminology of Freud, 'sublimated' by directing it into socially acceptable activity, which serves others.[187] It should also be purified into affection for an ideal of true womanhood which Rousseau would picture for Émile with all the eloquence and emotion he could compass, and this ideal he would personify and assign to it a name, the name Sophie. Before, however, introducing Émile to Sophie, Rousseau considers it necessary to describe the education in accordance with which the wife of Émile should be trained.

Émile's education is not even yet complete. Between his betrothal to Sophie and his marriage he is required to travel, the object being that he should get to know mankind in general.[188]

The education of woman had by most early educators been treated much after the manner of Locke;[189] Rousseau, however, at least paid woman the compliment of realising that her education demands independent treatment, and for this alone must be forgiven much.

Rousseau was congenitally even more unfitted than most other men to understand woman, and his views are accordingly even more contradictory. In his earliest writings his belief was that the hand that rocks the cradle rules the world; thus in the *Discourse on the Arts and Sciences* he maintains that men will always be what women choose to make them, and, in the *Discourse on the Origin of Inequality*, addressing 'the amiable and virtuous daughters of Geneva' he repeats: 'It will always be the lot of your sex to govern ours. . . . Continue, therefore, always to be what you are, the chaste guardians of our morals, and the sweet security for our peace.' Disillusioned, nevertheless, by his somewhat unfortunate experience of the sex, he came to modify his views and in *La Nouvelle Héloïse and Émile* to emphasise the training of the heart rather than of the head; the aim of woman's life as expressed in these works might be summed up in the popular precept, slightly modified: be good, sweet maid, and let who will, be clever. And for the place of woman in the scheme of things Rousseau might have quoted Milton to the effect that God made woman for marriage but marriage for man.[190] Thus in *La Nouvelle Héloïse*[191] Rousseau explains: 'Husband and wife were designed to live together but not to live in the same manner. They ought to act in concert, but not to do the same things. The kind of life which would delight the one would be insupportable to the other; the inclinations which nature has given them are as different as the occupations she has assigned them; they differ in their amusements as much as in their duties. In a word, each contributes to the common good by different ways, and the proper distribution of their several cares and employment is the strongest tie that cements their union.' In *Émile* he repeats:[192] 'The man should be strong and active; the woman should be weak and passive.' 'A man seeks to serve, a woman seeks to please; the one needs knowledge, the other taste'; ' "what will people think" is the grave of a man's virtue and the throne of a woman's'; and he even goes the length of affirming that woman is made for man's delight.[193] He wavers once, and admits the frailty of the male when he concedes: What is most wanted in a woman is gentleness; formed to obey a creature so imperfect as man, she should early learn to submit to injustice and to suffer the wrongs inflicted on her by her husband without complaint; she must be gentle for her own sake, not his.[194]

As men and women have different vocations, their education must be different: 'When once it is proved that men and women are and ought to be unlike in constitution and in temperament, it follows that their education must be different.'[195] Women's education is to be planned in relation to, and to be made subservient to, that of man. Its aim is: 'To be pleasing in his sight, to win his respect and love, to train him in childhood, to tend him in manhood, to counsel and console, to make his life pleasant and happy, these are the duties of women for all time, and that is what she should be taught while she is young.'[196] The woman's education is also conditioned by the fact that she never attains the age of reason; she is a case of arrested development! 'If women could discover principles and if men had as good heads for detail, they would be mutually independent.'[197] 'The search for abstract and speculative truths, for principles and axioms in science, for all that tends to wide generalisation, is beyond a woman's grasp; their studies should be thoroughly practical. It is their business to apply the principles discovered by men, it is their place to make the observations which lead men to discover those principles:'[198] 'Speaking generally if it is desirable to restrict a man's studies to what is useful, this is even more necessary for women, whose life, though less laborious, should be even more industrious and more uniformly employed in a variety of duties, so that one talent should not be encouraged at the expense of others.'

That Sophie's physical training should be different from that of Émile is understandable, the one aiming at grace, the other at strength,[199] but it is inexcusable to infer that since little boys should not learn to read, still less should little girls, and most ungallant to add the reason – most of them make a bad use of the fateful knowledge. As there is nothing so obviously useful, nothing which needs so much practice or gives so much opportunity for error as cyphering, it should precede reading.[200] The general principle to be followed in the education of girls is: 'Show the sense of the tasks you set your little girls, but keep them busy.'

The antithesis between the training of Émile and that of Sophie is strikingly illustrated with regard to religion. As Émile was considered incapable of forming any true idea of religion till adolescence, that was regarded as sufficient justification of the postponement of his religious teaching till this late stage; from the same premise Rousseau infers that we cannot speak of religion too soon to little girls, 'for if we wait till they are ready for a serious discussion of these deep subjects, we should be in danger of never speaking of religion at all'.[201] And he adds:[202] 'When you teach religion to little girls never make it gloomy or tiresome, never make it a task or a duty, and therefore never give them anything to learn by heart, not even their prayers. . . . It does not matter that a girl should learn her religion young but it does matter that she should learn it thoroughly, and still more that she should learn to love it.'

Sophie's religion is to be reasonable and simple, with few doctrines and fewer observances,[203] and the confession of faith which Rousseau formulates for her is simpler and more appropriate than that of the Savoyard Priest prescribed for Émile: 'There is a judge of human fate, that we are all His children, that He bids us all be just, He bids us love one another, He bids us be kindly and merciful, He bids us keep our word with all men, even with our enemies and His; we must know that the apparent happiness of this world is naught; that there is another life to come in which this Supreme Being will be the rewarder of the just and judge of the unjust.'

Two contrasted and almost contradictory schemes of education have been presented by Rousseau for Émile and for Sophie, but for individuals with similar natural endowment who, although their functions in society may be different, must nevertheless abide each other, some compromise would be necessary; the rational system of training Émile would have to be tempered by the somewhat conventional training of Sophie, if they were ever to live happily together. But Rousseau's scheme for the education of women ought properly to be regarded historically: his prescriptions – and proscriptions – ring strangely in modern ears.

Although Rousseau's books profited from the revival of interest in the Romantic imagination and were avidly read in France and Germany, his educational ideas were comparatively slow to achieve practical expression. He was deeply disappointed that the comprehensive scheme he drew up for national education in Poland was never adopted. The first attempt to teach by his theories was made in Germany by Johann Basedow (1724–90), who was so enthusiastic a disciple that he named his daughter Émilie. In the period immediately after the publication of his ideas reaction was much stronger than approval: he was so virulently attacked by the authorities that he felt obliged to quit France.

By degrees, however, his suggestions were adopted and put into practice by men who were themselves to exercise wide and profound influence. Rousseau's influence on his contemporaries may be assessed by Kant's confession.[204] 'I am by disposition an inquirer. I feel the consuming thirst for knowledge, the eager unrest to advance ever further, and the delights of discovery. There was a time when I believed that this is what confers real dignity upon human life, and I despised the common people who knew nothing. Rousseau has set me right. This imagined advantage vanishes. I learn to honour men, and should regard myself as of much less use than the common labourer, if I did not believe that my philosophy will restore to all men the common rights of humanity.' And the arresting impression made on the intelligentsia of Rousseau's own day by the publication of *Émile* may be inferred from the incident that only once did Kant miss his daily constitutional, namely, on the day when *Émile* arrived; the work so engrossed him that he read it to the end without a break.[205] The popular reception accorded it was just the reverse – it was condemned by the Archbishop of Paris immediately after publication as an irreligious work and ordered to be torn and burnt in Paris by the Public Executioner. Such a contradiction is only paralleled by Rousseau's own writings and in his life.

The liberty in which he believed was in fact a 'well-regulated' one, but what came to be remembered and repeated were his panegyrics, which had no qualifications: 'to renounce liberty is to renounce being a man, to surrender the rights of humanity and even its duties'.[206] On such statements, and on the belief, contrary to the Christian doctrine of original sin, that man is by nature good, were founded the beliefs of the French Revolution, which was to transform Western civilisation.

Not however immediately, at least in education. Authoritarianism maintained its position throughout most of the nineteenth century, and the work of many pioneer educators like Homer Lane and John Dewey was still required to transfer the focus of attention to the child, and look at educational problems from his point of view. Now that progressive education has triumphed in so many national systems, it is interesting to reflect that its most cherished features – child-centring, spontaneous activity, education by stages, the need for practice and the power of example, a determination to achieve all-round balance which produces anti-intellectualism on occasion – everything, indeed, except the fostering of the 'social virtues' and the liberation of women can be traced directly to the seminal ideas of Jean-Jacques Rousseau.[207] He stands to modern education as Plato to ancient education; the heading of almost every chapter in *The Schools of Tomorrow*[208] is a quotation from Rousseau.

8
Pestalozzi

JOHANN Heinrich Pestalozzi[1] was born in Zurich in 1746, into a family with social standing but little money. His father, a surgeon, died when he was five, and he was brought up by his mother and a faithful servant, Barbara Schmid;[2] it is not surprising that all his writings stress the importance of the maternal bond and the natural goodness of mankind. His consistent aim of improving the state of human society probably owed much to the attachment he formed to his grandfather, Andreas Pestalozzi, a pastor at Höngg with a lifelong record of social service.

He was sixteen when *Émile* and *The Social Contract* were published, and he was powerfully influenced in his most formative years by the ideas of Rousseau, notably his concept of 'natural education', his preference for practical rather than book learning, and the attention he paid to psychological development. Pestalozzi regarded the Genevan as 'the turning-point between the old and the new worlds of education'.[3]

His career, apparently a record of failure, was nevertheless remarkably influential. He never ceased to stand supremely self-confident in face of adversity, and the world, towards the end of his life, came to rate him more on his own valuation than that earned by some of his experiments: 'in his lifetime he was as much a legend as was, for example, Albert Schweitzer in the first half of this century'.[4] Undoubtedly he showed a streak of genius in recognising, well ahead of his time, the features of modern education, and sublime perseverance in the face of repeated rebuffs. Moreover, he had a singularly winsome nature, which attracted a devoted wife, Anna, eight years older than himself, and a succession of disciples of considerable skill; their contribution to the success of his methods ought never to be underestimated.

His career may be seen in five parts: (1) *The Neuhof ('New Farm'), 1774–80*. Intended for the ministry, then the law, he found that his advanced views precluded a public career, and settled in 1767 for farming, a decline in social status. After the failure of an attempt to farm by experimental methods, he and his wife, early in 1774, took in about a score of poor children for a simple education according to his theories. Some thrived, others exploited him, and the experiment was a financial failure.

(2) *Writing period, 1780–98*. Almost destitute at times, with an ailing wife and a physical and mental weakling of a son, Pestalozzi carried out no practical experiments for almost twenty years; he devoted all his time, reluctantly, to writing. His most influential educational publications of this period were *The Evening Hours of a Hermit* (1780) and a novel, *Leonard and Gertrude* (1781). For all the success of the latter,[5] he regarded this as the saddest time of his life. For over a decade he busied himself producing economic, social and political books and articles.

(3) *Stans, 1798–9*. After Napoleon's invasion of Switzerland had laid waste much of the canton of Unterwalden, a children's home was founded in the convent at Stans, and Pestalozzi was given charge. Despite serious handicaps as the representative of an unpopular central authority and a Protestant in a Roman Catholic community, he felt his work to be prospering – 'it is succeeding, it is succeeding in every way'[6] – when the return of the French in June 1799 saw the convent abruptly taken over by the Swiss commissar as a hospital and the experiment, which had become something of a nuisance to the authorities, abandoned.

(4) *Burgdorf, 1800–4*. For several months, from July 1799, Pestalozzi taught with success in a small school at Burgdorf, north of Berne. A castle there was intended by the Swiss authorities to become an educational institute and teacher training centre under a young official named J. R. Fischer. When Fischer died before it could be opened, Pestalozzi was appointed head, assisted by the first of his talented helpers, Hermann Krüsi; his assistants, in fact, did almost all of the classroom teaching. A two-man commission which inspected the school in 1802 was greatly impressed, but Pestalozzi was a poor administrator, and an attempt to combine his institute with another at the nearby town of Hofwil run by

Daniel von Fellenberg quickly failed. In the autumn of 1804, declining invitations from several countries, Pestalozzi moved to (5) *Yverdon, 1804–25*. Here he became world-famous, largely through the force of his theories and the charm of his personality, but also with the practical help of men like Johannes Niederer and Joseph Schmid. Many visitors, including Herbart, came to see his work. But he found some of his assistants difficult to control: the freedom he allowed attracted adventurous men but made them ungovernable. Schmid left in a fury, and launched a virulent attack on the institution, to which Niederer replied. A few years later there was a reconciliation, and Schmid returned, but when he took over the practical administration, the discipline became harsh, and other teachers left. In 1825 he was dismissed and Pestalozzi went with him. Two years later, at the Neuhof, in his eighty-second year, the master died.

Among the Great Educators Pestalozzi cuts a sorry figure; he appears a man afflicted with new ideas which he found himself unable to formulate or to put effectively into practice. This he was himself the first to confess. In his *Swansong* (1826) he admits:[7] 'My lofty ideals were pre-eminently the product of a kind, well-meaning soul, inadequately endowed with the intellectual and practical capacity which might have helped considerably to further my heartfelt desire. It was the product of an extremely vivid imagination which in the stress of my daily life proved unable to produce any important results.' Pestalozzi was a simple and sensitive soul who arrived at his principles mostly by intuition; a worse expounder of his own doctrines could hardly be imagined. In one work he describes his educational ideal in the form of a romance; in another, he is, as Herbart says,[8] metamorphosed into a pedantic drillmaster in arithmetic pleased with himself for having filled a thick book with the multiplication table. It was nevertheless fortunate that his reputation attracted philosophers like Fichte and Herbart, who not only critically examined his system but also published their versions of it. In fact, no great European educator has ever had such a succession of distinguished visitors to his schools, and from their reports we can reconstruct a picture of the man and his work.[9]

Pestalozzi's aim in life was to ameliorate the lot of the poor. As Herbart commented:[10] 'The welfare of the people is Pestalozzi's aim. . . . He did not seek the wreath of merit in your mansions but in their hovels.' His humanitarianism was reinforced in early youth by his reading of Rousseau's works. While this aim restricted his outlook, it compelled him to concentrate on the fundamentals of education, for, as Herbart remarks, 'the most pressing needs are the more universal'.[11] Pestalozzi was thus forced to formulate a practical scheme of education suitable for all, and, in spite of himself, to lay the foundation of our elementary-school system. Of this he became dimly conscious towards the end of his days, for in the *Letters to Greaves* he states:[12] 'It [the end held out as the highest object of all man's efforts] must embrace all mankind, it must be applicable to all, without distinction of zones, or nations in which they may be born. It must acknowledge the rights of man in the fullest sense of the word. . . . They embrace the rightful claims of all classes to a general diffusion of useful knowledge, a careful development of the intellect, and judicious attention to all the faculties of man – physical, intellectual and moral'.

Echoing Rousseau's dictum 'Life is the trade I would teach him',[13] Pestalozzi maintains[14] that the ultimate end of education is not a perfection in the accomplishments of the school but fitness for life, and in *How Gertrude Teaches Her Children*[15] he elaborates: 'We have spelling schools, writing schools, catechism schools, and we want – men's schools'.

Pestalozzi's efforts to realise his aim were a succession of failures. In his *Ansichten und Erfahrungen*[16] he explains that in the Neuhof in 1774 he not only tried to find work for the poor children, but also wished to warm their hearts and to develop their minds, and through self-instruction to elevate them to a sense of the inner dignity and worth of their nature; he also acknowledges his failure, admitting that he took upon his own shoulders a burden which he could not bear and which he should have left to others, and thereby exhausted himself, plunged himself into domestic confusion and brought indescribable suffering on himself.

According to Pestalozzi himself, *The Evening Hours of a Hermit* (1780) was intended to serve as a preface to all that he should write in the future, his 'first but fundamental survey of man's destiny'. In it he warns parents not to hurry their children into working at things remote from their immediate interests, and after the manner of Rousseau, not to anticipate the regular course of their development. The danger lies in children's lessons dealing with words before they have encountered the actual things. Here

Pestalozzi gives expression to a rejection of verbolatry as pronounced as that of Rousseau, also to his doctrine of *Anschauung*, the equivalent of Rousseau's dependence on things. Hermann Krüsi, one of Pestalozzi's coadjutors, in *My Educational Recollections*,[17] writes how before his meeting with Pestalozzi at Burgdorf he held the system in high estimation which by dexterous questions could elicit answers from the children. He continues: 'Having read in educational writings that Socrates had possessed this faculty in a high degree, the term "to Socratize" presented to me an almost magic charm. When I communicated my views on this subject to Pestalozzi he could not refrain from a knowing smile. "This art," he then said quite earnestly, "when applied at the proper time and place, has its own value, but it is utterly worthless for teachers and children in the public schools. Socrates was surrounded by young men who had a background in the knowledge of words and things. If you take pains to give your children first this background, then the necessary questions about things within their own observation will be naturally suggested. Without this background every attempt to elicit proper answers from the children by artfully put questions is merely thrashing of straw, and leads to sore deception or discouragement which may even deprive you of faith in yourself." '[18]

Leonard and Gertrude describes how, mainly by means of education, the regeneration of a small community was effected by the noble efforts of a pious woman, the wife of a village mason in humble circumstances. In the village of Bonnal, the home of Leonard becomes the model educational institution, and Gertrude, the mother of the children, the ideal educator. This home-education represents Pestalozzi's ideal,[19] and it was only the circumstances in which he laboured that compelled him in practice to adopt class-teaching methods. These he regarded as a necessary but temporary expedient till mothers in sufficient numbers should be adequately educated to superintend the instruction of their own children.

As yet there was no formal analysis of *Anschauung*, but the 'contact with realities' for which Pestalozzi pleaded in his *Evening Hours of a Hermit* is exemplified in the procedure of Gertrude. 'Yet she never adopted the tone of instructor toward her children; she did not say to them: "Child, this is your head, your nose, your hand, your finger"; or "Where is your eye, your ear?" but instead she would say: "Come here, child, I will wash your little hands", "I will comb your hair", or "I will cut your finger nails". Her verbal instruction seemed to vanish in the spirit of her real activity, in which it always had its source. The result of her system was that each child was skilful, intelligent, and active to the full extent that his age and development allowed.

'The instruction she gave them in the rudiments of arithmetic was intimately connected with the realities of life. She taught them to count the number of steps from one end of the room to the other, and two of the rows of five panes each, in one of the windows, gave her an opportunity to unfold the decimal relations of numbers. She also made them count their threads while spinning, and the number of turns on the reel, when they wound the yarn into skeins. Above all, in every occupation of life she taught them an accurate and intelligent observation of common objects and the forces of nature.' In everything order must be seen to reign.

The Stans experiment (December 1798 to June 1799) illustrated the truth of his view that education should be based on love. 'Even before the spring sun had melted the snows from our mountains, my children were no longer recognisable.' The great human sympathy for children with which Pestalozzi was endowed in a singular degree had prevailed. But affection, even when it is reciprocal, is not enough; the pupil must be trained to independence. As Herbart insists:[20] something more than a love for a subject is required of the youth; a well balanced, many-sided interest is demanded.

The Burgdorf period,[21] which followed, produced *How Gertrude Teaches Her Children* or *Letters to Gessner* (1801) – Pestalozzi's most important treatise on educational method. Reviewing this work, Herbart states:[22] 'It is his intention to place in the hands of wholly ignorant teachers and parents such writings as they need only to cause the children to read off and learn by heart, without adding anything of their own. What he believed could be carried into effect most immediately he preferred; he must have his levers sturdy enough not to break even in clumsy hands. The book in which, under the form of letters to a friend, he describes the outlines of such a plan, belongs really in the hands of such men as have influence on the organisation of the lowest schools and upon parents of the lowest social ranks. Such men would be able to spread his actual school books which are to be published in the future. What is faulty in the whole publication therefore is, perhaps, its title which brings it immediately into the hands of women, of mothers.'

Pestalozzi's intention, as he himself conceived it,[23] was to discover the nature of teaching itself, to found popular instruction on psychological principles, to produce a general methodology of instruction based on a psychological ordered sequence. But his method was not based on psychological generalisation: he never lost sight of the needs of real children: 'Inasmuch as the method is positive, it bases itself directly on the individual child which it has in its care; indeed there is nothing positive in education and in teaching but the individual child and the individual talents he has'.[24]

Although the title and the form of Pestalozzi's chief work are unfortunate, it is nevertheless the main source of his contributions to the psychology, sociology and philosophy of education. Of the Pestalozzian method Herbart says:[25] 'Its peculiar merit consists in having laid hold more boldly and more zealously than any former method of the duty of building up the child's mind, of constructing in it a definite experience in the light of clear sense-perception, not acting as if the child had already an experience but taking care that he gets one. . . . The Pestalozzian method, therefore, is by no means qualified to crowd out any other method but to prepare the way for it. It takes care of the earliest age that is capable of receiving instruction.' Herbart here refers to Pestalozzi's conception of *Anschauung*, a term for which there is no precise English equivalent, and the early translations of which seriously prejudiced the acceptance of Pestalozzi's doctrines in this country.[26] By *Anschauung* is to be understood the mere awareness of objects or of situations. Terms used by English and American writers to convey the same idea include: simple apprehension, direct acquaintance, spontaneous appreciation, concrete experience, personal contact, first-hand impressions, face-to-face encounter, the direct impact of things and persons.

Anschauung is the basis of all knowledge and experience. Kant remarks: 'All thought . . . must directly or indirectly go back to *Anschauungen*,' and 'Whatever the process and the means may be by which knowledge refers to its objects, there is one that refers to them directly and forms the ultimate material of all thought, namely, *die Anschauungen*'.[27] *Anschauung* is not, however, restricted to mere awareness of objects; it comprises also spontaneous appreciation of moral actions and direct realisation of situations. It emphasises the immediacy of the experience, but does not imply simplicity in the process; negatively it excludes the intervention of any object or process between the subject and his experience. Its primary purpose, for Pestalozzi, was to further the converse of man with his world.[28]

For Kant the forms of *Anschauung* were space and time. In his *Letters to Greaves*[29] Pestalozzi accepts Kant's classification. 'The relations and proportions of number and form constitute the natural measure of all those impressions which the mind receives from without. They are the measures, and comprehend the qualities of the material world; form being the measure of space and number the measure of time.' Earlier, and generally, he distinguished three aspects of *Anschauung*, namely, form, number and name. How he arrived at this division he records as follows:[30] 'Living, but vague, ideas of the elements of instruction whirled about in my mind for a long time. . . . At last, like a *Deus ex machina*, came the thought – the means of making clear all knowledge gained by sense-impression comes from number, form and language. It suddenly seemed to throw a new light on what I was trying to do.

'Now, after my long struggle, or rather my wandering reverie, I aimed wholly and simply at finding out how a cultivated man behaves, and must behave, when he wishes to distinguish any object which appears misty and confused to his eyes, and gradually to make it clear to himself.

'In this case he will observe three things:

(*i*) How many, and what kinds of objects are before him.

(*ii*) Their appearance, form or outline.

(*iii*) Their names; how he may represent each of them by a sound or word.

'The result of this action in such a man manifestly presupposes the following ready-formed powers:

(*i*) The power of recognising unlike objects, according to the outline, and of representing to oneself what is contained within it.

(*ii*) That of stating the number of these objects, and representing them to himself as one or many.

(*iii*) That of representing objects, their number and form by speech, and making them unforgettable.

'I also thought number, form and language are, together, the elementary means of instruction, because the whole sum of the external properties of any object is comprised in its outline and its number, and is brought home to my consciousness through language. It must then be an immutable law of the technique of instruction to start from and work within this threefold principle:

(*i*) To teach children to look upon every subject that is brought before them as a unit, that is, as separated from those with which it is connected.

(*ii*) To teach them the form of every object, that is, its size and proportions.

(*iii*) As soon as possible to make them acquainted with all the words and names descriptive of objects known to them.

'And as the instruction of children should proceed from these three elementary points, it is evident that the first efforts of the technique of instruction should be directed to the primary faculties of counting, measuring, and speaking, which lie at the basis of all accurate knowledge of objects of sense. We should cultivate them with strictest psychological technique of instruction, endeavour to strengthen and make them strong and to bring them, as a means of development and culture, to the highest pitch of simplicity, consistency and harmony.'[31]

On Pestalozzi's analysis of *Anschauung* much criticism has been expended.[32] One of Herbart's earliest essays on education was devoted to a consideration of it – *Pestalozzis Idee eines ABC der Anschauung* (1802),[33] and Fichte dealt at some length with it in the ninth of his *Addresses to the German Nation* on 'The Starting Point that Actually Exists for the New National Education' (1807–8),[34] Herbart objecting mainly to Pestalozzi's treatment of form, preferring the triangle to the quadrilateral as the basic geometrical figure, Fichte to the treatment of language, and both to some of the applications of the Pestalozzian method. To the objection that colour is a primary datum of *Anschauung* and should have equal recognition with form, Herbart replies[35] that the cardinal fault of uneducated sight consists in adherence to colour. 'More exactly speaking, it consists in being immersed in the pre-eminent colour, in losing weaker colours at the instance of the stronger. Correctness of sense-perception which is opposed to this fault, consists in synthetically connecting everything that pertains to the form of the thing. It is attention to form to which our vision requires to be especially educated.'

Apprehension of form was developed by Pestalozzi mainly through drawing, on the ground that children are ready at an earlier age for knowledge of proportion and for the guidance of the slate-pencil than for guiding the pen and making tiny letters.[36]

Pestalozzi, in fact, built all power of doing, even the power of clear representation of all real objects, upon the early development of the ability to draw lines, angles, rectangles and curves.[37] Thus he states[38] that 'by exercises in lines, angles and curves, a readiness in gaining sense-impressions of all kinds is produced in the children, as well as skill of hand, of which the effect will be to make everything that comes within the sphere of their observation gradually clear and plain.' Against the tendency for the means to obscure the aim, and for drawing to become an end in itself, Pestalozzi protested,[39] saying 'Nature gives the child no lines, she only gives him things, and lines must be given him only in order that he may perceive things rightly. The things must not be taken from him in order that he may see only lines.' And concerning the danger of rejecting nature for the sake of lines, on another occasion he angrily exclaimed:[40] 'God forbid that I should overwhelm the human mind and harden it against natural sense-impressions, for the sake of these lines and of the technique of instruction, as idolatrous priests have overwhelmed it with superstitious teaching, and hardened it against natural sense-impressions.'

By basing writing on drawing, separating the acquisition of the forms from the command of the writing instrument, and using the skill acquired in writing for the expression of significant ideas[41] Pestalozzi anticipated in many points the Montessori method of teaching writing. The defect of his method, as in language teaching, is that he carried his analysis to its ultimate limits, whereas what is psychologically simple to the child is not necessarily what remains when analysis cannot be carried further; in writing, the unit is the word or the letter, not the so-called element of the letter.

Scope for the application of Pestalozzi's principle of concreteness was readily found in arithmetic, which was the subject most highly developed at Yverdon, thanks to a special talent in

Pestalozzi's assistant, Schmid.[42] Reviewing Krüsi's development as a teacher, Pestalozzi writes: 'For instance, when he asked in arithmetic, How many times is seven contained in sixty-three? the child had no real background for his answer, and must with great trouble dig it out of his memory. Now, by the plan of putting nine times seven objects before his eyes, and letting him count them as nine sevens standing together, he has not to think any more about this question; he knows from what he has already learnt, although he is asked for the first time, that seven is contained nine times in sixty-three. So it is in other departments of the method.'[43] The general principle of *Anschauung* as applied to arithmetic Pestalozzi formulated in these terms:[44] 'That by exercising children beginning to count with real objects, or at least with dots representing them, we lay the foundation of the whole of the science of arithmetic, and secure their future progress from error and confusion.'

Whereas experiment has demonstrated that the apprehension of number-forms can be facilitated by modifications of the arrangement of the units proposed by Pestalozzi, and objection has been taken to the various devices based on the Pestalozzian number pattern on the ground that they involve counting,[45] experience has but confirmed the general principle that the concrete representation of number is indispensable to the beginnings of the teaching of arithmetic.

With the language aspect of *Anschauung* Pestalozzi concerned himself more particularly, although he did not quite regard the name as co-ordinate in rank with form and number.[46] Fichte complains[47] that acquaintance with the word-sign adds nothing to the knowledge of an object but simply brings it within the sphere of what can be communicated to others. Herbart nevertheless comes again to the defence of Pestalozzi contending[48] that to young children a word, a name, is not as to us merely the sign of a thing. The word itself is the thing. They linger upon the sound. Not until the latter has become commonplace to them do they learn to forget it in attention to the thing itself. Pestalozzi reasoned that the child must learn to talk before he can be taught to read,[49] and recognised the child's need of a full and facile vocabulary. Thus he affirms:[50] 'The advantage of a fluent and early nomenclature is invaluable to children. The firm impression of names makes the things unforgettable, as soon as they are brought to their knowledge; and the stringing together of names in an order based upon reality and truth develops and maintains in them a consciousness of the real relation of things to each other. Certain it is that when a child has made the greater part of a scientific nomenclature his own, he enjoys through it at least the advantage that a child enjoys who in his home, a great house of business, daily becomes acquainted from his cradle upwards with the names of countless objects.' Pestalozzi does not propose that the child should acquire a stock of names merely for their own sake but as a means to the mastery of things, a function which the name has had from the earliest times. He complained[51] that in the lower schools for more than a century there had been given to empty words a weight in the human mind that not only hindered attention to the impressions of nature, but even destroyed man's inner susceptibility to these impressions. His own method, he explains,[52] was 'like nature with the savage, I always put the picture before the eye, and then sought for a word for the picture'.

Pestalozzi's insistence upon the need of a training in language as an indispensable preliminary to an adequate education moved Herbart to ask:[53] 'What stands so long and universally in the way of human education as lack of language? Who is more surely excluded from the benefits of instruction conferred in human conversation than he who neither knows how to choose the appropriate expression nor how to appreciate the force of an expression well invented? Does even the educated man ever come to the end of the study of language, the creatress of all conversation, all society?'

Pestalozzi reduced language to words or names, and the latter he resolved into sounds. For each stage he constructed formal exercises, beginning with syllables which he regarded as the irreducible elements. The first exercises took the form, for example, a – ab – bab, etc., much after the manner of the present-day phonic methods of teaching to read. Lists of names of the most important objects in all divisions of the kingdom of nature, history, geography, human callings and relations he required to be memorised, and lastly sentences had to be formed in various ways. Pestalozzi's analysis was carried to extremes and evoked censure; the redeeming feature of his method was nevertheless that it based reading on sounds and not on spelling, and thereby prepared the way for modern methods. On the ground of content, too, it was condemned both by Fichte[54] and by Herbart[55] for, in *The Mother's Book,*[56] Pestalozzi was misled into beginning with the child's body, arguing that the first object of the child's knowledge must be the child himself.

Notwithstanding such objections the value of *Anschauung* as the basis of instruction remains unimpaired. *Anschauungsunterricht* became an established element in the German school curriculum; in an emasculated form it functioned in nineteenth-century English education as the object lesson.

Immediate experience is generally confused and must be made definite; it must likewise be generalised. This requirement was expressed by Kant in the oft-quoted statement: 'Gedanken ohne Inhalt sind leer, Anschauungen ohne Begriffe sind blind' – 'Thoughts without content are empty, *Anschauungen* without concepts are blind.'[57] And Kant adds: 'Therefore it is equally necessary to make our concepts sensuous [that is, to add to them the object of immediate experience] as to make our immediate experiences intelligible [*sich verständlich*], that is, to bring them under concepts.' In his *Letters to Greaves*[58] Pestalozzi explains: 'But if a mother is to teach by things, she must recollect also that to the formation of an idea more is requisite than bringing the object before the senses. Its qualities must be explained; its origin must be accounted for; its parts must be described, and their relation to the whole ascertained; its use, its effects or consequences must be stated. All this must be done, at least, in a manner sufficiently clear and comprehensible to enable the child to distinguish the object from other objects, and to account for the distinction which is made.' More technically expressed: *Anschauungen* must be made distinct by analysis according to form, number and name; they must then be made clear, and, for Pestalozzi, they are clear when they can be described. The final stage is to make them definite, that is, able to be defined, for, as Pestalozzi explains, the power of describing usually precedes that of defining which formally implies referring an object to its genius or species.

In this progressive development no step must be missed. There must be no gaps in instruction. This is Pestalozzi's principle of the sequential organisation of knowledge, second in significance only to his doctrine of *Anschauung*. It was this feature of his teaching that appealed to and was championed by Herbart:[59] 'I had long held this feeling of a clear apprehension to be the sole and genuine spice of instruction, and a regularity of sequence perfect and adequate in all respects was to me the grand ideal in which I saw the thorough-going means for securing to all instruction its rightful effect. The main endeavour of Pestalozzi, as I was given to understand, was exactly the same; namely, to find this sequence, this arrangement and combination of all things which must be taught either simultaneously or successively. On the supposition that he had found it, or at least that he was on the right way thither, every unessential addition, every adventitious aid would be an injury. It would be reprehensible, because it would distract attention from the main point. If he has not found that sequence, it still remains to be found, or at least to be amended and continued. But even in that case his method is correct; at least to the extent of throwing out the injurious additions. Its laconic brevity is its essential merit. Not a useless word is heard in his school; the train of apperception is never interrupted. The teacher pronounces for the children constantly. Every faulty letter is expunged from the slate immediately. The child never dwells on its mistakes. The right track is never departed from; hence every moment marks progress.'

Although *How Gertrude Teaches Her Children* is mainly concerned with the nature and development of knowledge, Pestalozzi would not have it thought that this is the aim of education, for he says: 'To have knowledge without practical power, to have insight, and yet to be incapable of applying it in everyday life, what more dreadful fate could an unfriendly spirit devise for us.'[60] And Fichte adds:[61] 'All this part of education is but a means and a preliminary exercise for the second essential part, the civic and religious education.' Reviewing *How Gertrude Teaches Her Children*, Herbart observes:[62] 'Without doubt the most necessary instruction must be that which teaches man what he most needs to know. Now what is needful to us is needful either to our physical or our moral nature. We need it either as sensuous beings to enable us to live or we need it as beings in the social relations of citizenship, family life, and so forth, in order that we may know and do our duty. Agriculture, manufacturing, commerce and all other gainful art and science pertain to the first class; religion, ethics, notions of civic right and obligations belong to the second.' Herbart's classification might be said to represent the main aspects of education in Pestalozzi's earlier efforts, the ideal education comprising for him a general introduction to the various forms of handicraft and to simple social relations. In his later work he was nevertheless inclined to regard the requirements of education as three in number – the training of the hand, the head and the heart.

Of the threefold division of the educational process – the physical, the intellectual, the moral-religious – the first comprises not merely physical culture but also artistic skill and technical dexterity since all involve the physical organs. Its aim is essentially moral – to develop perseverance, courage and self-control. Fichte approves[63] of the inclusion by Pestalozzi of the development of the pupil's bodily powers, quoting a passage from *How Gertrude Teaches Her Children,*[64] but complains that Pestalozzi has failed to supply a graduated scheme of physical exercises, an omission Pestalozzi had himself deplored.[65] While mental development in general consists in the inner organisation of impressions received from without, art reverses the process in so far as it modifies the external world by means of inner impulses and tendencies. The basis of all art is partly internal, partly external; partly mental, partly physical. Artistic skill comprises the effort to embody the products of the human mind, to give expression to the impulses of the human heart, to exercise the dexterities required in domestic and social life. Such is Pestalozzi's view of art as expounded in the *Swansong.*[66] The development of technical skill follows the same laws as the development of knowledge.[67]

Although Pestalozzi, following Rousseau, believes that the child is born good,[68] we must nevertheless take his education out of the hands of blind nature,[69] as the world he enters is a world spoilt alike for the innocent enjoyment of the senses and for the feelings of his inner nature.[70] The moral faculty is present in infancy. 'God has given the child a spiritual nature, that is to say, He has implanted in him the voice of conscience; and He has done more, He has given him the faculty of attending to this voice.'[71] The moral virtues originate in the relations existing between the child and his mother; indeed, by the time a child came to school the most effective part of his moral education was already over. In family relations too lies the whole essence of the natural germ of that state of mind which is peculiar to human dependence on the Author of our being.[72] An ABC of *Anschauung*, but a special type of *Anschauung* – an analogous or inner *Anschauung* – is necessary, as is also a perfect gradation of methods for developing the soul and feelings, 'the essential purpose of which should be to use the advantage of instruction and its mechanism for the preservation of moral perfection, to prevent the selfishness of the reason by preserving the purity of the heart from error and one-sidedness; and, above all, to subordinate my sense-impressions to my convictions, my eagerness to my benevolence, and my benevolence to my righteous will.'[73]

Pestalozzi has been criticised for neglecting formal religious teaching. In fact, there was a programme of religious education at Yverdon, but Pestalozzi's interest in the improvement of human society on this earth inevitably led him to give pride of place to moral training.[74]

It is worth observing that he parted company with Rousseau on the subject of discipline. He was not prepared to leave correction to circumstances; he believed in the positive virtue of hard work. Moreover, when it could not be avoided, corporal punishment was permissible on one condition – the pupil must understand the reason for his punishment. He would not then resent it: 'There are occasions when corporal punishment is undoubtedly the best thing; but it must be carried out with the greatest assurance from a parental heart, and the teacher who really reaches the point where he can act in the same spirit as a father or mother should have the right to act as they do in certain important cases, which demand such measures.'[75]

In his earlier writings Pestalozzi stressed the equality rather than the correlation of his three main divisions of education: the physical, the intellectual and the ethico-religious; or, to elaborate these, the physical, the technical, the aesthetic, the intellectual, the moral and the religious aspects of personality. In his later writings he insists that the three aspects should be co-ordinated by one spiritual principle. Thus in the *Swansong* he definitely characterises the relationship between them as one of harmony. 'The education of all three sides of our nature proceeds on common lines in equal measure, as is necessary if the unity of our nature and the equilibrium of our powers are to be recognised from the outset.'[76] And in the *Letters to Greaves*:[77] 'The powers of man must be so cultivated that no one shall predominate at the expense of another, but each be excited to the true standard of activity; but this standard is the spiritual nature of man.'

Earlier in *How Gertrude Teaches Her Children* the idea of harmonious development was mentioned:[78] 'The aim of all instruction is, and can be, nothing but the development of human nature, by the harmonious cultivation of its powers and talents, and the promotion of manliness of life.' Emphasis on harmonious development or on well-balanced training, it need hardly be remarked in the case of Pestalozzi, should not blind us to the fact that education while suppressing idiosyncrasy should respect individuality. In the *Swansong* Pestalozzi – in opposition to Rousseau, who believed that the great souls could find their way alone – advises: 'Unusual capacity should be given every possible chance, and, above all, it should be rightly guided.' A further danger in the quotation from *How Gertrude Teaches Her Children*, from which Pestalozzi was delivered by reason of the poverty of his pupils, is that it may be interpreted to support a mere training of the mental faculties without regard to the social value of the training and the social situations which the pupil will later encounter.

The institution at Yverdon reached its peak of influence about 1809.[79] But the days of Pestalozzi's astonishing popularity were also the days of his greatest mental distress; dissension persisted among his staff with which, by reason of his administrative incapacity, he was unable to cope. This explains why Froebel's estimate of Pestalozzi's work is so much at variance with that of Herbart. It was the earlier efforts of Pestalozzi in the adverse circumstances at Burgdorf,[80] where any measure of success was commendable, that Herbart approved, whereas Froebel later encountered the more ambitious enterprise at Yverdon only to have his great expectations disappointed.[81] Writing of his first visit,[82] Froebel says: 'What I saw was to me at once elevating and depressing, arousing and also bewildering. . . . The disappointing side of the teaching plan, against which I intuitively rebelled, although my own tendencies on the subject were as yet so vague and dim, lay, in my opinion, in its incompleteness and one-sidedness. Several subjects of teaching and education highly important to the all-round harmonious development of a man seemed to me thrust far too much into the background, treated in stepmotherly fashion, and superficially worked out.' This conviction was but confirmed by Froebel's second visit to Yverdon.[83] 'The powerful, indefinable, stirring and uplifting effect produced by Pestalozzi when he spoke, set one's soul on fire for a higher, nobler life,' writes Froebel, 'although he had not made clear or sure the exact way towards it, nor indicated the means whereby to attain it. Thus did the power and many-sidedness of the educational effort make up for the deficiency in unity and comprehensiveness; and the love, the warmth, the stir of the whole, the human kindness and benevolence of it replaced the want of clearness, depth, thoroughness, extent, perseverance, and steadiness. . . . On the whole I passed a glorious time at Yverdon, elevated in tone, and critically decisive for my after life. At its close, however, I felt more clearly than ever the deficiency of inner unity and interdependence, as well as of outward comprehensiveness and thoroughness in the teaching there.'

Pestalozzi's efforts in education were tentative, and although lacking the scientific precision demanded today, they were in the broad sense of the term experimental.[84] His results had not that consistency which obtains in a purely *a priori* scheme of education, nor did they command that respect which attaches to the conclusion of a philosophical theory;[85] as the products of hard-won experience they nevertheless possess a reliability which many other more pretentious systems do not. With Pestalozzi it may truly be said that necessity was the mother of invention, and this he himself recognised when he prayed:[86] 'God, I thank Thee for my necessity.' It was this necessity that constrained him to make *Anschauung* the common starting-point of all instruction, to insist that teaching should follow an orderly sequence, to formulate a general method based on psychological principles, to stress the importance and skill of a professional scho lmaster, to recognise the practical and emotional aspects of personality and to reinforce the democratic tradition in education.

Pestalozzi, according to his assistant, Hermann Krüsi, was a source of inspiration, able to teach and to stimulate, but not to organise. He never established a system;[87] it is his practical ideas that have endured, a fact which would have given him enduring pleasure. He laid no claim to originality: he took the ideas of a pioneer, Rousseau, and showed how they might develop in practice. With him 'education was to become at the same time more human and more scientific'.[88] His ideas were often strikingly in advance of their time, free, for instance, of sentimentality. He did not subscribe to the fashionable theory of compensatory talents, but suggested, as modern research does, that to those who have is frequently given; the brilliant scholar is also the all-rounder. His insistence on the need to centre attention on the child has remained valid, though it was recognised very slowly, through all the changes in the world since his day. It was to be, for example, at the heart of the thinking of writers as diverse as Froebel and Dewey. The consequence was a psychological approach: he laid the same stress as Freud on the importance of the relationship between mother and child, and his concept of 'readiness' has long since become an educational cliché. His 'stages' of child development were to reappear in the work of Herbart and, more recently, that of his fellow-Swiss, Jean Piaget. His doctrine of *anschauung* reappeared in the 'object lesson'. It is not too much to claim that Pestalozzi, with his unremitting care for social democracy, laid the foundation for our elementary-school system.

9
Herbart

WHEN Johann Friedrich Herbart[1] was born in 1776 Rousseau was still alive; he died in 1841, only eighteen years before the birth of Dewey. As with so many of the 'Great Educators' the clue to many of his opinions is to be found in the details of his upbringing. His father, a judicial and administrative councillor in the small Hanoverian town of Oldenburg, was a diligent, rather frosty man, with no gift for radiating family warmth. By contrast, his mother, the energetic if charmless daughter of a local physician, had been 'born to command', and as long as she lived played an abnormally large part in her son's affairs: in 1794, when he went to the University of Jena at the age of eighteen, she insisted on accompanying him! Until he was twelve his education had been conducted at home by her and by a tutor, Hermann Uelzen, whose philosophical bent awoke an early interest in Herbart for ethics, metaphysics and psychology; the boy also displayed a remarkable memory and talent both for composing and performing music. For six years thereafter he attended the Latin school at Oldenburg; several years younger than most of his classmates, he proved zealous and successful in his studies.

Although his father probably intended him for the law, his own inclination and the prevailing intellectual climate in Jena turned him towards philosophy. The influence of Kant was still powerful, and Herbart found himself more in sympathy with the Kantian system than with that of his own professor, Fichte. From an early stage in his career he regarded himself as fundamentally a philosopher, his principal role a teacher of philosophy, and in these tasks he had no little conventional success. From 1802 to 1809 he taught in Göttingen, from 1809 to 1833 in Königsberg, from 1833 to 1841 in Göttingen again. Although his lectures were known to be far from easy, they were extremely popular, often crammed with visitors as well as his own students; when he died the latter walked with his cortège in torch-light procession to the graveyard. On the other hand he spent his professional career as a rebel against the idealism so fashionable in Germany in his time, and his work failed to impress men of influence like Goethe and Humboldt, the Prussian minister for education, whose adverse opinion probably cost him the chair on which he had set his heart, that once held by Hegel at Berlin.

In 1797, when he was twenty-one, he took a post in Switzerland as tutor to the three sons of Karl Friedrich von Steiger, Landvogt of Interlaken. During a stay of almost three years he met Pestalozzi and visited his establishment at Burgdorf. The experience had a profound effect on Herbart, planting a life long interest in education and reinforcing the attraction he had always felt towards the study of psychology. When he accepted the chair at Königsberg he stipulated that pedagogy should be included in his duties, and during all his twenty-four years there he ran a seminar in the subject, including a period of practical teaching. This seems, however, to have been 'the least successful of his enterprises',[2] perhaps because his own experience was restricted to work as a tutor with a handful of pupils: he remained unsatisfied, for example, with his own much-quoted ideas about discipline. He wrote copiously, though not lucidly. His most famous educational works were translated under the titles *Textbook of Psychology*[3] and *The Science of Education*.[4] In his own mind his pedagogy was no more than his philosophy in action; he would have regarded any attempt to separate the two as simplistic and inevitably false.

'Pedagogy as a science', says Herbart,[5] 'is based on ethics and on psychology. The former points out the aim of culture, the latter the way, the means and the obstacles.' Likewise in *The Application of Psychology to the Science of Education*: 'Education is related to ethics by the conception of the aim which the educator has in view. By the consideration of means and obstacles it is forced back on psychology.'[6] In *Observations of a Pedagogical Essay* he further explains: 'I have for twenty years employed metaphysics, mathematics, and side by side with them self-observation, experience and experiments, merely to find the foundations of true psychological insight. And the motive for these not entirely effortless investigations has been, and is, in the main my conviction that a large part of the enormous gaps in our pedagogical knowledge results from lack of psychology.'[7] As the negative or critical aspect of Herbart's psychology is better known in educational circles than the positive or constructive, we shall deal with it first.

Locke, as we have indicated in a previous chapter, had not only refuted the doctrine of innate ideas but had also challenged the existence of mental faculties. Herbart agreed in discarding mental faculties, and quite definitely rejected formal training. Stout[8] regarded Herbart's uncompromising polemic against innate faculties, activities and predispositions as the most striking negative feature of his psychology. 'The soul', says Herbart,[9] 'has no innate tendencies nor faculties.' Again,[10] 'it is an error, indeed, to look upon the human soul as an aggregate of all sorts of faculties.' Commenting on this rejection of the faculties Stout remarks: 'The human mind has always been prone to mistake abstractions for realities, even when the corresponding concretes stand out in clear and definite detail. This propensity becomes almost irresistible in a case in which concrete details are shadowy and evasive. Hence we find that the faculty psychologists, unable to make legitimate use of their generalisations in the explanation of particular phenomena, treated them as if they were real forces producing these phenomena. Thus in their hands psychology became transformed into a kind of mythology which was none the less mischievous because scarcely anyone overtly and explicitly professed to believe in it.'

On the training of the faculties Herbart in his *Brief Encyclopaedia of Practical Philosophy*[11] remarks: 'Those, however, who have no proper insight seldom grasp anything about the rules of education. They cling to the old idea that there are certain powers or faculties in the soul which have to be exercised, and it does not matter what they are exercised on. The exercises might well belong to the same category as gymnastic exercises, because men have only one kind of muscle, and by gymnastics the muscles of the body become strong and pliable. In actual fact every apperceptive system comprises elements of imagination, memory and reason, though naturally not all in equal proportions. In one and the same person there can quite easily be, and usually is, an apperceptive system composed predominantly of intellectual elements while another is rich in imagination, while in a third memory plays the greatest part. Intense feeling may colour one apperceptive system, whereas apathy characterises another. What educators call formal training is accordingly a complete chimera, since it presupposes the exercise of powers existing only in the imagination of those who hold such views on psychology.' And in the *Textbook of Psychology* he illustrates:[12] 'Memory and imagination agree in this, that in every man their special strength is limited to certain classes of subjects. For him who wishes geometrical imagination, exercises in the so-called art of poetry would be quite useless; and he who retains without any trouble the technical terms of a science which interests him, has often a bad memory for village gossip.'

Herbart is frequently accused not only of disposing of mental faculties but even of presenting us with 'a psychology without a soul'. Herbart could admit the charge, but would plead in extenuation that this was merely a methodological expedient. The soul was a metaphysical necessity, but it was only as it entertains presentations[13] and thereby becomes mind that psychology can profitably deal with it; 'we may regard the mind as the soul endowed with the power of presentation,'[14] he says, and,[15] 'so far as it possesses presentations or conceives, the soul is called mind; so far as it feels or desires it is called the heart'. At the outset of the *Textbook of Psychology* Herbart had explained: 'the treatise of psychology may very well be allowed to precede that on metaphysics, and in this way the metaphysical idea of the soul (the substance of the mind) may be dispensed with at first. By this, the beginner lightens his task, partly because he can tarry longer in the circle of experience, and partly because the manifold relations of psychology to morals, pedagogy, politics, philosophy of history and of art, heighten the interest in the study.' Stout,[16] however, notes that the incompatibility of the soul as a simple unitary entity and the mind as a concrete multiplicity escaped Herbart: 'in Herbart's procedure there is one – and only one – fundamental incoherence. His metaphysical speculation conducted him to the doctrine that the soul is an absolutely simple being; for psychological purposes he substituted, instead of the conception of simplicity, that of systematic totality. In doing so he was inconsistent, but the inconsistency was necessary and praiseworthy. Without it no psychology would have been possible for him.'

A further charge levelled against Herbart is the intellectualism of his psychology, ideas and their relation to one another being, it is said,[17] the sole origin of all other mental activities such as feeling and will. In his *Textbook of Psychology* Herbart nevertheless devotes a chapter to the 'Faculty of Feeling'.[18] There he explains that if we restrict our account of mental processes to presentations and their origin we are by no means able to indicate all that goes on in our minds; we must also consider feeling and desire. 'Feeling', he tells us,[19] 'is not a separate, independent faculty of the soul, but only a consequence of the mutual interaction of ideas.' In the mental life when a presentation in process of realising itself is inhibited by another presentation, an unpleasant feeling is aroused, but if its realisation is facilitated, pleasure ensues. Herbart distinguishes feelings from emotions, pointing out that the latter have a physical component, and, as he adds, act upon the body with remarkable, often dangerous, power; thus courage and timidity are very often dependent upon health and sickness.

Herbart's view of the integration of feeling and emotion with ideas has important consequences educationally. There can be no education of the feelings *per se*.[20] Herbart would accordingly not be content to rely for moral training on the emotionalism of Rousseau or the sentimentalism of Pestalozzi. He demands a surer foundation, and, as we shall see, finds it in 'the circle of thought'; as he himself puts it:[21] 'The disposition of the heart has its source in the mind.'

The intellectualism of Herbart's psychology is intensified by the ambiguity of the term *Empfindung* to signify both sensation and feeling. Thus in the introduction to *The Science of Education* he says that out of thoughts arise feelings (*Empfindungen*), and, from these, principles and modes of action. Professor Rein of Jena (1847–1929), the last of the great German Herbartians, explained the statement thus.[22] 'It is to be regretted that we Germans unfortunately employ the term *Empfindung* in two senses. First, we understand by it *Gefühl*, i.e. feeling – we speak of a man with fine *Empfindungen* (sensibility) and mean thereby a man with fine feelings. On the other hand we understand by *Empfindung* the mental reaction to an external stimulus, what the Englishman understands by sensation. Herbart here by *Empfindungen* was thinking of *Gefühl* (feeling) which can be so intimately and so vitally associated with presentations (*Vorstellungen*) that out of them arise volitional acts which, by reason of their comprehensiveness and worth, rank as principles or moral ideas. The circle of thought is, according to Herbart, no mere intellectual structure but is interwoven throughout with feelings and volitional impulses. The task of educative instruction is to anchor in the youth's soul this circle of thought.'

Herbart's positive contribution to psychology lies in the emphasis placed on the subjective factors in the mind, in the recognition of activities, not themselves in consciousness which form an integral functional part of mind.[23] Herbart's view of mind and his method differ from that of his English associationist predecessors. They regard mind as a succession of mutually exclusive mental states, and their method is the introspective. Herbart holds that mental states, while each has its own intrinsic quality, act and react on one another in manifold ways and constitute a single concrete system.

The English associationists also sought to formulate in a few simple laws – similarity, contrast, contiguity – the conditions under which certain mental experiences were revived or recalled: Herbart, on the other hand, sought to account for the disappearance of presentations from consciousness instead of for their reinstatement in consciousness. He posed the problem in these terms:[24] 'Our presentations recede from consciousness and return again. For which shall we seek explanation – the receding or the returning? The question must first be directed towards the former although in the past it is usual to discuss only the latter.' Herbart explains the disappearance of presentations from consciousness after this fashion.[25] To preserve his metaphysical concept of the soul as a unity Herbart concludes that contrary presentations of the same sensory modality, e.g. red and blue, sour and sweet, conflict and tend to suppress each other. The presentation that is repressed[26] is not annihilated, otherwise it could not later be recalled. What happens is that it is transmuted into a force,[27] becoming a tendency in the subconscious, the special feature of which is its constant striving to reassert itself in consciousness as a presentation. This is a condition of the reproduction of ideas. It should be added that a presentation once produced is never quite lost.[28]

Only antithetical presentations suffer eclipse and are resolved into subconscious mental activities. The reciprocal arrest does not arise with presentations of different sensory modalities, for example, with a tone and a colour, nor with presentations of different quality but compatible with one another, for example, with the several attributes which together constitute an object. Such a unity Herbart terms a 'complex', a term reintroduced later by Jung to characterise a constellation of ideas in the unconscious. Herbart's significant contribution to psychology is accordingly the recognition of a system of forces operating in the subconscious, in addition to presentations in the mind. Stout[29] designates the two spheres 'presentative activities' and 'presented content'.

Another conception which Herbart finds necessary to introduce is the threshold of consciousness (*Schwelle des Bewusstseins*). A presentation which is in consciousness is said to be *above* the threshold; if the arresting forces are just sufficient and no more than to secure eclipse, it is said to be *on* the threshold; if the forces of repression are sufficient to secure total eclipse, the presentation is said to be *below* the threshold. Herbart further distinguishes[30] the static threshold (*die statische Schwelle*) from the dynamical (*mechanische*) threshold. With the former the conditions of equilibrium of presentations are established and presentations below the static threshold are without influence on conscious processes: with the latter, equilibrium is not established, and presentations below the dynamical threshold operate as important factors in determining the course of events within consciousness. These two thresholds Ernest Jones claims correspond topographically with the position of Freud's two censorships; the former where an inhibited idea is robbed of its activity and can enter consciousness only when the inhibition is lifted; it is therefore not unlike a suppressed idea in the preconscious;[31] the latter type of threshold is where wholly repressed ideas are still in a state of rebellious activity and succeed in producing, e.g., feelings of oppression.

Presentations related together in the past tend to cohere and form what Herbart calls 'an apperception mass'. Such an organised system of presentations exercises a selective function, facilitating the assimilation of congruent ideas while reacting to exclude incompatible ideas. As Stout explains:[32] 'Attention and apperception reciprocally determine each other. It is through apperception that presentation acquires the significance and interest which enables it to attract attention. On the other hand the heightened intensity which accrues to it as an object of attention enables it to react with increased energy upon the mental system to which it belongs.' The modern psychologist[33] adds that the environment that the child encounters for intellectual growth is also in part conditioned by the inner organisation of the child's mind. Thus what we notice depends not so much on the strength of the external stimulus or on the susceptibility of the subject as on the context, the mental system[34] dominant at the time. This accounts for the fact that different people, or the same person at different times, have different perceptions under the same external conditions. As Herbart remarks of *Anschauung*:[35] even in the same surroundings every man has his own world. In literature the principle finds expression in various forms. Carlyle says: The eye sees what it brings the power to see; and Browning: 'Tis the taught already that profit by teaching.

Apperception thus emphasises the significant part that old knowledge plays in the acquisition of the new, how new knowledge should always be a development of previous knowledge. Stout[36] regards it as the main principle which psychology lends to the theory of education as its starting-point. James, on the other hand, in his *Talks to Teachers*,[37] to discount the exaggerated significance attributed to the principle at one time in American educational circles, contends that it means nothing more than the act of taking a thing into the mind, but how children take a thing into their minds is just what teachers would like to know. In fact, though Herbart, at the height of his fame, was most widely acclaimed for his doctrine of apperception, he did not rely as heavily on it as might be inferred.[38]

Following the precedent set by Herbart himself,[39] we shall proceed from this consideration of his psychology to deal with his educational doctrines before considering his ethics or 'practical' philosophy. Both were dependent on his pyschology, and precedence of publication was accorded to the *Allgemeine Pädagogik* since it suffered less from the lack of psychology.

Although psychology provides the means, philosophy dictates the end of education. While Herbart confesses that education has no time to make holiday till philosophical questions are once for all cleared up,[40] in the same work[41] he admits: 'To teach completely how life is determined by its two rulers, Speculation and Taste, we must seek for a system of philosophy, the keystone of instruction,' and he also claims[42] that the true perfection of education is philosophy.

In the opening sentences of *Abhandlung über die ästhetische Darstellung der Welt als das Hauptgeschäft der Erziehung* (Dissertation on the presentation of the world from the aesthetic standpoint as the main task of education)[43] he affirms: 'The one and the whole work of education may be summed up in the concept – morality.' But he goes on to explain that while morality is the *highest* aim, to set up morality as the *whole* aim of humanity and education an expansion of the concept is required, as is also a proof of its necessary presuppositions and the conditions of its actual possibility. And in the *Allgemeine Pädagogik* he repeats:[44] 'I therefore believe that the mode of consideration which places morality at the head is the most important, but not the only and all-embracing standpoint of education'. The aesthetic coherence of the world may also be regarded as the ideal of education.[45]

Neither ethics nor aesthetics can, however, determine fully the end of education. This Herbart admitted, although his admission has usually been ignored, both by his critics and by his expositors. Education must include the ideals of truth and of righteousness as well as of goodness and beauty. Intellectual inquiry and religious reverence are as natural to man and as necessary to him for the full realisation of his personality as are ethical endeavour and aesthetic enjoyment; and the aim of education as of life itself cannot be formulated in any more succinct phrase than that of Eucken, namely, to exalt personality.

Herbart is sometimes accused of ignoring the individuality of the pupil. In the *Umriss*[46] he nevertheless affirms that we need not go further than experience to see that there is a great diversity in intellectual talents, and in the introduction to that work declares that the assumption of unlimited plasticity is inadmissible and that the educability of the child is limited by his individuality. In the *Minor Pedagogical Works*[47] he says it is a chief requisite of a good pedagogical plan that it be flexible enough to fit the various capacities. What Herbart, however, seeks to avoid is that individuality should develop into eccentricity. Where this occurs, a state of society results in which 'each brags of his own individuality, and no one understands his fellows'.[48] It should also be noted that he does not, as did T. Percy Nunn[49] later, make the development of individuality the aim of education. Individuality is one of the data of education, not the end. It has to be fashioned into personality, and this is achieved through the development of a variety of interests and their integration.

Human activity, for Herbart, has two main aspects: many-sided interest and moral character. Many-sided interest is further qualified by 'well-balanced' – *gleichschwebende Vielseitigkeit.*[50] This is equivalent to the popular statement – the harmonious expansion of all the powers of the individual. Many-sidedness is opposed not only to one-sidedness but also to versatility;[51] it must be distinguished, Herbart says in the *Allgemeine Pädagogik,*[52] from its exaggeration – dabbling in many things.

Interest in its turn has two aspects – a subjective or psychological, and an objective. The objective comprises the various activities in which the individual participates or the different aspects of the environment, physical and social, to which he reacts; it consists of the two main divisions (1) knowledge and (2) sociability.[53]

Knowledge he classifies into (1) actual phenomena, (2) scientific laws, (3) aesthetic relations (or the empirical, the speculative and the aesthetic), representing different attitudes to our natural environment or different aspects of experience; and sociability into (1) individual, (2) civic and (3) religious, representing different attitudes in interpersonal relations or different aspects of our spiritual environment. These constitute the six facets of a many-sided interest, and when fully exploited provide a liberal training or an all-round education.

Existing mental contents originate from two main sources – experience and social participation.[54] Through experience we acquire knowledge, and through intercourse we develop social sensitivity. While we cannot dispense with experience and intercourse we must realise how limited are the opportunities which circumstances afford. They must be supplemented by instruction, for as Herbart claims,[55] experience seems, as it were, to expect that instruction will follow to analyse the material amassed and to collect and arrange the scattered and formless fragments. He thus sums up: 'Interest arises from interesting objects and occupations. Many-sided interest originates in the profusion of these. To create and develop this interest is the task of instruction which carries on and completes the preparation begun by intercourse and experience.'[56] Instruction alone, he adds,[57] can lay claim to cultivate a well-balanced, all-embracing many-sidedness. It is for this reason that Herbart keeps reiterating that he has no conception of education without instruction; conversely, he does not acknowledge any instruction which does not educate.[58] Instruction thus acquires the place of first importance in Herbart's educational theory. 'The chief means of positive education lies in instruction taken in its widest sense', he claims.[59] In *How Gertrude Teaches Her Children* Pestalozzi lamented that men do not apply their skill to found education upon principles and to bring instruction and education into harmony. The latter task is what Herbart, if anyone, has achieved. For Locke instruction was the least part of education: for Herbart it was the chief.

Not all instruction is, however, educative; the types of instruction which in Herbart's opinion[60] are not educative are those which afford only temporary excitement or light entertainment, and such studies as remain isolated and inert.

Instruction may take two main forms – synthetic and analytic.[61] The child's experience may be augmented through the teacher's description of events or activities; this is narrative instruction and, according to Herbart,[62] has but one law – to describe in such a way that the pupil believes he sees what is described. Or the teacher may avail himself of the pupil's experience, eliciting the facts which he requires for his exposition. These facts may have to be supplemented, but whether supplied by the teacher or the pupil they require to be organised according to the purpose the teacher has in view. Both these forms of exposition – narration and eduction – are classed by Herbart as synthetic. The pupil's experience may not only be inadequate; it may even be erroneous, in which case the teacher must dissect it to utilise the elements in a new systematic whole; this Herbart terms analytic instruction, and he adds:[63] 'The pupil ought properly to provide the material for analytic instruction, especially in later years.' The various forms of presentation or exposition are not mutually exclusive, but may be combined as occasion requires in the same lesson.[64]

Herbart in his *Allgemeine Pädagogik*[65] illustrates how the analytic and synthetic types of instruction may be employed in the respective fields of interest already enumerated – empirical, scientific, aesthetic, human, civic and religious, but his treatment, he acknowledges, is too general to provide a curriculum which must arrange the opportunities provided in accordance with the needs of the pupils and the talents of the individual teacher. Earlier, Herbart had suggested as a guide to the organisation of teaching material the principle of recapitulation, a doctrine which, common to many educators from Plato to Montessori and Dewey, plays a prominent part in Herbartian literature:[66] 'If pupils would continue the work of their forefathers they must have travelled the same way; above all, they must have learned to recognise these forefathers as their own from their early years.'

The interests which constitute the main divisions of education Herbart[67] reminds us are interests of one person, and he warns us: 'Do not forget interest among interesting things.' It is with the doctrine of interest in this sense, although it occupies only a minor place in his writings, rather than with the doctrine of instruction that Herbart's name has come to be associated in Britain and in America mainly through its exposition by Adams in his *Herbartian Psychology Applied to Education* and by Dewey in his early essay, 'Interest in relation to Training of the Will'. Even the aim of the project method, Kilpatrick admits,[68] is to reaffirm the old doctrine of interest.

The doctrine of interest is implied in a passage in Plato's *Republic*[69] quoted earlier. Rousseau in *Émile* had declared: 'Present interest, that is the motive power, the only motive power that takes us far and safely.' And in one of his *Letters to Greaves*,[70] Pestalozzi explains: 'This interest in study is the first thing which a teacher . . . should endeavour to keep alive. There are scarcely any circumstances in which a want of application in children does not proceed from a want of interest; and there are, perhaps, none under which a want of application in children does not originate in the mode of treatment adopted by the teacher. I would go so far as to lay it down as a rule that whenever children are inattentive and are apparently taking no interest in a lesson, the teacher should always first look to himself for the reason.' Herbart sums up Pestalozzi's complaint in the dictum that weariness is the cardinal sin of instruction,[71] and explains:[72] 'The word interest stands in general for that kind of mental activity which it is the business of instruction to create. Mere information does not suffice; for this we think of as a supply or store of facts which a person might possess or lack, and still remain the same being. But he who lays hold of this information, and reaches out for more, takes an interest in it.'

Interest is thus a concomitant of mental activity. Herbart is, however, no advocate of 'activity for activity's sake' even though it is mental activity, nor of 'activity leading to further activity'. 'Interest', he says,[73] 'means self-activity. But not all self-activity, only the right degree of the right kind is desirable, else lively children might very well be left to themselves. There would be no need to educate or control them. It is the purpose of instruction to give the right *direction* to their thoughts and impulses, to incline these toward the morally good and the true.' Interest he opposes to apathy. It displays a preference over mere perception for certain objects by arousing in the mind analogous presentations and involuntarily suppressing others. It differs from certain other mental processes by depending on its object and referring to the present.[74]

By requiring that interest should be a result of instruction we do not, as is popularly supposed, emasculate education; interest is not to be confused with amusement, and it is not for lack of warning by Herbart that their identification has gained currency. 'The teacher', he says,[75] 'should not be misled into turning instruction into play, nor designedly into work; he sees before him a serious business and tries to forward it with gentle but steady hand.' 'That which is too simple', he repeats,[76] 'must be avoided'; and again,[77] 'Instruction must be comprehensible and yet difficult rather than easy, otherwise it causes *ennui*', or, as his British expositor explains,[78] 'we find that so far from enervating the pupil, the principle of interest braces him up to endure all manner of drudgery and hard work. . . . The theory of interest does not propose to banish drudgery but only to make drudgery tolerable by giving it a meaning.'

'Interest depends partly on native capacity which the school cannot create; but it depends also on the subject-matter of instruction.'[79] Not only, however, on the selection of the appropriate subject-matter, but also on its arrangement. We must know both what we are teaching and how to teach it.

When presentations arise spontaneously in the pupil's mind, the pupils are said to be attentive, and the instruction has an interest for them.[80] When attention had to be enforced, it is doubtful whether an interest in the subject can ever be evoked. Or, as A. N. Whitehead says in *The Aims of Education*:[81] 'In training a child to activity of thought, above all things we must beware of what I will call "inert ideas" – that is to say, ideas that are merely received into the mind without being utilised, or tested, or thrown into fresh combinations'. The distinction between 'animate' as against what might be called 'inanimate' knowledge is not absolute, for the knowledge generally regarded as inanimate can become animate if the teacher relates it to some topic that has real significance for the pupil; as Herbart explains:[82] 'Presentations that must by effort be raised into consciousness because they do not rise spontaneously, may become spontaneous by gradual strengthening. But this development we cannot count on, unless instruction, advancing step by step, brings it about.'

Knowledge is likewise likely to be inanimate if it remains detached or dissociated from a general system of ideas. In his *Umriss* Herbart warns us – 'If the facts of knowledge are allowed to fall asunder. . . .instruction endangers the whole of education.'[83] And Whitehead elaborates:[84] 'The results of teaching small parts of a large number of subjects is the passive reception of disconnected ideas, not illuminated with any spark of vitality. Let the main ideas which are introduced into a child's education be few and important, and let them be thrown into every combination possible.' As whatever remains isolated has little significance, Herbart emphasises the correlation of studies.[85]

No matter what subject-matter is selected or what method of exposition – analytic or synthetic – is adopted, the same sequence must be followed in instruction if interest is to ensue. Herbart insisted that teaching procedure should be adapted to the stages discernible in the learning process. He first distinguished two phases – an intensive and an extensive. *Vertiefung* – concentration on, or to be engrossed in, a subject – and *Besinnung* – integration and organisation of the results of *Vertiefung*.[86] In one of his *Aphorisms*[87] he explains that *Vertiefung* – concentration – occurs when a thought so dominates the mind that it suppresses the usual contents of consciousness, and *Besinnung* – organisation – when the usual contents assert themselves and incorporate the new; integration is essential not only to organise the effects of concentration but also to prevent a lopsided development.

As these two concepts are too general for practical purposes

Herbart finds it necessary to subdivide concentration into clearness and association, and organisation into system and method. Clearness, association, system and method thus become Herbart's formal steps in teaching,[88] under one name or another: Herbart's nomenclature was not always consistent.

'In order always to maintain the mind's coherence', he contends,[89] 'instruction must follow the rule of giving equal weight in every smallest possible group of its objects to concentration and reflection; that is to say, it must care equally and in regular succession for clearness of every particular, for association of the manifold, for organising what is associated, and for a certain practice in expansion through this arrangement. Upon this depends the distinctness which must rule in all that is taught.'

Under clearness Herbart includes the analysis and synthesis of the given. It is equivalent to the so-called Herbartian step of presentation. Through association the new knowledge presented to the pupil is connected with the old; and association accordingly implies the apperceptive process and is analogous to the preparation stage of the Herbartian five formal steps. Its purpose is to secure a proper orientation of the subject to be taught. 'For association', Herbart tells us,[90] 'the best mode of procedure is informal conversation, because it gives the pupil an opportunity to test and to change the accidental union of his thoughts, to multiply the links of connection, and to assimilate, after his own fashion, what he has learned. It enables him, besides, to do at least a part of all this in any way that happens to be the easiest and most convenient.' Association prepares the way for system, which is 'the perfect order of a copious co-ordination'. 'By exhibiting and emphasising the leading principles', Herbart adds, 'system impresses upon the minds of pupils the value of organised knowledge.'[91] In the Herbartian tradition system is termed generalisation. Furthermore, a system is not to be learned merely, it is to be used, applied, and often needs to be supplemented by additions inserted at appropriate places.[92] This application Herbart terms 'method' whereas by his successors the self-explanatory term 'application' has been appropriated to denote the extension of the formulated principle.

These various steps are believed by Herbart to be requisite, one by one, in the order given for every section small or large, of subjects to be taught.[93] While various educationists have attempted to substantiate this claim,[94] the procedure can be said to be valid only for that form of instruction which Herbart had mainly in view, the aim of which is the acquisition of knowledge; when the aim of the lesson is the development of skill, a different procedure will doubtless be found to be more appropriate.

Herbart's formal steps apply to method-wholes, instructional units or centres of interest, not to individual lessons, that is, they are stages in the exposition of a topic which has a unity and completeness in itself. It was the mechanical application of the formal steps in each and every lesson that brought the Herbartian method into discredit, and for this formalism there was no warrant in the writings of Herbart.

In introducing the concept of many-sidedness of interest Herbart had intimated that one aspect of human activity was being neglected, namely, action, and, what immediately impels thereto – desire.[95] The two spheres of human activity are accordingly interest and desire, knowing and willing. They are nevertheless not unconnected, being linked through instruction.[96] Just as instruction creates a many-sided interest, so it has also the task of developing what from the standpoint of character training Herbart now calls 'the circle of thought'. The section dealing with the influence of the circle of thought on character[97] is the central point of the *Allgemeine Pädogogik*: it is, in Herbart's own words,[98] the vantage point from which the whole should be viewed.

Herbart's firm conviction is that the chief seat of the cultivation of character lies in the circle of thought and that in the formation of the circle of thought the main business of education consists.[99] Character training, he claims,[100] is unable to accomplish its work unless in conjunction with instruction. 'It will be seen when the task of setting forth the whole of virtue is reviewed in its completeness that the main things are accomplished by instruction.'[101] In the Introduction to the *Allgemeine Pädagogik* he affirms:[102] 'Those only wield the full power of education who know how to cultivate in the youthful soul a large circle of thought closely connected in all its parts, possessing the power of overcoming what is unfavourable in the environment, and of dissolving and absorbing into itself all that is favourable.' In his reply to Jackmann's review he repeats: 'Instruction will above all form the circle of thought and education the character. The latter is nothing without the former – herein is contained the whole sum of my pedagogy'; and in his *Brief Encyclopaedia* [103] he takes credit for introducing the term 'an educative instruction'. This principle of the determination of the inner aspect of character by means of instruction is Herbart's chief contribution to educational thought, and proves how futile it is from his standpoint to oppose education or the training of character to instruction. 'Moral education', he sums up, [104] 'is not separable from education as a whole.'

While instruction is thus the central theme of Herbart's doctrine he never allows us to forget that man's worth lies not in his knowing but in his willing. [105] Before, however, proceeding with the task of harmonising the ethical endowment of the pupil with the moral ideal Herbart disposes of a conception which, though he sometimes does not even regard it as a part of education, is a precondition of it, namely, *Regierung* (orderliness or teacher's control of pupil's behaviour). This is one of the three chief concepts, *Regierung* (orderliness), *Unterricht* (instruction), *Zucht* (character training or self-discipline), according to which his whole doctrine is treated. [106] 'It may be doubted', he explains, [107] 'whether the treatment of discipline in the sense of keeping order belongs to pedagogy or should not more appropriately be appended to those parts of practical philosophy which treat of authority in general.' He adds in the *Umriss* [108] that moral improvement is not brought about by the enforcement of authority, and that education can only begin after order has been restored. [109] Later on in the *Allgemeine Pädagogik* he nevertheless concedes [110] that orderliness may have both an indirect and a direct bearing on character; it partly helps to make that instruction possible which will influence the subsequent formation of character, and it serves to create through action or inaction a beginning of character. The separation of the concepts, as Herbart observes, [111] serves to aid the reflection of the educator who ought rather to know what he is about than make a perceptible difference between them in practice.

The distinction between *Regierung* and *Zucht* can be presented in a series of antitheses. The former serves primarily the needs of the teacher, the latter those of the pupil. 'To maintain quiet and order in the lessons, to banish every trace of disrespect to the teacher is the business of *Regierung*; direct action on the temperament of youth with a view to character training is *Zucht*.' [112] *Regierung* secures merely external conformity, whereas the work of *Zucht* is not to secure a certain mode of external behaviour but rather to develop insight and the appropriate volition in the mind of the pupil.[113] '*Regierung* takes into account the results of actions, later on *Zucht* must look to unexecuted intentions.'[114] *Regierung* is intermittent, whereas *Zucht* is persistent, lasting, slowly insinuating and only abating gradually.[115] The aim of *Regierung* lies in the present, whereas *Zucht* has in view the future adult.[116]

Discipline need not be repressive, and Herbart reviews the various means of maintaining order – supervision, the threat of punishment, compulsion – and concludes: when the environment is so arranged that childish activity can spontaneously discover the road to the useful and expend itself thereon, then discipline is most successful,[117] and in the *Umriss*[118] he sums up: the foundation of control consists in keeping children employed.

Regierung – control or restraint – is, as Herbart from his own experience as a tutor was forced to recognise,[119] a necessary evil, doubtless better than anarchy, but its defect is that it weakens while education seeks to strengthen. It is negative and inhibitive, whereas education should be positive and purposive. Although Herbart's main contribution to the history of school discipline in Britain and America has been through his doctrine of interest, his distinction between *Regierung* and *Zucht,* between good behaviour secured by administrative regulations and gentlemanly conduct exercised by voluntary self-restraint has significance in education, since the term 'discipline' is in English generally employed to convey what was by Herbart characterised as *Regierung.* A 'well-disciplined' school may be the worst possible institution for the development of character, since it may leave no opportunities to practise such actions as are initiated by the pupils' own motives nor afford occasion for the exercise of self-discovery and self-imposed discipline. It does not train the pupils to the right use of such freedom as they will later enjoy; it secures an immediate appearance of docility by paralysing the pupils' power of initiative, and it invites an equally violent reaction that destroys any unity of character that the pupils might otherwise develop. Discipline in Herbart's sense of *Zucht,* not in the sense of *Regierung,* should be the aim of every teacher who desires to play his part in the formation of character.[120]

Before dealing with character training Herbart has to dispel a confusion regarding transcendental freedom. Both Herbart and

Kant recognised that morality was the highest aim of mankind, and, accordingly, of education. Freedom is, however, the indispensable postulate of morality. For Kant the only principle that could determine the will without infringing its freedom was pure respect for the law. Any external influence, inclination or desire entering into the motive would deprive the moral law of its sanctity. If therefore pure respect for the law is the only valid motive in morality, the teacher's efforts to influence the character of his pupils would be stultified, for they would import into his pupils' decisions those empirical elements which Kant was at pains to exclude.

This was the dilemma that confronted Herbart. He rebutted it by distinguishing between, and retaining, both the metaphysical and the genetic views of freedom. He supports Kant's metaphysical justification of freedom:[121] Kant's axiom remains eternally true – no practical (moral) principle must require the actuality of any object whatever. Kant, who strictly opposes the empirical to the pure reason, is, he says, right. In the *Allgemeine Pädagogik* he adds.[122] 'It was certainly a mistake to *begin* ethics with this categorical imperative. The purely positive must here take precedence, and many things be unfolded in their relation and sequence which Kant had not thought of. But they who forget themselves so far as to desire the release of mankind from the categorical imperative make a still graver mistake.' The educator must adopt a different standpoint from that of the critical philosopher – for the teacher morality is an occurrence[123] – as Kant himself recognised in his lectures *On Education*.

Herbart rejected the transcendental freedom which implies the possibility of action without motives – 'the will that wills naught would be a self-contradiction'[124] – for this would make the pupil's choice arbitrary and wholly indifferent to the influence which education or environment might exert, and render futile all moral training: 'Not the slightest breath of transcendental freedom may blow through any cranny into the domain of character.'[125] But he did this without denying true freedom of the will for he declares:[126] 'Freedom is of the utmost direct importance to the formation of character, provided it issues in well-weighed and successful action.'[127] Education, he also states, would be tyranny if it did not lead to freedom. He concludes:[128] 'I must beg some readers not to identify inner freedom with *transcendental* freedom.'

The great paradox for Herbart, as for all educators, is to determine the child to the free choice of the good, to render freedom and discipline compatible. The educator is in this sense, as Herbart admits,[129] unavoidably a determinist. Kant in his lectures *On Education* recognised this difficulty: 'One of the great problems of education is how to unite submission to the necessary restraint with the child's capability of exercising his freewill – for restraint is necessary.' And Herbart confesses:[130] 'The author believes he will never be understood by those to whom the coexistence of determinism and morality is still a riddle.' The problem has been formulated by a modern French philosopher:[131] 'The task of the educator is a strange one: to act on mind and conscience in such a way as to render them capable of thinking and judging, of themselves, to determine initiative, arouse spontaneity, and fashion human beings into freedom.'

Just as there was an objective and a subjective aspect of the many-sided interest, so, for Herbart, there is an objective and a subjective side of moral character – that which determines, and that by which it suffers itself to be determined. But, as Herbart reminds us[132] both what determines and what is determinable have their origin in the circle of thought.

The objective aspect, that which determines the character, comprises the 'practical' or moral ideas. Instead of six types of interests, there are five moral ideas. These are (1) *Innere Freiheit* (inner freedom), (2) *Vollkommenheit* (perfection or proficiency), (3) *Wohlwollen* (benevolence), (4) *Recht* (justice), (5) *Billigkeit* (equity or retribution). The first two deal only with the form and not with the content of moral action; the other three lie at the base of social order. Distinguishing between inner freedom and transcendental freedom in *The Science of Education*[133] Herbart explains that we are conscious of the former whenever we force ourselves to do our duty against our inclinations. The idea of perfection, he states,[134] implies a high regard for both body and mind and their systematic cultivation; perfection nevertheless does not connote the complete realisation of the moral ideal but merely the proficiency with which the will is obeyed. Benevolence implies consideration of, or sensitiveness to, others. The idea of justice demands that the pupils abstain from contention, and the idea of equity is especially involved in cases where the pupil has merited punishment as requital for the intentional infliction of pain. This last moral idea of equity, he believes, is the one which has been most commonly overlooked, since it is concerned with something more than mere right.[135] The motto of right is 'To every man his own'; of equity, 'To every man what he deserves'.[136] Of these five moral ideas the first to be comprehended by children is perfection, the next right and equity, which they perceive in their relationships with each other. Concepts of benevolence and inner freedom are formed only slowly, and in some children may not appear at all.[137]

Virtue is the perfect conformity of the will to the moral ideas; duty is enjoined to overcome hindrances in the attainment of virtue. The moral ideal is, for Herbart, as it was for Plato, not a single virtue but a system of virtues.

Corresponding to the four formal steps in intellectual instruction are the four stages for training in corporate life; these are *Merken* (to register), *Erwarten* (to anticipate), *Fordern* (to desire), *Handeln* (to act).[138] Although Herbart affirms[139] that character is the embodiment of the will, he does not include the will as a separate function among the subjective aspects of character training. He is in this quite logical, for he had denied the existence in the mind of independent faculties and had likewise rejected the 'transcendental' freedom of the will. 'There is no such thing as an independent faculty of will.'[140] The will, for him, is not something apart from desire; 'action generated out of desire is will'.[141] The teacher's task is accordingly to assist the pupil to acquire the right desires, for when opportunity presents itself and the pupil realises that he can attain his end, action follows: 'will is desire combined with the assurance of the attainment of what is desired'.[142] This definition accords almost precisely with that given by a psychologist like Stout who defines volition as 'a desire qualified and defined by the judgment that so far as in us lies we shall bring about the attainment of the desired end because we desire it'.[143] The conviction that the desire is capable of fulfilment is based on the success attending previous efforts in similar circumstances, for 'from success springs the confidence of will whereby desire ripens into decision'.[144]

Volition has ultimately its roots in the circle of thought, not indeed in the details one knows, but certainly in the combinations and total effect of the acquired presentations.[145] Herbart further explains: the circle of thought comprises the contents that by stages can mount from interest to desire, and desire through its realisation in action constitutes volition. The whole inner activity, indeed, has its abode in the circle of thought.[146] As instruction forms the circle of thought it plays a part both in intellectual and in moral training: 'It will be seen that when the task of setting forth the whole of virtue is reviewed in its completeness the main things are accomplished by instruction.'[147] And the test of a perfect instruction, Herbart concludes,[148] 'is exactly this – that the store of knowledge and concepts which it has raised by clearness, association, system and method to the highest flexibility of thought is, by virtue of the complete interpenetration of all its parts, at the same time capable as an organisation of interests of compelling the will with its utmost energy. Because this is wanting culture is often the grave of character.'[149]

Educators previous to the time of Herbart had made the training of character the end of education while others had recognised the importance of instruction, but it was left to Herbart to connect instruction with character training through interest and to provide techniques based on psychological considerations for the attainment of both. He made the proper selection of the content of instruction and the right method of presenting the selected content moral duties incumbent on the teacher, and contributing factors to the achievement of the aim which he had envisaged.

It is a convention of literary criticism that when a writer dies his works immediately drop out of notice, but if they hold something of continuing value enjoy a revival within the next few decades. The fate of Herbart seems to extend this dictum classically in the field of education. For a quarter of a century after his death in 1841 his pedagogical ideas slipped into oblivion, but from the middle sixties, and especially the eighties, until the first decade of the twentieth century (and even later in some countries) they exerted major influence in Western Europe and the United States.

Part of this, as Dunkel has shown, is undoubtedly due to his followers, Professor Tuiskon Ziller of Leipzig and Wilhelm Rein, director of the practising school at Jena. Ziller's *Foundation of the Doctrine of Educational Instruction*,[150] published in 1865, is generally held to have launched the Herbartian movement, but it communicated Herbart's system through Ziller's eyes, and Rein amended it still further. The effect was to formulate doctrines acceptable to the 'advanced' educational thinking of the time, in short, to 'keep Herbart up to date'.

In his own day and immediately after his death, Herbart's influence was limited. His philosophical doctrines battled against the contemporary current, his books received consistently unfavourable reviews. His pedagogical ideas, which advocated an individualist approach, were unacceptable to Prussian authoritarianism; moreover, on the purely practical level, his seminars could not be demonstrated to have produced efficient teachers. Unlike Pestalozzi's, his rather chilly personality attracted no circle of faithful disciples. It was his ideas, particularly the 'five steps', the 'apperceptive mass' and the 'threshold of consciousness', that appealed to educationists of the late nineteenth century, and many of them were interpreted in ways Herbart would have repudiated. The steps are examples of this process: it was in Rein's fivefold system of Preparation, Presentation, Association, Generalisation and Application, not Herbart's tight, fourfold organisation, that they gained general approval, and then as a practical scheme for the planning of lessons rather than a psychological statement of the stages in the learning process.

In its amended form Herbartianism spread in the late eighties to the United States, where there was a National Herbart Society for the Scientific Study of Teaching;[151] Herbartian books by Charles DeGarmo and the brothers Charles and Frank McMurry became educational best-sellers. Dunkel suggests, plausibly, that Americans, in a period of rapid expansion, adopted the theory because it was both academically respectable and practically simple. In the first decade of the twentieth century, however, when the new pedagogical doctrines of 'child-centring' and 'learning before teaching' began to hold sway, Herbartian theory quickly faded. The name was dropped in 1902 from the title of the National Society, and within a year or two the doctrine was dead.

In Britain the movement's influence persisted longer. By far the most influential publication was *The Herbartian Psychology Applied to Education*, by John (later Sir John) Adams, a writer of great felicity and influence.[152] The practical aid offered to embryo teachers by Rein's version of Herbartianism appealed greatly in the training colleges,[153] and Herbart was still an important name in college education departments in Britain at the outbreak of the Second World War, thanks in some degree to the influence of books like Adams's and the early editions of this present volume.

10
Froebel

FRIEDRICH Froebel[1] was the last of the group of Swiss and German educators who, in the last half of the eighteenth century and the first quarter of the nineteenth, transformed Western education. He was born in Thuringia in 1782, and, like Comenius, lost his parents when he was young. Brought up by an uncle, he had an unremarkable career in the village school of Stadt-Ilm; indeed, dreamy and uninterested, he was generally regarded as rather backward. From 1797 to 1799 he was apprenticed to a forester, and found in the peace of the Thuringian woodland a setting ideally suited to his contemplative temperament; it was then, he believed, that he formulated his philosophy of the unity of all nature, after an experience as mystical and powerful in its own way as that of St Ignatius of Loyola two and a half centuries before. Like Ignatius he felt grossly undereducated for his life's work, and he enrolled in the University of Jena to study natural science. Unfortunately, being very short of funds, he was imprisoned for a small debt and had to leave the university. At home in Thuringia, he took a succession of jobs – surveyor, accountant, private secretary – and at the same time educated himself.

In his early twenties he again attempted formal education, studying architecture at Frankfurt-on-Main. There he met the director of a model school run on the lines laid down by Pestalozzi, and accepted a post in it. From 1807 to 1809 he went on to work at Yverdon, and absorbed many of the Swiss pioneer's ideas, but he found them deficient in the natural science he advocated. His educational apprenticeship was interrupted in 1813 by the War of Liberation, in which he fought as a soldier in Lützow's corps. It was to be a rewarding experience, for he met two young men,

Langethal and Middendorf, who were to become his faithful followers.

After a short period as curator of a museum of mineralogy in Berlin, he set up his first school in 1816 at Griesheim on the Ilm. Shortly afterwards he moved to Keilhau in his native Thuringia, where he and his disciples married and formed a new educational community. In time, despite lengthy periods of hardship, his experiments won acceptance: the Swiss Government sent young teachers to learn his methods, and he moved to Burgdorf, thirty years after Pestalozzi had founded his school there.

His work made him increasingly sure that many of his pupils had been warped and even ruined for educational purposes before they reached him, and he came to concentrate on the first seven years of life. His great work, *The Education of Man,* is evidence of this, and his last great educational achievement was the foundation, at Blankenburg in 1837, of the first 'garden of children', the *Kindergarten.* His last years were unhappy. In 1848, when he might have had hopes of support for his libertarian ideas, his nephew Karl published books suspected of socialism, and Froebel found himself tarred by reactionaries with the same brush, and forbidden to practise his experimental ideas. He died in 1852.

With as much justification as Herbart, Froebel might have claimed that his educational principles were nothing apart from his philosophy;[2] in fact, when von Raumer issued his rescript in 1851 prohibiting the establishment of kindergartens in Prussia as dangerous to society – with their 'three-year-old demagogues', as a comic paper of the day commented – he did so on the ground that the principle consisted in laying at the foundation of the education of children a highly intricate theory.[3]

The philosophy which Froebel inherited, and by which through his attendance at the University of Jena[4] he could not but be influenced, was the idealism initiated by Kant, and developed by Fichte, Schelling and Hegel. A short excursus into this philosophy is requisite to obtain the proper orientation for an adequate appreciation of Froebel's doctrines although at the outset it must be premised that, by reason of his irregular training, Froebel neither adopted nor developed a consistent philosophic attitude. He continued without ceasing, as he himself explains in a letter to Krause,[5] 'to systematise, symbolise, idealise, realise and recognise identities and analogies amongst all facts and phenomena, all problems, expressions and formulae; and in this way, life with all varied phenomena and activities became more and more free from contradictions, more harmonious, simple and clear, and more recognisable as a part of the life universal'.

The task which Kant set himself was to determine the conditions which made knowledge or experience possible. Locke had assumed that experience was a mere reflection of nature in the form of unrelated impressions, but Hume had demonstrated that this position when logically developed ended in scepticism. The other alternative was that nature must conform to our method of conceiving it. The world of science is found to be arranged in space and time, and its phenomena are connected in a causal series; this arrangement and determination, Kant maintains, results from the fact that the mind is so constituted that it is only thus that experience is possible for it. The world apprehended by the forms of space and time and conceived in accordance with the categories of substance, cause, etc., Kant terms the phenomenal world. He leaves open the possibility of another form of experience by postulating the existence of the noumenal world, a world which cannot be known through perception and understanding, but which might be experienced by an intuitive intelligence.

When we attempt to apply the forms of perception and the categories of the understanding beyond the sphere of the phenomenal world, that is, beyond the range of science, we find that such application gives rise to antinomies or conflicting conclusions apparently logically deduced. We can prove, for example, both that the world had a beginning, and that it had no beginning; that it had a First Cause, and that it had no First Cause; that the soul is a simple substance, and that it is not so. The conclusion which Kant draws from the antinomies is that the conceptions of cause, substance, etc., are valid only within the phenomenal sphere; it is their application beyond this sphere that creates the antinomies; causality is, for example, limited to the scientific world; in another form of experience or in another sphere, for example, the moral, freedom may be possible.

Kant in his *Critique of Pure Reason* thus restricts the application of the conceptions of space, time, substance, cause, etc., to the scientific realm, reserving nevertheless the possibility of the existence of another realm where freedom would be possible, and the immortality of the soul and the existence of God would not be self-contradictory conceptions. Opposed to the phenomenal world he sets the noumenal world, noumena being regarded as mere limiting conceptions implying the possibility of a form of experience other than the material and scientific.

In the *Critique of Practical Reason* Kant maintains that the noumena which in the first *Critique* were merely possible objects in a non-scientific world have positive significance and content. We find in the ethical sphere the conception of duty, a positive conception which in its nature implies freedom. Thus for Kant there are two spheres in which man lives, the phenomenal or scientific world governed by the conception of cause, and the noumenal or ethical world characterised by freedom. Kant fails to relate these two spheres satisfactorily to each other, but to him is due the credit of demonstrating that either alone is incomplete. He made materialism and naturalism as adequate philosophical explanations untenable, and by establishing the priority of the ethical life and the reality of the spiritual realm laid the foundation of modern idealism. The educational corollary of Kant's doctrine[6] is that in opposition to, but not incompatible with, a mechanical concatenation of external phenomena stands the free inner synthetic or creative activity of mind.[7]

The task set to his successors was to resolve the dualism inherent in Kant's system. His naturalistic and realistic interpreters, on the one hand, relying mainly on the first *Critique,* insisted on the connectedness and completeness of the phenomenal world, and resolved the realities of the noumenal or intelligible world – God, freedom and immortality – into mere serviceable illusions. Fichte, on the other hand, relying on the supremacy of the practical (moral) reason, emphasised the noumenal character of the intelligible world to such an extent as to reduce the phenomenal world to a mere appearance or illusion. The free activity of reason or self-consciousness could not, in Fichte's view, be conditioned by anything alien to itself. He consequently assumed that the object which consciousness demanded as a necessary condition of its own existence and progressive realisation was not a mere sensuous element externally 'given', but a product of the self-estranging process of consciousness itself.

While Schelling's standpoint was at the outset practically identical with that of Fichte, in his later writings he sought to correct the overstatement of Fichte which tended to reduce nature to a nonentity, by insisting that the Absolute manifests itself equally in nature and in spirit, and that the intelligence could find itself in nature as well as in itself. That Froebel was influenced by Schelling is beyond doubt, for in his *Autobiography*[8] he admits that he was acquainted with Schelling's work *On the World Soul*, stating 'what I read in that book moved me profoundly, and I thought I understood it'. In this work 'Schelling', it is said,[9] 'seeks mainly for a principle which shall reduce the whole of nature to unity. This principle must not be sought in any transcendental, supernatural region, whether called God or Fate, but in nature itself. A principle such as is sought Schelling seemed to find in a conception of matter as a unity of opposite forces, and hence he naturally attempted to reduce all the varied phenomena of nature to the single principle of a force that always manifests itself in opposite directions. Accordingly nature must no longer be divided up into separate groups of phenomena, with a special kind of force for each – mechanical, chemical, electrical, vital – but in all must be seen the same force in various forms, the same unity in duality. . . . In making the idea of force the supreme principle of nature. Schelling has manifestly stripped that conception of its purely mechanical connotation, and thus it becomes practically identical with the idea of nature as an eternal process or manifestation of self-activity.' Schelling takes the aesthetic view of nature according to which reality is regarded as a living whole, as the expression throughout of spirit, the highest reach of thought, and the final attitude of speculation; Froebel likewise employs aesthetic metaphor to explain the relation of the world to God. Thus he states:[10] 'The relation of nature to God may be truly and clearly perceived and recognised by man in the study and elucidation of the innermost spiritual relation of a genuine human work of art to the artist.'

In Hegel[11] the idealism of Kant finds its consummation and completest expression. Instead of two realms – a natural and a spiritual – as with Kant, there is, for Hegel, only one form of existence, the spiritual, and it comprises the natural. The ultimate source of all being and of all knowing is Mind or the Absolute. It is analogous to Plato's 'Idea of the Good', and it is significant that in introducing the couplet – 'the real is the rational and the rational is real' – Hegel refers to Plato.[12] 'The Absolute', he explains,[13] 'is Mind (Spirit) – this is the supreme definition of the Absolute. To find this definition and to grasp its meaning and burthen is, we may say, the ultimate purpose of all education and all philosophy.'[14]

The dedication of Froebel's *The Education of Man*[15] – '*Ihm*' – might refer to Hegel's Absolute, while the opening paragraph expresses in vague terminology the Hegelian standpoint: 'The whole world – the All, the Universe – is a single great organism in which an eternal uniformity manifests itself. This principle of uniformity expresses itself as much in external nature as in spirit. Life is the union of the spiritual with the material. Without mind or spirit matter is lifeless; it remains formless, it is mere chaos. Only through the entrance of the spiritual into the material does the cosmos originate. Spirit manifests itself in order. Every creature, every object is matter informed by spirit. . . . God is the presupposition, the condition of their existence. Without God they would not exist. God is the one ground of all things. God is the all-comprehending, the all-sustaining. God is the essential nature, the meaning of the world.'

As the truth for Hegel is the whole, Mind or the Absolute cannot be contained within any fragmentary form of existence, and the effort to realise itself more and more adequately by successive stages follows a definite pattern, the dialectical movement. For Plato, as we have seen, dialectic was a search after the true and the real; the mediaevalists, unmindful of Plato's warning that dialectic was not a suitable study for the young, included it in the *trivium*, the earlier of the scholastic disciplines, with the result, as Plato predicted, that it degenerated into an exercise of solving intellectual riddles; it became a method of disputation instead of a method of discovery.[16] The Hegelian dialectic is a movement of thought of a unique type.[17] The impasse which results when categories applicable in one sphere are indiscriminately applied in other spheres, illustrated by Kant's antinomies, Hegel regarded as characteristic not only of Kant's Ideas of Reason but even of all thought. 'Collisions, in fact, belong to the nature of thought, the nature of consciousness and its dialectic.'[18] A transition into its opposite is the result of extending a conception beyond its legitimate sphere. This 'law of opposites' Froebel freely exploited. 'Everything and every being comes to be known only as it is connected with the opposite of its kind, and as its unity, its agreement with its opposite, is discovered.'[19] Opposites have nevertheless significance only within a more inclusive unity; there can be no opposition between something in this room and something in next week. Hence the triadic structure of the Hegelian dialectic: the 'thesis'; this necessarily calls forth its opposite, 'the antithesis'; and the reconciliation of thesis and antithesis in a more comprehensive concept, the 'synthesis'. Froebel exemplifies this dialectical movement in his various writings: the child is a child of nature, a human child and a child of God.[20] Morality mediates between religion and practical efficiency.[21] The selection of objects constituting the second 'gift' is determined by the same sequence of triads. 'The sphere and the cube are pure opposites. They stand to each other in the relation of unity and plurality, but especially of movement and rest, of round and straight. The law of connection demands for these two objects of play a connecting one, which is the cylinder. It combines unity complete in itself in the round surface, and plurality in the two straight ones.'[22]

When the close analogy between his law of opposites with their reconciliation in a higher unity and the dialectical movement of thought in Hegel's philosophy was indicated by a visitor to his kindergarten at Liebenstein in 1851, Froebel, while not disclaiming acquaintance with Hegel's principle, is reported[23] to have replied that he did not know how Hegel had formulated and applied this law, as he had had no time for the study of the latter's system. This may well have been the case, since the idea of antitheses and their reconciliation in a higher synthesis is not peculiar to Hegel but is common to Fichte and Schelling.

With Krause, a philosopher almost unknown to English students of philosophy, Froebel was acquainted and maintained a correspondence. To one of Froebel's letters to Krause[24] we owe a knowledge of many of the autobiographical details of Froebel's life; that Krause's writings and his acquaintance with Froebel had an influence upon the latter, is acknowledged by Baroness B. von Marenholz-Bülow in her *Reminiscences of Friedrich Froebel*. 'The theory in which Froebel and Krause agreed especially', she says,[25] 'is the idea of the analogy existing between organic development in nature and organic development in the spiritual world, and according to which the historical development of mankind had proceeded, obeying the same laws as those of nature and its organisms. The same logic of the one all-penetrating Divine Reason rules in both, unconscious in the one (nature), conscious to itself in the other (mind). Therefore are the opposites ruling everywhere, not absolute, but relative, and always find connection or solution in the process of life.'

In direct contrast to Locke and Herbart, who assume that the mind is built up out of presentations, Froebel maintains that the mind unfolds from within according to a predetermined pattern. 'All the child is ever to be and become, lies, however slightly indicated, in the child, and can be attained only through development from within outward.'[26] The pattern followed is that known as preformation according to which the germ contains in miniature the fully developed plant or animal, point for point. Thus in *The Pedagogics of the Kindergarten* he says: 'The tree germ bears within itself the nature of the whole tree'; 'the development and formation of the whole future life of each being is contained in the beginning of its existence'.[27] The development of the individual also parallels the course of development of the race. 'In the development of the inner life of the individual man the history of the spiritual development of the race is repeated.' It is also a continuous process. 'It is highly important', Froebel affirms,[28] 'that man's development should proceed continuously from one point, and that this continuous progress be seen and ever guarded. Sharp limits and definite subdivisions within the continuous series of the years of development, withdrawing from attention the permanent continuity, the living connection, the inner living essence, are therefore highly pernicious, and even destructive in their influence.'

All creatures have one function only – to express the spiritual, the Divine, that slumbers in them. The aim of education accordingly consists solely in so treating man as to awaken in him his spiritual nature. 'Surely the nature of man is in itself good', Froebel declares.[29] This view of the innate goodness of the child Froebel doubtless acquired from Rousseau, with its corollary for the early stages of development – negative education. Were man's inner and divine nature not marred by untoward external influences, the ideal education would be passive, non-interfering. 'Indeed, in its very essence education should have these characteristics; for the undisturbed operation of the Divine Unity is necessarily good – cannot be otherwise than good.'[30]

This ideal condition of affairs but seldom obtains. 'Nature', Froebel admits,[31] 'rarely shows us that unmarred original state, especially in man; but it is for this reason only the more necessary to assume its existence in every human being until the opposite has been clearly shown; otherwise that unmarred original state where it might exist contrary to our expectation, might be easily impaired.' When, however, it is clearly established that the original nature of the individual has been marred,[32] then Froebel does not hesitate to prescribe categorical, mandatory education in its full severity.

As Kant's imperative was categorical, and his moral law was valid only for a free being who voluntarily imposed it on himself, so for Froebel 'in its inner essence the living thought, the eternal spiritual ideal, ought to be and is categorical and mandatory in its manifestations. . . . The ideal becomes mandatory only where it supposes that the person addressed enters into the reason of the requirement with serene, childlike faith, or with clear, manly insight. It is true, in word or example, the ideal is mandatory in all these cases, but always only with reference to the spirit and inner life, never with reference to outer form.'[33]

As freedom is obedience to a law which is in conformity with our highest nature and as such is self-imposed, or, as Hegel puts it, as 'freedom is the truth of necessity', so for Froebel[34] 'in good education, in genuine instruction, in true training, necessity should call forth freedom; law, self-determination; external compulsion, inner free-will; external hate, inner love. Where hatred brings forth hatred; law, dishonesty and crime; compulsion, slavery; necessity, servitude; where oppression destroys and debases; where severity and harshness give rise to stubbornness and deceit – all education is abortive. In order to avoid the latter and to secure the former, all prescription should be adapted to the pupil's nature and needs, and enlist his cooperation. This is the case when education in instruction and training, in spite of its necessarily categorical character, bears in all details and ramifications the irrefutable and irresistible impress that the one who makes the demand is himself strictly unavoidably subject to an eternally ruling law, to an unavoidable eternal necessity, and that, therefore, all despotism is banished.'

While Froebel emphasises the principle of continuity in development, this does not deter him from recognising well-marked stages in development and agreeing with Rousseau that each stage should be fully exploited before advance is made to the succeeding stage, otherwise difficulties will be created which it will be impossible later to rectify. The stages recognised by Froebel, namely, infancy, childhood, boyhood, youth, corresponded to Rousseau's divisions in *Émile*. For Rousseau the activity characteristic of infancy is habit; for Froebel it is sensory development. Froebel's account of sensory development is highly artificial, the result of an attempt to impose on it the dialectical form. Childhood, the second stage, is distinguished from infancy by the appearance of language; it is then the child begins to represent the internal outwardly. Actual education now begins, attention and watchful care being less directed to the body than to the mind.[35] Speech training should now be begun. Each object should be given its appropriate name, and each word should be uttered clearly and distinctly. Pestalozzi was criticised by Fichte for regarding the name as an attribute of *Anschauung,* but on pedagogical grounds Froebel supports Pestalozzi, maintaining that to the child a name is still one with the thing,[36] and that the name creates the thing for the child.[37] He adds in *The Pedagogics of the Kindergarten*[38] that the name defines the object by connecting it with something familiar. The pre-eminent activity of the childhood stage of development is nevertheless play, and it is in treating of childhood in *The Education of Man* that Froebel enters a plea for the place of play in education.

Play is the characteristic activity of childhood: it is, says Froebel,[39] 'the highest phase of child-development – of human development at this period; for it is self-active representation of the inner – representation of the inner from inner necessity and impulse. Play is the purest, most spiritual activity of man at this stage, and, at the same time, typical of human life as a whole – of the inner hidden natural life in man and all things. It gives, therefore, joy, freedom, contentment, inner and outer rest, peace with the world. It holds the source of all that is good.'

To have educative value the play of the child must not be a purposeless activity; his play impulses must be directed and controlled by the employment of definite material necessitating an orderly sequence in the feelings engendered and in the activities exercised. 'Without rational, conscious guidance', Froebel is reported to have said,[40] 'childish activity degenerates into aimless play instead of preparing for those tasks of life for which it is destined. . . . In the kindergarten the children are guided to bring out their plays in such a manner as really to reach the aim desired by nature, that is, to serve for their development. . . . Human education needs a guide which I think I have found in a general law of development that rules both in nature and in the intellectual world. Without law-abiding guidance there is no free development.'[41]

It was on the transition to adolescence that Rousseau inverted his procedure, experience henceforth to be acquired at second-hand, not first-hand. At a stage earlier than Rousseau, namely, at the transition from childhood to boyhood, Froebel proposes a similar inversion. Whereas the period of childhood is characterised as predominantly that of life for the sake of living, for making the internal external, the period of boyhood is predominantly the period for learning, for making the external internal.[42] Here we have an illustration of Froebel's law of opposites. Education is no longer to be determined by endowment; it is to be environmentally determined. It is no longer to be child-centred; it is henceforth to be curriculum-centred. Actually it is both endowment and environmentally determined from the outset, and in *The Pedagogics of the Kindergarten*[43] Froebel virtually admits this through his recognition of a third or synthesising stage. 'Another fundamental idea is that all knowledge and comprehension of life are connected with making the internal external, the external internal, and with perceiving the harmony and accord of both.'

While play is the characteristic activity of childhood, work is that of boyhood. Interest in the process gives place to interest in the product. 'What formerly the child did for the sake of the activity, the boy now does for the sake of the result or product of his activity.'[44] 'If activity brought joy to the child, work now gives delight to the boy.'[45] Whereas during the previous period of childhood the aim of play consisted simply in activity as such, the aim lies now in a definite, conscious purpose.[46] The contrast is forced. Work is regarded as directed and purposive, whereas, in disregard of his previous statements on play, play is now simply an 'activity as such'. The distinction is likewise invalid. The more extended range of the pupil's environment has provided him with new patterns of activity in the shape of vocational occupations to be imitated; for the boy these are another form of play, not work in the sense of his parents' work. The pupil's activities at the boyhood stage are self-selected, their products have no economic significance, and their features are characteristic of play. In childhood the pupil imitates domestic activities, in boyhood neighbourhood occupations. This supports the conclusion that his development is determined, as indicated above, by the widening range of environment rather than by a sudden transition from inner experience to outer. There is, however, for Froebel a unity transcending the opposition between play and work, for both he regards as means to the individual's self-realisation. 'Man works', he affirms,[47] 'only that his spiritual divine essence may assume outward form, and that thus he may be enabled to recognise his own spiritual, divine nature and the innermost being of God.'[48]

The activities in which the boy engages have all the characteristics of projects – practical problems involving co-operative effort and affording intellectual and moral training. 'If in his former activity (in childhood) he emulated phases of domestic life, in his present activity (in boyhood) he shares the work of the house – lifting, pulling, carrying, digging, splitting.'[49] Even building a hut is instanced, and this justifies the claim of an American writer that Froebel, particularly in his *Education of Man,* has given the world no mean anticipation of Dewey's own school.[50]

The other main feature of boyhood education is instruction. It too serves to mark the transition from making the internal external to making the external internal. 'Instruction is conducted not so much in accordance with the nature of man as in accordance with the fixed, definite, clear *laws* in the nature of things, and more particularly the laws to which man and things are equally subject. It is conducted in accordance with fixed and definite conditions lying *outside* the human being.'[51]

Although Rousseau had dispensed with a predetermined curriculum, in sketching Émile's development he incidentally indicates his attitude to the teaching of various subjects. Froebel in describing his pupil's life and education from the developmental standpoint likewise proposes various educational occupations and reveals his attitude to these. In addition he provides a more independent and systematic treatment of the subjects of the curriculum than did Rousseau. The subjects, it must be premised, are not to be regarded as ends in themselves; they are merely instrumental to the full realisation of the pupil's personality.

Froebel was an early advocate of the inclusion of manual

instruction in the school curriculum. Manual work is a necessary condition of the realisation of the pupil's personality; through it he comes to himself. 'Every child, boy, and youth, whatever his condition or position in life, should devote daily at least one or two hours to some serious activity in the production of some definite external piece of work. . . . Children – mankind, indeed – are at present too much and too variously concerned with aimless and purposeless pursuits, and too little with work. Children and parents consider the activity of actual work so much to their disadvantage, and so unimportant for their future conditions of life, that educational institutions should make it one of their most constant endeavours to dispel this delusion. The domestic and scholastic education of our time leads children to indolence and laziness; a vast amount of human power thereby remains undeveloped and is lost.'[52]

In addition to manual instruction Froebel also recommends the introduction of such subjects as drawing, nature-study and school gardening. He insists, like Herbart, on an all-round development as the aim of education, and the main divisions of an educational curriculum he designates thus: (1) religion and religious instruction, (2) natural science and mathematics, (3) language, (4) art and objects of art, remarking[53] that human education requires the knowledge and appreciation of religion, nature and language; and with reference to instruction in art he states the aim:[54] 'Its intention will not be to make each pupil an artist in some one or all of the arts, but to secure to each human being full and all-sided development.'

Froebel did not complete *The Education of Man* by treating of adolescence but devoted the later part of his life to founding the kindergarten[55] on which his fame mainly rests. Froebel considered 'childhood as the most important stage of the total development of man and humanity',[56] and in his *Reminiscences*[57] he gives his reason: 'The earliest age is the most important one for education, because the beginning decides the manner of progress and the end. If national order is to be recognised in later years as a benefit, childhood must first be accustomed to law and order, and therein find means of freedom'. For this stage of childhood he devised his gifts, the first being the soft ball, the second the sphere, the cube and the cylinder.

Not only does Froebel in his gifts anthropomorphise playthings and assume that children will be able to appreciate the symbolism involved,[58] but he also believes that the quasi-philosophic conceptions which underlie the games will impress themselves on the child's mind and determine his attitude to life. So obsessed is Froebel with his philosophical formulae that his psychological insight cannot save him from such absurdities as assuming that the child when dealing with the second gift, that is, during the second half of the first year of his life, has some dim perception of the nature and destiny of man.[59] In his account of the same gift he affirms:[60] man himself 'in play, even as a child, by play should perceive within and without how from unity proceed manifoldness, plurality, and totality, and how plurality and manifoldness finally are found again in and resolve themselves into unity and should find this out in life'. In reviewing the first gifts he observes:[61] 'In and by means of the ball (as an object resting in itself, easily movable, especially elastic, bright, and warm) the child perceives his life, his power, his activity, and that of his senses, at the first stage of his consciousness, in their unity, and thus exercises them. . . . The ball is therefore to the child a representative or a means of perception of a single effect caused by a single power. The sphere is to the child the representative of every isolated simple unity; the child gets a hint in the sphere of the manifoldness as still abiding in unity. The cube is to the child the representative of each continually developing manifold body. The child has an intimation in it of the unity which lies at the foundation of all manifoldness, and from which the latter proceeds. In sphere and cube, considered in comparison with each other, is presented in outward view to the child the resemblance between opposites which is so important for his whole future life, and which he perceives everywhere around himself, and multifariously within himself.'

By his methodological arrangement of the gifts and occupations[62] Froebel nevertheless founded a new type of educational institution, and although his system too readily lent itself to formalism with later generations of teachers who had not the spirit of the master, it ameliorated the lot of countless children. On the ground of its excessive symbolism his theory is open to criticism. Although, as Dewey says,[63] his love of abstract symbolism often got the better of his sympathetic insight, 'Froebel's recognition of the significance of the native capacities of children, his loving attention to them, and his influence in inducing others to study them, represent perhaps the most effective single force in modern educational theory in effecting widespread acknowledgment of the idea of growth.'

Although his establishments, like those of Pestalozzi, were inspected by visitors from several countries, Froebel's ideas were not especially quick to spread. Less than a score of kindergartens had been opened when he died. But, like Pestalozzi, he was fortunate in his disciples. His widow became head of an establishment in Hamburg to train teachers on his principles. His 'most brilliant pupil', the Baroness von Marenholtz-Bülow, lectured all over Europe and founded a similar institution in Berlin. His grand-niece, Henrietta Breyman, later Frau Schröder, was very active in Belgium and Switzerland, and set up a 'Pestalozzi – Froebel-Haus' in Berlin. By 1877, a quarter of a century after his death, schools using his system had sprung up in most of the countries of western and central Europe, as well as Canada, Japan and the United States.

It was in America that his theories, like those of many other pioneers, were most enthusiastically received. The demonstration kindergarten at the Philadelphia Exhibition of 1876 brought them to the notice of many willing enquirers, who proceeded to experiment with them, first in private seminaries, then in the public schools. The effect was to revolutionise infant education, and it endured until the appearance of the more structured Montessori system in the early years of the following century. Both systems were well fitted to play their part in the attempts at social welfare which flourished in the two decades immediately before the Great War: both contributed largely, for example, to the nursery school movement fostered by pioneers like the sisters Rachel and Margaret MacMillan. For some years Montessori prevailed, but Froebelianism, with its emphasis on free play and the liberty of the child, continued to rule the early years and does so to this day.

11
Montessori

FROEBEL died in 1852, Montessori[1] in 1952. The intervening century brought about a complete change in the social background of education, Froebel's kindergarten being founded at Blankenburg – charmingly situated at the entrance to the Schwarza Tal, one of the most picturesque and beautifully wooded valleys of Thuringia – Montessori's House of Childhood in the slums of a European capital. The contrast determined their respective standpoints. In an ideal rural environment Froebel centred attention mainly on the endowment and development of the child. Montessori on the other hand placed the centre of gravity of her system in the environment. Thus in *The Secret of Childhood* she affirmed:[2] 'Our own method of education is characterised by the central importance that we attribute to the question of environment; . . . it is well-known how our pedagogy considers the environment so important as to make it the central point of the whole system.'

Maria Montessori was by nature a pioneer. Her parents intended her to be a teacher, but her own preferences were more assertive. Seeking a career as an engineer, she went to a boys' technical high school, but in 1896, at the age of twenty-six, became the first woman to graduate in medicine from the University of Rome, indeed the first in Italy. On the staff of the university's psychiatric clinic, she specialised in work with medically deficient children, travelling to London and Paris to study the methods of Jean Itard and Edouard Séguin. Two years of success with backward children fostered an interest in general education, and she returned to Rome as a student of philosophy, psychology and anthropology, at the same time assisting on the staff of the city's training college for women. In 1904 she became Professor of Anthropology.

Less than three years later her main life's work began. To remove the social evils of the poorest quarters of Rome, the Association of Good Building was formed, its plan being to acquire tenements, remodel them, put them into a productive condition and administer them in the interests of the occupier.[3] The care of the reconstructed tenements was given to the tenants, and they did not abuse their trust. Difficulties nevertheless arose with young children under school age. Left to themselves during the day, and unable to appreciate the motives which led their parents to respect the property, such children spent their time defacing the buildings. To cure this evil it occurred to the Director General of the Roman Association for Good Building 'to gather together in a large room all the little ones between the ages of three and seven belonging to the families living in the tenement. The play and the work of these children were to be carried on under the guidance of a teacher who should have her own apartment in the tenement house.'[4] Thus came to be instituted the House of Childhood – the school within the tenement. The expenses of the new institution were met, in accordance with the general self-supporting principle of the reconstruction scheme, by the sum that the Association would otherwise have been forced to expend upon redecoration and repairs.

Towards the end of 1906[5] the Director General of the Roman Association of Good Building entrusted to Montessori the organisation of the infant schools in the model tenements in Rome. The method adopted by her was determined by her training and previous experience. Montessori, having graduated in medicine, was for a time in charge of the training of mentally defective children. Her success with these was remarkable. She taught a number of such children so efficiently to read and write that they were able to be presented for examination with normal children of the same age, and this phenomenal result was attributed to the fact that her pupils had been taught by an improved method. She accordingly conjectured that if the methods employed with defective children were applied in the training of normal children, they would yield even more surprising results.[6]

To be successful these methods should obviously be applied with children at a mental level corresponding somewhat to the stage of development of deficients, that is, they should be employed in the training of infants; at this period of life the child has not acquired the co-ordination of muscular movements necessary to enable him to perform deftly the ordinary acts of life, his sensory organs are not fully developed, his emotional life is still unstable and his volitional powers irresolute. The significance of the pedagogical experiment for which the institution of the House of Childhood afforded the facilities lies in this, Montessori explained:[7] 'It represents the results of a series of trials made in the education of young children, with methods already used with deficients.'

Such an application to normal children of the methods found successful with deficients was contemplated by the earliest workers engaged in the education of the feeble-minded. Thus, at the laying of the foundation stone of the first American schools for defectives in 1854, the Rev. Samuel J. May, basing his argument on the theological or metaphysical doctrine that evil is never an end in itself but always a means to some higher good, ventured to declare with an emphasis somewhat enhanced, he admitted, by a lurking distrust of the prediction, that the time would come when access would be found to the idiotic brain, the light of intelligence admitted into its dark chambers and the whole race be benefited by some new discovery on the nature of mind.[8] This hope had been anticipated by Séguin in his treatise on idiocy published in 1846:[9] 'If it were possible that in endeavouring to solve the simple question of the education of idiots we had found terms precise enough that it were only necessary to generalise them to obtain a formula applicable to universal education, then, not only would we in our humble sphere have rendered some little service, but we would besides have prepared the elements for a method of physiological education for mankind. Nothing would remain but to write it.'[10]

Before proceeding to elaborate the principles underlying the Montessori method we should perhaps recall the fact that the child under school age usually acquires unaided an education which, if somewhat unsystematic in character, is nevertheless not inconsiderable in amount. When such early education is consciously controlled and systematically directed, the results may be remarkable.

By discovering the main characteristics of the training of defective children we shall have the key to the Montessori method.

The first principle is to train the pupil to be independent of others with regard to the ordinary practices of life; it appears also to necessitate approach to the child mind at a lower level than can be adopted with normal children, an appeal to the senses rather than to the intellect. With physically defective children it implies training one sense to function vicariously for another; for example, with deaf children, teaching words not by hearing the sounds but by feeling the vibrations of the larynx of the speaker. The ultimate reference is to the sense of touch, which is regarded as fundamental and primordial. The Montessori system accordingly becomes an 'education by touch'. Montessori maintained that the sense of touch is fundamental, that it undergoes great development during the early years of life, and that, if neglected at this age, it loses its susceptibility to future training.

Séguin, of whom Montessori claimed to be a disciple, had designated his treatment of the feeble-minded as the physiological method. Recognising the advance which Montessori made, and her adaptation to the training of normal children of a procedure specially devised for deficient children, we may characterise her method as the psychological method. Pestalozzi had sought to psychologise education, but as in his day there existed no psychology of the school child, he ended by mechanising instruction, and the methods which were successful with him failed with teachers of a later age.

The psychological method in education implies that the educative process is adapted to the stage of mental development of the child, and to his interests, and is not wholly subordinated to the necessities of a curriculum or to the teacher's scheme of work. 'By education', said Montessori,[11] 'must be understood the active help given to the normal expansion of the life of the child.' The 'psychological moment' in the educative process comes when consciousness of a need arises in the child's experience. There are, in Montessori's terminology, 'sensitive periods', when the child shows 'an intense interest for repeating actions at length, for no obvious reason, until – because of this repetition – a fresh function suddenly appears with explosive force.'[12] Montessori schools identified sensitive periods for sensory learning, for language, for movement, for the appreciation of order.[13] 'It is necessary then', in the Montessori method, 'to offer those exercises which correspond to the need of development felt by an organism, and if the child's age has carried him past a certain need, it is never possible to obtain, in its fulness, a development which missed its proper moment;'[14] and, if a child fails to perform a task or to appreciate the truth of a principle, the teacher must not make him conscious of his error by repeating the lesson; she must assume that the task has been presented prematurely, and, before again presenting the stimulus, await the manifestation of the symptoms which indicate that the need exists. The duration of a process is determined not by the exigencies of an authorised time-table, but by the interval which the child finds requisite to exhaust his interest. Thus in a Montessori school we may find a pupil working unremittingly at a self-imposed task for several days on end. Nevertheless, Montessori conceived the child's development as proceeding by stages, each of about three years except the last, which extended from twelve to eighteen.[15]

A further consequence of the adoption of the psychological standpoint is that there are in the Montessori system no prizes: 'Heaven forbid that poems should ever be born of the poet's desire to be crowned in the capital'.[16] The pupil's sense of mastery is his highest reward: 'His own self-development is his true and almost his only pleasure.'[17] He works for the enjoyment of working, not, as the adult works, for the sake of the result. Such correction as is admitted in the Montessori system comes from the material, not from the teacher. 'From the "Children's Houses" the old-time teacher who wore herself out maintaining discipline of immobility and wasting her breath in loud and continual discourse, has disappeared, and the didactic material which contains within itself the control of errors is substituted, making auto-education possible to each child.'[18] This is the principle of Rousseau and of Spencer, not, however, as by them confined to moral misdemeanours, that the child should meet with no obstacles other than physical; it is an intellectual 'discipline by consequences'.

The psychological method implies the perfect freedom of the child, the freedom which consists in absolute obedience to the laws of the development of his own nature. 'The method of observation (that is, the psychological method) is established upon one fundamental base – the liberty of the pupils in their spontaneous manifestations.'[19] This liberty necessitates independence of action on the part of the child: 'Whoever visits a well kept school is struck by the discipline of the children. There are forty little beings from three to seven years old, each one intent on his own work; one is going through one of the exercises for the senses, one is doing an arithmetical exercise, one is handling the letters, one is drawing, one is fastening and unfastening the pieces of cloth on one of the wooden frames, still another is dusting. Some are seated at the tables, some on rugs on the floor.'[20] To many this scene would suggest licence, not liberty; but, as Herbart explained:[21] 'When the environment is so planned that childish activity is directed along the lines of the useful and expends itself thus, the result is the most effective form of discipline (*Regierung*).'

As instruction should be adapted to the stage of development of the pupil, Montessori advocated that the environment should likewise be so adjusted: 'Give the child an environment in which everything is constituted in proportion to himself and let him live therein. Then there will develop within the child that "active life" which has caused so many to marvel because they see in it not only a simple exercise performed with pleasure but also the revelation of a spiritual life.'[22] Such an environment not only makes the liberty of the child possible but it is also necessary 'that the environment should contain the means of auto-education'.[23] 'He who speaks of liberty in the schools, ought at the same time to exhibit objects – approximating to a scientific apparatus, which will make such liberty possible.'[24]

Montessori was convinced of the inter-relationship of mental and physical powers in human beings: 'mental development *must* be connected with movement and be dependent on it. It is vital that educational theory and practice should become informed by this idea.'[25] She therefore laid great emphasis on the practices of her method, which fall into three classes: (1) the exercises of practical life; (2) the exercises in sensory training; and (3) the didactic exercises. Although Montessori described these exercises in detail and provided specific material, she did not lay down precise methods of using them, fearing that this would inhibit learning. Their function was to liberate the child by giving him the necessary tools to learn for himself when he was ready.[26]

The main task in the training of feeble-minded children is to teach them to take care of themselves. This is likewise the first phase in the training given in the House of Childhood. It is a training in liberty; for freedom, according to Montessori, does not consist in having others at one's command to perform the ordinary services, but in being able to do these for oneself, in being independent of others. Thus in the House of Childhood the pupils learn how to wash their hands, using little washstands with small pitchers and basins, how to clean their nails, brush their teeth, and so on. Exercises are also arranged to train the child in the movements necessary in dressing and undressing. The apparatus for these exercises consists of wooden frames, mounted with two pieces of cloth or of leather, which are fastened by means of buttons and buttonholes, hooks and eyes, eyelets and lacings or automatic fasteners. After some practice in fastening and unloosening the pieces of cloth with the various types of fasteners, the child finds that he has acquired a dexterity which enables him to dress and undress himself; and, not content with the satisfaction derived from such independence, his consciousness of the possession of a new power excites in him a desire to assist in dressing the whole family.[27] All the furniture in the House of Childhood, tables, chairs, etc. – for there are no fixed desks – are of such a size and construction that the pupils can handle them easily; they learn to move them deftly and without noise, and are thus afforded a training in motor adjustment.

Montessori also devised certain formal gymnastic exercises to develop in the child coordinated movements. She disapproved of the child practising the ordinary gymnastic exercises arranged for the adult. 'We are wrong', she maintained,[28] 'if we consider little children from their physical point of view as little men. They have, instead, characteristics and proportions that are entirely special to their age.' A new set of exercises must consequently be devised, and, in accordance with the general Montessori principles, this was accomplished by observing the spontaneous movements of the child. One piece of apparatus, namely, the little round stair, may be instanced.[29] A wooden spiral stairway enclosed on one side by a balustrade on which the children can rest their hands, the other side being left open, enables the children to habituate themselves to ascending and descending stairs without holding on, and teaches them to move up and down with movements that are poised and self-controlled. The steps are very low and shallow, and the children can thereby learn movements which they cannot execute properly in climbing ordinary stairways in their homes, in which the proportions are suited to adults. The general result of the new exercises is to give the pupils of the House of Childhood a gracefulness of carriage which distinguishes them from other children.

For the methods and the apparatus of her scheme of sensory training Montessori was largely indebted to the apparatus and tests employed by the experimental psychologist.[30] The standpoints of experimental psychology and of sensory training are nevertheless different. Experimental psychology measures the sensory capacities; it does not attempt to improve these, whereas Montessori was not interested in measuring the capacities but in furthering their development. In the application of tests by psychologists, especially when the investigation extends over a long period, practice-effects frequently disclose themselves. These practice-effects are to the psychologist disturbing factors which he must estimate and eliminate, but it is just these practice-effects that sensory education strives to secure.[31]

The psychological techniques for determining sensory acuity and sensory discrimination had been applied by Montessori in training the feeble-minded. In applying them to normal children she found that they required modification. With deficient children the exercises had to be restricted to stimuli which were strongly contrasted; normal children can, however, proceed to finely graded series. Normal children manifest great pleasure in repeating exercises which they have successfully accomplished; deficient children when they succeed once are satisfied, and show no inclination to repeat the task. The deficient child when he makes mistakes has to be corrected; the normal child prefers to correct his own mistakes. The differences were summed up by Montessori in the statement that the didactic material which, used with deficients, makes education possible, used with normal children, provokes auto-education.[32]

'To make the process one of self-education,' Montessori explained in *The Advanced Montessori Method*,[33] 'it is not enough that the stimulus should call forth activity, it must also direct it. The child should not only persist for a long time in an exercise; he must persist without making mistakes. All the physical or intrinsic qualities of the objects should be determined not only by the immediate reaction of attention they provoke in the child but also by their possession of this fundamental characteristic, the control of error, that is to say, the power of evoking the effective collaboration of the highest activities (comparison, judgment).'

In sensory training Montessori, like Rousseau, believed in isolating the senses whenever that is possible. This procedure, it will readily be inferred, was suggested by the education of physically deficient children. Blind people, it is popularly assumed, acquire a very fine discriminative ability in the sphere of touch. We are not surprised then to find that in the training of their tactual sense the pupils of the Montessori schools are blindfolded, a feature of the training which seems to add zest to their efforts. The auditory exercises are given in an environment not only of silence, but even of darkness.

The material used in the sensory training recalls the apparatus of the psychological laboratory. For perception of size, series of wooden cylinders varying in height only, in diameter only or in both dimensions at once, are employed, likewise blocks varying regularly in size, and rods of regularly graded lengths; for perception of form, geometrical insets in metal, in wood or the shapes of the insets drawn on paper; for discrimination in weight, tablets of wood similar in size but differing in weight; for touch, a highly polished surface and a sandpaper surface; for sense of temperature, small metal bowls with caps; for auditory acuity, cylindrical sound boxes containing different substances; for the colour sense, graded series of coloured wools.

The procedure adopted may be illustrated from the method followed in the training in colour discrimination. Montessori accepted from Séguin the division of the lesson into three stages or steps: (1) the association of the sensory percept with the name. For example, the child is shown two colours, red and blue. When the red is presented, the teacher says simply, 'This is red'; when the blue, 'This is blue'. (2) The second period or step involves recognition of the object when the name is given. Thus the teacher says to the child, 'Give me the red', 'Give me the blue'. (3) The third step involves recalling the name corresponding with the object. Thus the child is asked, the object being shown, 'What is this?' and he responds, 'Red' or 'Blue'. Recall, as ordinary experience abundantly exemplifies, is more difficult than recognition.

This procedure follows the methods employed for testing the colour-vision of children; but, as indicated above, instead of using the techniques for testing, Montessori employed them for training the sensory activities of her pupils.

Similar methods were adopted in developing the child's tactual acuity, and in training him to discriminate differences in temperature and in weight. In these exercises the child was blindfolded or enjoined to keep his eyes closed during the tests; he was encouraged to do so by being told that he would thus be able to feel the differences better.

To the three periods or steps in a lesson recommended by Séguin, Montessori in certain sensory modalities added a preparatory series of exercises which represents the real sense education or auto-education, and by which the pupil acquires an extraordinary ability to differentiate finely graded stimuli. For the colour sense these exercises require the sorting and grading of sixty-four cards of various coloured wools, and are preparatory to the naming step or period in the lessons on sense training.

The exercises which are directed to the development of form play such an important part in the Montessori system as to entitle them to separate treatment. The first exercise is to sort into heaps bricks and cubes such as are employed by Froebel. Young children come to recognise the forms of these merely by grasping them; they do not require to trace the contour. This exercise may be varied by the use of different materials, as, for example, by the use of coins, and so expert do the children become that they can distinguish between small forms which differ but little from one another, such as corn, wheat and rice.[34]

The real training in the perception of form begins, however, when the child passes to the exercises of placing wooden shapes in spaces made to receive them, or in superimposing such shapes on outlines of similar form.

Geometric insets of various designs, the initial ones strongly contrasted, the later ones merely dissimilar forms of the same figure, as for example, the triangle, are mixed up and have to be sorted out by the children and fitted into the frames made to receive them. The frames furnish the control necessary to test the accuracy of the work. Ordinary solids, for example, cubes, spheres, prisms, are not employed as is usually the case in the teaching of form, but, instead, insets representing solid objects with one of the dimensions greatly reduced and with the two dimensions determining the form of the plane surface made most evident; they differ in this respect from the Froebelian gifts, the reason being that the choice of material in the Montessori method is determined purely from the pedagogical standpoint, and that the objects most commonly met with in practical life, table tops, doors, window frames, etc., are of this form. In learning to fit the geometric insets into the spaces provided for them the child employs not only the visual sense but also the tactual and muscular senses; he is taught to run the index finger of the right hand round the contour of the form and to repeat this with the contour of the frame into which the inset fits. It is frequently observed that children who cannot recognise a shape by looking at it, do so by touching it. The association of the muscular-tactual sense with that of vision, Montessori maintained, 'aids in a most remarkable way the perception of the forms and fixes them in memory'.

From the exercises with the solid insets in which the control is absolute, the child passes to exercises in the purely visual perception of form. The wooden insets have to be superimposed on figures cut out of blue paper and mounted on cards. In a further series of exercises the figures are represented by an outline of blue paper, which for the child represents the path which he has so often followed with his finger. Finally, he is required to superimpose the wooden pieces on figures whose outlines are represented merely by a line. He thus passes from the concrete to what is relatively abstract, from solid objects to plane figures represented merely by lines and perceived only visually.

Through such exercises the forms of the various figures, circles, ellipses, triangles, rectangles, etc., come to be known, and, when the need of them becomes urgent, the names of the figures are given. As no analysis of the forms is undertaken, no mention made of sides and angles, it may legitimately be contended that at this stage the teaching of geometry is not being attempted.[35]

The methods adopted in training the perception of form, involving as they do the extensive employment of tactual and motor imagery, prepare the way for the teaching of writing and other didactic processes. Before considering the didactic exercises it may be opportune to estimate the value of sensory training in the education of the child. Montessori maintains, like Aristotle, that 'there is nothing in the intellect which was not first in the senses', and that if we multiply the sensations and develop the capacity for appreciating fine differences in stimuli we refine the sensibility and multiply man's pleasures.[36] Such a claim would be difficult to substantiate. To the practical exercises in the Montessori system no objection can be taken, for in addition to affording sensory training they are of direct value in enabling the child to meet the social situations which arise in everyday life. Nor can objection be urged against such exercises in sensory training as subserve the didactic processes of writing, etc.; but one may question the value of a specific training of the sensory powers for their own sake. While lack of certain forms of sensory training may prejudicially affect an individual's advancement in specific occupations and professions, high intellectual attainments may be compatible with serious sensory deficiency, as the well-known case of Helen Keller illustrates. It is also doubtful whether the results of a sensory training in a specific sphere can be transferred even to other sensory spheres; the assumption that they do transfer involves the doctrine of formal training or transfer of training. It has likewise to be added that the development of certain senses might not be socially advantageous; and in this connection we need only instance the sense of smell which Montessori significantly ignored. What Montessori designated sensory training should have been termed perceptual training, involving as it does judgment and comparison. This would have obviated some of the criticisms levelled against the early versions of the system.[37]

It was by the success attending the application of the didactic processes of writing, reading and numbers, that popular interest was aroused in the Montessori method, but at the inception of the system it was not intended that such exercises be included, and the results were incidental.

In the Montessori system the teaching of writing precedes the teaching of reading. Montessori maintained[38] that in normal children the muscular sense is most easily developed in infancy, and this makes the acquisition of writing exceedingly easy for children. It is not so with reading, which requires a much longer course of instruction and which calls for a higher level of intellectual development, since it treats of the interpretation of signs, and of the modulation of the voice in the accentuation of syllables in order that the word may be understood. Reading is mainly a mental task, whereas in writing to dictation the child translates sounds into material signs and performs certain movements, the latter process being easy and usually affording pleasure to the child.

To her predecessors Montessori owed little with regard to the teaching of writing unless by way of warning. The apparatus used by Séguin with deficient children was found inconvenient, and of his method Montessori remarked: 'We have Séguin teaching geometry in order to teach a child to write,'[39]

In accordance with her general principle Montessori adopted with regard to writing what we have termed the psychological standpoint. 'Let us observe an individual who is writing and let us seek to analyse the acts he performs', she proposed; and again: 'It goes without saying that we should examine the individual who writes, not the writing; the subject, not the object.'

The procedure followed in the teaching of writing emerged from the experience of teaching a feeble-minded girl to sew. Montessori discovered that weaving kindergarten mats enabled this child to acquire such control over the movements of the hand that she could execute sewing which she had previously been unable to perform. The general principle which she deduced from this was that 'preparatory movements could be carried on, and reduced to a mechanism, by means of repeated exercises, not in the work itself, but in that which prepares for it. Pupils could then come to the real work, able to perform it without ever having directly set their hands to it before.'[40]

Writing, according to the Montessori view, is not a mere copying of headlines, but significant writing, the writing of words which express ideas. In writing are involved two diverse types of movement, the movement by which the forms of letters are reproduced and that by which the instrument of writing is manipulated; in addition to these movements there is also necessary for the writing of words to dictation the phonetic analysis of spoken words into their elementary sounds. Preparatory exercises for each of these elements must, in accordance with the general principle enunciated above, be devised and practised independently before writing is actually commenced.

As the children had already learned to know the forms of the geometric insets by running their fingers round the contours, so, to teach the forms of the letters, it occurred to Montessori to get the pupils to trace with the finger the shapes of the letters cut out in sandpaper and pasted on cards, the roughness of the sandpaper providing a control for the accuracy of the movements. The children, indeed, as soon as they have acquired facility in this tracing of the forms of the letters, take great pleasure in repeating the movement with closed eyes. Thus the forms of the letter are not learned and impressed on the minds of the pupils by visual analysis and retained by visual imagery, but by tactual and motor experiences and grapho-motor imagery.

The phonetic sounds of the letters are taught at the same time as the tracing of the forms, the steps in the lesson following the three-stage procedure already illustrated. The audio-motor imagery helps to reinforce the grapho-motor and to facilitate the retention of the forms of the letters. The children are also practised in analysing the spoken word into its sounds and in reconstructing the word with sandpaper letters. The way is thus prepared for reading.

The control of the pen is also attacked indirectly. Recourse is had for this training to the geometric insets, of which mention has already been made. Taking one of the metal frames into which the inset fits, the child draws on a sheet of paper with a coloured crayon around the contour of the empty frame. Within the figure which results he places the metal inset, and with a crayon of a different colour traces the outline of the inset. Thus are reproduced in different colours upon the paper the two figures. With another crayon of his own selection, held as the pen is held in writing, the pupil fills in the figures which he has outlined. In making the upward and downward strokes he is taught not to pass outside the contour. Variety is lent to the task by the choice of different coloured crayons and by the use of different insets, the employment of the latter also training him to make upward and downward strokes of various lengths. Gradually the lines tend less and less to go outside the enclosing boundary until at last they are perfectly contained within it, and both the centre and the frame are filled in with close and uniform strokes. The child is now master of the writing instrument; the muscular mechanism necessary to its manipulation is established.

The moment arrives when the partial processes are perfected, when the three prerequisites to writing are at the pupil's command, that is, when he has acquired control of the writing instrument, when he can reproduce the forms of the letters moving his fingers in the air, and when the composition of words out of the isolated sounds of letters can be effected mentally. At this point the imitative tendency in the child arouses in him the impulse to write, and a pupil who has given no previous indication of having developed ability in this direction begins straightway to write. The spontaneous emergence of this writing activity is recorded by the directress much after the fashion that the appearance of the first snowdrop or primrose would be recorded by a botanist. The children, not perceiving the connection between the preparation and the combined achievement, are possessed by the delusion that, having now grown to the proper size, they know how to write.[41]

In her first efforts Montessori brought several of her pupils at the same time to the completion of the preparatory training; thereupon what might be termed a pedagogical Pentecost possessed the school. The scene was thus described by Montessori:[42] 'One beautiful December day when the sun shone and the air was like spring, I went up to the roof with the children. They were playing freely about, and a number of them were gathered about me. I was sitting near a chimney, and said to a little five-year-old boy who sat beside me, "Draw me a picture of this chimney," giving him as I spoke a piece of chalk. He got down obediently and made a rough sketch of the chimney on the tiles which formed the floor of this roof terrace. As is my custom with little children, I encouraged him, praising his work. The child looked at me, smiled, remained for a moment as if on the point of bursting into some joyous act and then cried out, " I can write! I can write!" and kneeling down again he wrote on the pavement the word "hand". Then full of enthusiasm he wrote also "chimney", "roof". As he wrote he continued to cry out, "I can write! I know how to write!" His cries of joy brought the other children, who formed a circle about him, looking down at his work in stupefied amazement. Two or three of them said to me, trembling with excitement, "Give me the chalk. I can write too." And indeed they began to write various words: mama, hand, John, chimney, Ada . . .

'After the first word, the children, with a species of frenzied joy, continued to write everywhere. . . . . In these first days we walked upon a carpet of written signs. Daily accounts showed us that the same thing was going on at home, and some of the mothers, in order to save their pavements, and even the crusts of their loaves upon which they found words written, made their children presents of paper and pencil. One of these children brought to me one day a little notebook entirely filled with writing, and the mother told me that the child had written all day long and all evening, and had gone to sleep in his bed with the paper and pencil in his hand.'

Montessori reported[43] that the average time that elapsed between the first trial of the preparatory exercises and the first written word was, for children of four years, from a month to a month and a half. With children of five years the period was much shorter, being about a month. The pupils were generally expert after three months.

The teaching of reading is prepared for in the Montessori system by the procedure adopted in the teaching of writing. Included in the exercises preparatory to writing is word-building with sandpaper script characters representing the sounds of the spoken word. Reading demands the inverse process, that is, the reproduction of the sounds from the symbols and the fusion of these sounds into words. There is also necessary for the correct enunciation of the word the proper accentuation of the syllables, and this comes only with recognition of the meaning. Montessori consequently refused to give the name 'reading' to anything less than this. Just as, in her system, writing is something more than mere copying pot-hooks and head-lines, so reading is not a mere 'barking at print' but the recognition of the meanings represented by the visual characters. 'What I understand by reading,' she said, 'is the interpretation of an idea from the written signs'; and again: 'Until the child reads a transmission of ideas from the written words he does not read.'[44]

The didactic material for the lessons in reading consists of slips of paper or of cards upon which are written, in clear large script, words and phrases.

The lessons begin with the reading of names of objects which are known or which are present. There is no question of restricting the selection of words to those that are easy, for the child already knows how to read the sounds which compose any word. The procedure is as follows: The child is given a card on which a name is written in script. He translates the writing slowly into sounds, and if the interpretation is exact the directress restricts herself to saying 'Faster'. The child reads more quickly the second time, but still often without understanding. The teacher repeats, 'Faster, faster'. The child reads 'faster' each time, repeating the same concatenation of sounds; finally the word emerges in consciousness.

When the child has pronounced the word, he places the card under the object whose name it bears, and the exercise is finished. It is a lesson which proceeds very rapidly since it is only presented to a child who is already prepared through writing.[45]

Sentences describing actions or expressing commands are likewise written on slips of paper, and the children select these and carry out the requests contained in them. It is to be noted that the child does not read the sentences aloud.[46] The aim of reading is to teach the child to discover ideas in symbols, hence the reading should be silent and not vocal. 'Reading aloud,' according to the Montessori analysis, 'implies the exercise of two mechanical forms of language – articulate and graphic – and is a complex task. The child, therefore, who begins to read by interpreting thought should read mentally.' 'Truly,' claimed Montessori,[47] 'we have buried the tedious and stupid ABC primer side by side with the useless copybooks!'

The success of this method of teaching reading may be judged from the following incident related by Montessori,[48] which also indicates that the system was in its application in Italy not confined to the children of the poor. 'A four-year-old boy, educated in a private house, surprised us in the following way. The child's father was a Deputy, and received many letters. He knew that his son had for two months been taught by means of exercises apt to facilitate the learning of reading and writing, but he had paid slight attention to it, and, indeed, put little faith in the method. One day, as he sat reading, with the boy playing near, a servant entered, and placed upon the table a large number of letters that had just arrived. The little boy turned his attention to these, and holding up each letter read aloud the address. To his father this seemed a veritable miracle.'

As to the average time required for learning to read, it appears that the period intervening between the commencement of the writing process and the appearance of the ability to read is about a fortnight. Facility in reading is, however, arrived at much more slowly than in writing. Normal children trained according to the Montessori method begin to write at four years of age and at five know how to read.

The Italians start these processes with an undoubted advantage as their language is practically phonetic. The irregular system of representation of the English language handicaps teachers who seek to apply the method in English-speaking countries; nevertheless 'individual English children who have been taught by the Montessori system have learned to read and write as rapidly as the Italian children in the Montessori schools.'[49] Tozier tells of a little boy, aged only three and a half years, who, without realising that he had done anything more than play, could read and write both in English and in Italian.[50]

Montessori's treatment of the teaching of number has not received the same general approval as her method of teaching writing and reading. This is, however, not surprising, for teachers have generally assumed that the concept of number in the child's mind originates in counting, whereas the Montessori procedure is based on a comparison of lengths, and is a long way on the road to the structural arithmetic proposed by Stern.[51]

The device of which greatest use is made in the teaching of number in the Montessori system is the 'long stair', a set of ten rods, the first being one metre in length, the last one decimetre, the intermediate rods diminishing in length by decimetres. The rods are divided into decimetre parts, the spaces on the rods being painted alternately red and blue. When arranged in order they form what is called the 'long stair'. They are utilised in the sensory exercises for training the children in discrimination of length. In these exercises the rods are mixed up, and the teacher grades them in order of length, calling the child's attention to the fact that the stair thus constructed is uniform in colour at one end. The child is then permitted to build it for himself.

After the child has had practice in arranging the rods in order of length he is required to count the red and the blue divisions, beginning with the shortest rod, thus: one; one, two; one, two, three; always going back to one in the counting of each rod and starting from the same end. He is then required to name the various rods from the shortest to the longest, according to the total number of divisions each contains, at the same time touching the rods on the side on which 'the stair' ascends. The rods may then be called 'piece number one', 'piece number two', and so on, and finally they may be spoken of in the lessons as one, two three.

The graphic signs for the numbers are cut in sandpaper, and by the three-period lesson arrangement previously illustrated the pupil is taught to associate the names of the numbers with their graphic forms. The graphic signs are then related to the quantity represented.

Addition may then be attacked, and is taught by suggesting to the child to put the shorter rods together in such a way as to form tens; 1 is added to 9, 2 to 8 and so on. Subtraction, multiplication and division can also be introduced by means of the same didactic material, and later on the child is allowed to express graphically his operations with the rods.

The means and methods of dealing with the larger denominations of number and the higher arithmetical processes are dealt with in *The Advanced Montessori Method*,[52] as is also the teaching of drawing, music, grammar and prosody.

The system was originally criticised, notably by Kilpatrick,[53] for its neglect of literary training and the training of the imagination. Unfortunately the critics identified these two imputed defects. In defence of Montessori, or in explanation, it may be said that she accepted the recapitulation principle in education: 'The child follows the natural way of development of the human race. In short, such education makes the evolution of the individual harmonise with that of humanity.'[54] To one who accepts this doctrine it would be open to contend that just as in the early development of mankind practical activities must have figured more largely than the literary, so the early education of the child should be more realistic than humanistic. In *The Advanced Montessori Method*, however, Montessori rejects the recapitulation principle, dismissing it as 'a materialistic idea now discredited'.

While Montessori was probably in error in regarding imagination as a substitute for the real and not an independent line of activity related to the real as play is to work, those who would employ fairy tales to train the imagination are in deeper error; for not only does their position imply the faculty psychology and the doctrine of formal discipline, but the training which they desiderate is also of the free or uncontrolled imagination, whereas the imagination that is of value is of the controlled constructive type – the creative imagination of science[55] and of art based on truth.[56] The proper defence of fairy tales is that they form part of the literary heritage of a people and as such ought to be known.[57]

The Montessori method necessitates the employment of

teachers who are possessed of a training in child-psychology and in its application to young children. On this Montessori repeatedly insisted: 'The broader the teacher's scientific culture and practice in experimental psychology, the sooner will come for her the marvel of unfolding life, and her interest in it.'[58] 'The more fully the teacher is acquainted with the methods of experimental psychology, the better will she understand how to give a lesson.'[59] The training of the teacher should enable her to know when to intervene in the child's activities, and, what is more important, when to refrain from intervening. 'In the manner of this intervention lies the personal art of the educator.'[60]

As the function of the teacher in the Montessori system is different from that of the teacher in the ordinary school system, being confined mainly to observing the mental development and to directing the psychical activity of the child, Montessori substituted for the title 'teacher', the term 'directress'; 'instead of facility of speech she has to acquire the power of silence; instead of teaching she has to observe; instead of the proud dignity of one who claims to be infallible she assumes the vesture of humility.'[61]

Montessori has been criticised, with reason, for overstressing the cognitive and neglecting the social aspects of a child's development.[62] Her later apologists make a good deal of the social opportunities offered by her method, but their illustrations are seldom convincing in suggesting that such opportunities will inevitably be grasped. She herself would probably have rested her fame on the introduction into early education of the special devices for sensory training. The significance of these she may have overrated. The permanent elements of her method are more likely to be the practical activities and the exercises subsidiary to the didactic processes. But the most significant feature of the system is the individualisation of instruction. Although this is characteristic of most recent advances in educational practice, Sir John Adams[63] considered himself justified in attributing to Montessori the credit for sounding the knell of class teaching.

Maria Montessori gained international recognition within a comparatively short time. *The Montessori Method*, published in 1909, only two years after the opening of the House of Childhood, was immediately successful, translated into many languages. In 1912 she visited the United States, and was received by the President; an American Montessori Association was founded. In

1922 she was appointed Inspector of Italian Schools, but steadily fell out of favour with the Fascist regime, which she regarded as seeking to exploit her international reputation. In 1934 she left to make her home in Spain; later she moved to Holland, with long absences on missionary visits. Trapped in India at the outbreak of the Second World War, she was interned there until its end. She died in the Netherlands in 1952.

At first, since her system, like those of Rousseau, Pestalozzi and Froebel, rested on faith in the potential of each child, she was widely regarded as a pioneer of progressive education. In Europe her methods had a great vogue in the period between the two world wars, when she travelled untiringly lecturing on them. 'Montessori schools' sprang up in many countries, especially under the aegis of the Roman Catholic church. But her insistence on the exclusive use of the 'right' material – 'liberty within limits' – was suspect among libertarian thinkers, who feared that it would foster slavish habits of reliance and obedience. In the United States her influence faded much earlier, mainly through the opposition of William Kilpatrick, whose critique, *The Montessori System Examined*, was published in 1914. In his view her methods were out of date; they belonged essentially to the mid-nineteenth century. He attacked her for neglecting social training, for providing inflexible materials which lacked variety, for failing to stimulate the imagination, and for relying too much on the exploded doctrine of the transfer of training. Her success with very young children, since the same effect could be achieved with no great loss by six-year-olds, amounted to a party trick. 'Stimulating she is; a contributor to our theory, hardly, if at all.'[64]

By 1918 her influence had disappeared in the United States. In Europe it did not flag until after the Hitler War. Her revival in America came in the late fifties, as part of the reaction against 'freedom methods' and the disenchantment with lack of quantifiable results. She was identified as the exponent of discipline in the interest of freedom, and a number of the psychological discoveries of Piaget were held to confirm her ideas – the role of sensory-motor training in cognitive development, the child's natural inclination to proceed from the concrete to the abstract, the phenomenon of 'stages' and 'sensitive periods'. In 1958 a new Montessori School was founded in Greenwich, Connecticut by Nancy Rambusch; by the early seventies there were several hundred. Her philosophy of the value of work (as 'fun') instead of uncontrolled and unchannelled play, and of respect for the environment in an age of pollution was commended by disciples like Rambusch,[65] Lillard[66] and Orem.[67]

Her influence, however, failed to win a long battle in Europe with the freer ideas of the Froebelians, and it was from them, notably Susan and Nathan Isaacs, that the most persistent criticism of her ideas came. As Nathan Isaacs pointed out, just before he died,[68] 'however sharply her scheme differs in *method* from conventional education, it fully accepts the latter's assumptions and aims'. Each piece of material had its specific use. The child would not be allowed to work with it until he was ready, and readiness meant recognising that use and no other. 'It is of course understood', Madame Montessori wrote, 'that here we do not speak of useless or dangerous acts, for these must be suppressed, destroyed'.[69]

The main attraction of such a scheme was the speed and efficiency with which even apparently dull children were able to learn the things society wanted them to learn. The disadvantage was the lack of creative work: convinced Froebelians wrote that it was 'practically non-existent', with many children spending their whole time 'wandering round after the teacher'. 'Unfortunately', wrote Susan Isaacs,[70] 'she has given her genius for devising techniques to the narrow ends of the scholastic subjects'. A teacher like Montessori could prevent dullness from seeping in by the power of her personality, but many of her less gifted followers could not avoid a mechanistic monotony. Individual methods were not in themselves progressive; the result might be, in Nathan Isaacs's words, 'just another old-fashioned claim to have found the real elixir of pedagogic life, the one true pedagogy'.[71]

Montessori's disciples, needless to say, rebut all these criticisms. The method, they claim, makes ample provision for creative activity, and gives full rein to social impulses. In the opinion of Orem,[72] 'Montessori schools are preparing competent, self-confident learners respectful of themselves and others. . . . Such children may represent our greatest hope for the seventies.' The conflict is one area of the most persistent education debate of the present day – freedom and trust the child or discipline and trust the teacher.

12
Dewey

It has become a cliché to point out that, in material circumstances at least, the world has changed more in the last hundred years than in all previous recorded history. Those who try to educate their younger fellows have found their task immensely complicated by such change, and have owned themselves desperately in need of guidance. The man who has produced most guidance in the last hundred years is John Dewey.[1]

He was born in the epoch-making year, 1859, in which Darwin published *The Origin of Species*; in due course one of the principal aims of his philosophical system would be to come to terms with the implications of the doctrine of evolution. His father was a storekeeper in the small town of Burlington, Vermont, a community which, like others in New England, seems to have come close to living by the principles of Jeffersonian democracy, even to the extent of holding a regular town meeting. Dewey was brought up to regard class distinctions as artificial; his religion was Congregationalist, and he saw – or believed he saw – evidence of the practical efficiency of rational, tolerant discussion.

His education was orthodox. From the town high school he went before he was sixteen to the University of Vermont, whence he graduated in 1879 without notable distinction. He did however show a special bent for philosophy, coming top in his senior year, and after a little over two years teaching high school classes in Pennsylvania and Vermont, returned to the study of the subject, this time at the new university founded by Johns Hopkins in Baltimore. In 1884 he was appointed instructor in philosophy at the University of Michigan, where he came under the powerful influence of William James and also developed a deep and abiding interest in pedagogy. Ten years later he moved as head of philosophy to the new, high-powered University of Chicago, and entered on the most productive period of his career, which was to extend over almost half a century in Chicago and New York. In the former, a huge metropolis which had grown up in his own lifetime, he had harrowing experience of the crippling social and industrial problems caused by rapid change. The philosophical system he developed was an attempt to design a blueprint for solutions, and his pedagogical system was the cutting edge of his philosophy. He was the founder and controller of the university's 'laboratory school', which opened for elementary pupils in 1896 and threw up a secondary department in 1903. Its curriculum and methods tried to give practical expression to his experimental doctrines, and there was general agreement on their success, especially at the elementary stage.

In its early days the school programme owed much to Herbartian ideas;[2] visiting lecturers included Charles deGarmo and the McMurry brothers. It was also possible to discern the influence of Rousseau, Pestalozzi and Froebel in the doctrines of child-centring and interest, and of Comenius in the emphasis on children learning from each other. None of this is surprising: as Malcolm Skilbeck points out,[3] 'of all the great educational theorists Dewey was by far the best read in the history of educational thought'. But although he drew heavily on his precursors, he also criticised them trenchantly, and the system he produced was ultimately his own.

In 1904 he accepted the chair of philosophy at Columbia, and moved to a central position in American, and international, educational thought. We have to return to Pestalozzi to find an educationist who so dominated the educational stage as John Dewey did throughout the first half of the twentieth century, and he played this part by virtue of the fact that in him were concentrated in a special degree the progressive tendencies of his age and country. Writing of the democratic way of life and the significance in it of intelligence, Dewey explained that he did not invent this faith but acquired it from his surroundings, and the same explanation might be offered for the other features of his philosophic and educational outlook. Until his retirement in 1930 and for some years afterwards he wrote and travelled widely. His ideas were taken up in many countries, notably the young Soviet Union, which was faced in the 1920s with building a new heaven and a new earth, and looked among educationists for suitable architects. Dewey's strong libertarian principles – he was active, for example, in the movement to free Sacco and Vanzetti – and his attacks on the brutalising features of capitalism made him an appropriate candidate. In Britain his theories were introduced in the first years of the twentieth century by Professor J. J. Findlay of Manchester, but they were slow to take hold. At home his influence was pervasive, spread by gifted and eloquent followers like Sidney Hook, G. H. Mead and W. H. Kilpatrick. His ideas were taken up with fervour, but often, inevitably, distorted. He died in 1952, just before a virulent reaction set in.

Dewey was a great educationist because he was a great philosopher; no one since the sophists has so intimately identified philosophy and education as Dewey has done. In fact, he himself declared that the most penetrating definition of philosophy which can be given is that it is the theory of education in its most general phases.[4] To put it the other way, 'education is the laboratory in which philosophical distinctions become concrete and are tested'. His philosophy, as might be expected of one who forthrightly rejected any situation, and condemned any institution that was static, underwent constant revision. He was fully conscious of this trait and confesses:[5] 'I seem to be unstable, chameleon-like, yielding one after another to many diverse and even incompatible influences; struggling to assimilate something from each and yet striving to carry it forward in a way that is logically consistent with what has been learned from its predecessors.'

At the outset of his career, under the influence of his teacher of philosophy and later colleague at Michigan University, Professor George S. Morris, Dewey accepted the Hegelian standpoint in philosophy.[6] With the introduction, however, of the Darwinian conception of evolution in the very year Dewey was born, idealists were faced with the alternative of replacing the Hegelian dialectic by the evolutionary view of development or of abandoning idealism completely. British Hegelians, to whom Dewey admitted he owed much, adopted the former alternative maintaining resolutely the supremacy of spirit as the essential feature of idealism. Dewey on the other hand gradually abandoned idealism in favour of Darwinian naturalism with the concepts of adaptation and the struggle for existence; the tail started to wag the dog. At this stage Dewey was inclined to designate his philosophic position 'experimental idealism'. He came to believe that with the evolution of his intelligence man had acquired an ability to control and shape his social environment.[7]

Hegelianism nevertheless left 'a permanent deposit' in Dewey's thinking. Hegel's synthesis of opposites – of subject and object, spirit and matter, the divine and the human – had a special attraction for him, and throughout his later writings we find him constantly contesting all dualisms.

Dewey was next to fall under the influence of William James (1842–1910) and pragmatism.[8] While pragmatism has always been the popular philosophy of the common man in England, it became a recognised doctrine in American schools of philosophy. It was initiated by C. S. Peirce (1839–1914) as a logical method whereby from its practical effects we could ascertain the meaning of an abstract conception, but it was generalised and popularised by William James in the form that the test of the truth of an idea is to be found in the consequences of the acts to which the idea leads.[9] It was not so much the pragmatic strain in James's philosophy that attracted Dewey as the return to the biological conception of the *psyche* which he discerned in James's psychology; *that* he found most stimulating – 'the most distinctive factors in his [James's] general philosophic view, pluralism, novelty, freedom, individuality, are all connected with his feeling for the qualities and traits of that which lives. Many philosophers have had much to say about the idea of organism; but they have taken it structurally and hence statically. It was reserved for James to think of life in terms of action.'[10]

In any activity which is in process of evolution we can define the end only in terms of the means and account for the means only by reference to the end. Dewey, not content with recognising the relativity of ends to means, subordinated the ends to the means, and even abolished the distinction between them. The end, for him, was merely a series of acts viewed at a remote stage, and the means are merely the series viewed at an earlier one; the end is a name for a series of acts taken collectively, means a name for the same series taken distributively.[11] In a sense, therefore, education has no end beyond itself, 'growth leading to further growth', a concept which was to have liberating effects for millions of children in restrictive classrooms.

The result of thus disposing of ends is to render life meaningless;

an aimless life is accordingly something to be commended rather than condemned; education, as it only too often unfortunately is, becomes an endless round – activity for activity's sake, like the cat chasing its own tail – and the whole process tends ultimately to disintegrate. Human ends are rather projections in imagination of a better state than the present; they determine the selection and organisation of the means and economise effort; they control the whole process. It is just the presence of this imaginative foresight in man, his capacity to create ideal ends, that distinguishes human action and conduct from the behaviour of animals, unawareness of the end or outcome of the process being characteristic of instinctive activity. But Dewey, although he does not, as many naturalists do, revert in philosophy to instinct as the ultimate principle of explanation of man's behaviour, nevertheless insists on the continuity of animal and human life; the same principles of explanation are common to both; he recognises no difference between the protozoon and the creature who has been made a little lower than the angels; he refuses to acknowledge another dimension of experience in man than that assigned to animals; culture, art, morality and religion are all explicable on biological principles; there exists for him no 'realm of ends'. Everything is provisional; nothing ultimate. Knowledge is always a means, never an end in itself; it is purely instrumental, hence the title of Dewey's philosophy – Instrumentalism.[12]

An organism so long as it lives is subject to change and even after death to disintegration. Change accordingly becomes one of Dewey's most fruitful categories. In pre-Socratic days Heraclitus propounded the doctrine of the flux of things; matter was unceasingly undergoing transmutation; all life was involved in continual decomposition and renewal.[13] In protest Socrates sought in the definition something stable which would render discussion possible, and Plato found in the 'idea' the permanent element that made things what they are.

For Dewey there are no fixed beliefs; the quest for certainty on which philosophers and men of science have been engaged ever since the time of Socrates is an illusion diverting man's attention and abilities from the possible and practical realities within his comprehension – it is dismissed as a 'compensatory perversion'.[14] There are no easy formulae for solving ethical problems; 'growth itself is the only moral end'[15] Idealism, on the other hand, contends that spiritual values are indestructible. It acknowledges 'the eternal realities which do not change and the beauties that do not fade'.[16] The great achievements of history are credited to men who have faith in some fundamental principle. It is of such Fichte wrote.[17] 'These men, and all others of like mind in the history of the world won the victory because eternity inspired them, and this inspiration always does, and always must, defeat him who is not so inspired.' Mankind too in its long history down the ages has here and there succeeded in hitting the right trail. There are spheres in which the procedures that man has adopted are never likely to be abandoned; although the methods may be modified and expanded, the pursuit will continue in the same direction; we do not anticipate change out of all recognition. A. N. Whitehead in *The Aims of Education* declares[18] that the process [of science] is a search for permanence, uniformity and simplicity of logical relation. In *Science and the Modern World* he elaborates:[19] Apart from recurrences, knowledge would be impossible, for nothing could be referred to our past experience. Also apart from some regularity of recurrences measurement would be impossible. But there is a complementary fact – nothing ever recurs in exact detail. Men expected the sun to rise, but the wind bloweth where it listeth. There are thus two principles inherent in the very nature of things, the spirit of change and the spirit of conservation. There can be nothing real without both.

Dewey himself cannot remain faithful to the principle of change. In *How We Think*[20] he refers to 'securely established facts and principles', and recognises that if thinking is to be possible at all 'the standard of reference must remain the same to be of any use. The concept signifies that a meaning has been stabilized, and remains the same in different contexts.' In *Freedom and Culture*,[21] referring to Jefferson's speeches and letters Dewey explains that it is the *ends* of democracy, the rights of *man* – not of men in the plural – which are unchangeable. In *A Common Faith*[22] he went so far as to assert that 'ours is the responsibility of conserving, transmitting, rectifying and expanding the heritage of values we have received'. And his disciple W. H. Kilpatrick in spite of devoting a section to the 'Philosophy of Change' in *Education for a Changing Civilisation* concedes:[23] 'Consider chemistry. It changes, but the tested results remain reliable.'

An exclusive dependence on change would render reference to the past useless, and planning ahead futile; one could only wait till the necessity should arise. Participation in, rather than preparation for, life became the watchword of education. It led to the incredible extravagances of some progressive schools which did not believe in teaching facts because facts are constantly changing and regarded the reaching of geography as useless because maps alter so rapidly. It would justify the student who, to his tutor's query why he was not working for an examination, replied that he wanted to come fresh to it!

The issue of permanence or progress in education was raised by Kant in his *Lectures on Education*: 'Children', he says,[24] 'ought to be educated, not for the present, but for a possibly improved condition of man in the future.' Plato having established his ideal state would allow no innovations; his ideal was permanence. Herbert Spencer,[25] on the other hand, rejects government control as conservative, and regards education as a progressive force in society. 'All institutions have an instinct of self-preservation growing out of the selfishness of those connected with them. Being dependent for their vitality upon the continuance of existing arrangements, they naturally uphold these. Their roots are in the past and the present, never in the future. Change threatens, modifies them, eventually destroys them; hence to change they are uniformly opposed. On the other hand, education, properly so-called, is closely associated with change – is its pioneer – is the never-sleeping agent of revolution – is always fitting men for higher things, and *unfitting* them for things as they are. Therefore, between constitutions whose very existence depends upon man continuing what he is, and true education, which is one of the instruments for making him something other than he is, there must always be enmity.' Both permanence and progress are essential, and Dewey by his emphasis on change has challenged the mediaevalism that would shackle education to the past.

In addition to the naturalistic bias, Dewey derived from James the doctrine of pragmatism but not without qualification. Dewey, in fact, accuses James of a paradoxical habit of merely turning things upside down – instead of the thought being father to the deed, the deed is father to the thought. By contrast Dewey affirms that the essence of pragmatic instrumentalism is to conceive of both knowledge and practice as means of making good –

excellencies of all kinds – secure in experienced existence, and he explains:[26] 'It does not imply that action is higher and better than knowledge, and practice inherently superior to thought. Constant and effective interaction of knowledge and practice is something quite different from an exaltation of activity, for its own sake. Action when directed by knowledge, is method and means, not an end. The aim and end is the securer, freer and more widely shared embodiment of values in experience by means of that active control of objects which knowledge alone makes possible.'

Notwithstanding this disclaimer there are numerous statements throughout Dewey's writings which are scarcely, if at all, distinguishable from the pronouncements of James. Thus, in *Democracy and Education*,[27] dealing with the development of the experimental method he says: 'It means that we have no right to call anything knowledge except where our activity has actually produced certain physical changes in things, which agree with and confirm the conception entertained.' In *Human Nature and Conduct* he maintains[28] that the act comes before the thought, and that a motive does not exist prior to an act and produce it. In *The Quest for Certainty* he declares that the experimental procedure is one that installs doing at the heart of knowing, that the validity of the object of thought depends upon the consequences of the operations which define the object of thought; and he repeats – the test of ideas, of thinking generally, is found in the consequences of the acts to which the ideas lead.[29]

An objection urged against hedonism in ethics is that we cannot tell beforehand how much pleasure a given course of action will yield. So with pragmatism; we cannot tell till the deed is done what the consequences may be and whether the idea on which we acted is right. We can be wise only after the event. As Whitehead says:[30] 'If we wait for the necessities of action before we commence to arrange our ideas, in peace we shall have lost our trade, and in war we shall have lost the battle.' Dewey himself in another connection concedes[31] that the final outcome can never be foreseen: 'The point is the intervention of an indefinite number of indefinitely ramifying conditions between what a person does and the consequences of his actions, including even the consequences which return upon him. The intervals in time and space are so extensive that the larger number of factors that decide the final outcome cannot be foreseen. Even when they can be anticipated, the results are produced by factors over which the average person has hardly any more control than he has over those which produce earthquakes.'[32]

Anticipating such a self-contradictory dogma, John Ruskin in *Unto This Last*[33] has robustly formulated the idealist position, 'No man ever knew, or can know, what will be the ultimate result to himself, or to others, of any given line of conduct. But every man may know, and most of us do know, what is a just and unjust act. And all of us may know also, that the consequences of justice will be ultimately the best possible, both to others and ourselves, though we can neither say what is best, or how it is likely to come to pass.' If we accept Dewey's statements that the test of truth lies in the consequences to which it leads, and that we can never know what these consequences are, we are convicted of pure scepticism.

The pragmatists' exaltation of practice over theory, of experimental inquiry over speculation, of action over contemplation is historically untenable. Ideas are more powerful and lasting than actions, the influence of which is limited to a particular time and place. Ideas have the capacity of perpetual self-reproduction which Plato's *Symposium* declared was the characteristic of immortality. Apart from the teaching of the great religious leaders, ideas have changed the course of the world's history; we need only instance Rousseau's *Social Contract* and the French Revolution or Karl Marx's *Das Kapital* and modern communism. Dewey's view[34] that practice inspires theory, that educational practices and direct experience in the field originate and determine educational ends and theories is contradicted by the history of education; almost all the great educators have been philosophers, and have not been renowned for their skill in practical teaching – in fact, some of them take an impish delight in confessing their failure as practitioners.

Some mental activities cannot be said to have any practical consequences, for example, the pursuit of a subject for its own sake which is just its cultural value, the appreciation of a work of art or the enjoyment of a symphony. These are not instrumental; they are autotelic or, to use Dewey's term, 'consummatory'; they have intrinsic worth; they are ends in themselves. In a democratic society the individual too has to be treated as an end in himself. Dewey tries to evade this conclusion by designating certain excursions into higher mathematics as 'playing with concepts', but play itself is just another autotelic experience.

Pragmatism, laying stress on consequences, ignores or disparages motives. Thus Dewey says:[35] 'We call a biting dog ugly, but we don't look for his motive in biting. . . . It is absurd to ask what induces a man to activity generally speaking. He is an active being and that is all there is to be said on the score.' Yet courts of law in judging whether the accused committed a murder do not hesitate to consider the motive of the crime.

Tried by every practical test – its own criterion – pragmatism fails to account for the facts; as it has been said, it is not a philosophy, but a way of trying to do without philosophy. Its value in education might be expressed in the words of Francis Bacon:[36] 'But this is that which will dignify and exalt knowledge; if contemplation and action may be more nearly and straitly conjoined than they have been.'

Pragmatism is reflected in Dewey's curriculum, if in his educational philosophy we dare speak of a curriculum. Indeed, he regarded *Democracy and Education* as the book in which his philosophy was most fully expounded, for 'education is the laboratory in which philosophic distinctions become concrete and are tested'.[37] In *The Dewey School*[38] the main hypothesis was that life itself, especially the occupations and associations which serve man's chief needs, should furnish the ground experience for the education of the child. An occupation like cooking or carpentry 'supplies the child with a genuine motive'.[39] Herbert Spencer in *Education: Intellectual, Physical and Moral*,[40] answering his own question 'What knowledge is of most worth?', adopted the same principle, and anticipating by a century certain modern writers, oriented education from the scientific standpoint, claiming that a curriculum based on science would satisfy all the requirements of a liberal education.[41] He classified the activities which constitute human life in order of importance as follows: the biological, the social and political and the cultural, adding that accomplishments, the fine arts, *belles-lettres* as they occupy the leisure part of life, should be subordinate to that instruction and discipline on which civilisation rests. Modern curriculum makers would classify these activities in the order of frequency, a criterion which Dewey rightly rejects, claiming that while the principle contributes at most to the more efficient practices in some subjects, it does not give any help in larger questions of curriculum reconstruction and methods.[42]

Dewey, however, unlike Spencer and modern curriculum makers, maintains that it is impossible to classify human activities for educational purposes. We cannot establish a hierarchy of values among studies, he affirms.[43] 'It is futile to attempt to arrange them in an order beginning with one having least worth and going on to that of maximum value. In so far as any study has a unique and irreplaceable function in experience, in so far as it marks a characteristic enrichment of life, its worth is intrinsic and incomparable . . . the only ultimate value which can be set up is just the process of living itself.' This view that there are no ultimate ends to which the concrete satisfactions of experience are subordinate dispenses with a predetermined curriculum, the result being thus stated by the President of Yale University: 'To-day the young American comprehends the intellectual tradition of which he is a part and in which he must live only by accident.' 'The crucial error', he adds, 'is that of holding that nothing is any more important than anything else, that there can be no order of goods and no order in the intellectual realm. There is nothing central and nothing peripheral, nothing primary and nothing secondary, nothing basic and nothing superficial.'[44]

Dewey himself had earlier scented this danger, for in an article entitled 'How Much Freedom in the New Schools'[45] he issued the warning that it is the absence of intellectual control through significant subject-matter which stimulates the deplorable egotism, cockiness, impertinence and disregard for the rights of others apparently considered by some persons to be the inevitable accompaniment, if not the essence, of freedom, and he challenged the progressive schools to furnish a new type of subject-matter. 'And this subject-matter can be provided in a way which will obtain ordered and consecutive development of experience only by means of the thoughtful selection and organisation of material by those having the broadest experience – those who treat impulses and inchoate desires and plans as potentialities of growth and not as finalities.'

In spite of his contention that we cannot classify human activities for educational purposes Dewey does indicate an order of preference; the curriculum, he says,[46] echoing Spencer, must be planned with reference to placing essentials first and refinements second. And his answer to the questions, What are the essentials? What are men's chief needs? is biased by his pragmatic philosophy: 'Men's fundamental common concerns center about food, shelter, clothing, household furnishings, and the appliances connected with production, exchange and consumption. Representing both the necessities of life and the adornments with which the necessities have been clothed, they tap instincts at a deep level; they are saturated with facts and principles having a social quality.' While Spencer with his insistence on pure science and individualism is typical of the nineteenth century, Dewey with his insistence on applied science and industrial arts and on the social factor is representative of the twentieth century. Both nevertheless tend to underrate the importance in man's life of the spiritual values, on which T. Percy Nunn insisted in defining the essentials of life:[47] 'Among the strains or currents in a national tradition the highest value belongs to those that are richest in the creative element. These are themselves traditions of activity, practical, intellectual, aesthetic, moral with a high degree of individuality and continuity, and they mark out the main lines in the development of the human spirit. Consider what man has made of poetry, and what poetry has made of him; what a noble world he has created out of the sounds of vibrating reeds, strings and brass; think of the expansion of soul he has gained through architecture and the arts of which it is the mother and queen; of the achievements of his thought, disciplined into the methods of mathematics, the sciences and philosophy. Do we not rightly measure the quality of a civilisation by its activities in such directions as these? and if so, must not such activities be typically represented in every education which offers the means to anything that can properly be called fullness of life?' Dewey evidently plumps for food and furniture, Nunn for poetry and philosophy – an illustration of the age-long conflict in human thought between the materialistic and the idealistic views of life.

Not content with maintaining that consequences are the ultimate test and criterion of meaning and validity, Dewey complemented the pragmatic principle by emphasising origins, claiming that thinking arises out of practical needs, that only through action is knowledge acquired and progress made possible. He was, in fact, more interested in the means or instrumentality of attaining knowledge than in testing its validity. The method whereby this is attained is the experimental. 'That western civilisation is increasingly industrial in character is commonplace; it should be an equally familiar fact that this industrialization is the direct fruit of the growth of the experimental method of knowing.'[48] So impressed is Dewey with its efficacy that he is led to assume that it is the only method of knowing. Thus in *How We Think*[49] he maintains that from the scientific side, it is demonstrated that effective and integral thinking is possible only where the experimental method in some form is used. This contention has suggested the alternative title to his philosophy, namely, Experimentalism. In his laboratory school at the University of Chicago it was applied assiduously in the teaching of history and science; in literature, where it fitted less conveniently, the rationale was not so clear.[50]

On both counts Dewey's thesis is inadequate. While necessity is the mother of invention, pure intellectual curiosity likewise stimulates the extension of knowledge. Aristotle in his *Metaphysics*[51] affirmed that philosophy originated in wonder, but all that we need do to discount Dewey's assumption is to examine the instances of operational thinking cited by Dewey himself in *How We Think*.[52] Two of the three originate in theoretical curiosity not in practical needs, namely 'A Case of Reflection upon an Observation', the significance of a long white pole bearing a gilded ball at its tip which projects nearly horizontally from the upper deck of ferryboats; and the cause of bubbles appearing on the outside of the mouth of tumblers and going inside when the tumblers are washed in hot soapsuds and then placed mouth downwards on a plate. The third instance, 'A Case of Practical Deliberation', namely, to decide which of several routes to take to enable him to keep an appointment does arise out of practical needs. The ratio of the theoretical to the practical is evidently not in Dewey's favour.

There are, as Whitehead has said,[53] two kinds of logic – one of which, however, Dewey ignores – the logic of discovery and the logic of the discovered. 'The logic of discovery consists in the weighing of probabilities, in discarding details deemed to be irrelevant, in divining the general rules according to which events occur, and in testing hypotheses by devising suitable experiments. This is inductive logic. The logic of the discovered is the deduction of the special events which, under certain circumstances, would happen in obedience to the assumed laws of nature. Thus when the laws are discovered or assumed, their utilisation entirely depends on deductive logic. Without deductive logic science would be entirely useless. It is merely a barren game to ascend from the particular to the general, unless afterwards we can reverse the process and descend from the general to the particular, ascending and descending like the angels of Jacob's ladder. When Newton had divined the law of gravitation he at once proceeded to calculate the earth's attraction on an apple at its surface and on the moon. We may note in passing that inductive logic would be impossible without deductive logic. Thus Newton's calculations were an essential step in his inductive verification of the great law.'

The history of science does not support Dewey. Advances in the mathematical sciences have come about mainly by deduction: 'Humanity has waited centuries for the revelation of certain properties of the circle and the ellipse which we know were nevertheless implicitly contained in the definition of these curves, since we can deduce them from it by syllogisms and with the help of a small number of postulates and of axioms recognised as valid at all times. But for the circle and the ellipse we use no experiments. Of what avail could they be since it is a question of purely rational deduction?'[54] In view of the difficulty of applying experiment in astronomy Dewey shifts his position and explains[55] that the progress of inquiry is synonymous with advance in the invention and construction of physical instruments for producing, registering and measuring changes. Physics is the field where experiment has been pre-eminently successful, but even here progress is not exclusively dependent on experiment, some scientific principles having been arrived at by deductive reasoning.[56] And Whitehead adds:[57] 'The paradox is now fully established that the utmost abstractions are the true weapons with which to control our thought of concrete fact.' While in the biological sciences the scope of experiment is being considerably extended, the great change of outlook in biology in the nineteenth century – Darwin's doctrine of evolution – was not achieved by experiment but by observation and deduction. In psychology the most significant advance since the time of Aristotle – Freud's disclosure of the 'Unconscious' – was not the result of experiment but of clinical observation.[58] In the social sciences the complexity of the factors makes experiment difficult, and leads Dewey to confess:[59] 'What purports to be experiment in the social field is very different from experiment in natural science; it is rather a process of trial and error accompanied with some degree of hope and a great deal of talk.'

Although the verdict on Dewey's appeal on behalf of experiment as the essential feature of all productive thinking is 'Not Proven', this should not detract from the credit of insisting that in the acquisition of knowledge acquaintance with the process is essential to the full understanding of the result to which it leads.[60] The virtue of the heuristic method[61] lay in this rather than in following the order of the original discoveries. The experimental method that Dewey proposes is a definitely planned procedure; it is not, as he warns his too ardent disciples,[62] 'just messing around nor doing a little of this and a little of that in the hope that things will improve'. Vocational education must concentrate on underlying industrial principles, not merely on the acquisition of job skills.[63] The stages of the method are those of any logical induction – formulation of problem, suggestion of hypothesis, testing hypothesis, formulation of principle – but expressed by Dewey as follows:[64] 'They are first that the pupil have a genuine situation of experience – that there be a continuous activity in which he is interested for its own sake; secondly, that a genuine problem develop within this situation as a stimulus to thought; third, that he possess the information and make the observations needed to deal with it; fourth, that suggested solutions occur to him which he shall be responsible for in an orderly way; fifth, that he have opportunity and occasion to test his ideas by application, to make their meaning clear and to discover for himself their validity.'[65]

The two aspects of thinking – that thinking arises out of practical needs and the testing of results by their practical consequences – are combined in the project method.[66] The method is a natural corollary to his teaching, although Dewey repeatedly warns us of its limitations. Thus in *Democracy and Education* he mentions that projects may be too ambitious and beyond the pupil's capacity to accomplish: 'It is quite true that children tend to exaggerate their powers of execution, and to select projects that are beyond them';[67] and in *The Way Out of Educational Confusion*[68] he indicates the opposite defect that projects may be too trivial to be educative.

In view of the title of Dewey's main educational work *Democracy and Education,* we cannot conclude our review without reference to his political doctrines. He himself was brought up in 'a classless society',[69] and any form of authoritarianism was foreign to his nature. He accepted Aristotle's principle[70] that 'that which most contributes to the permanence of constitutions is the adaptation of education to the form of government', hence a democratic state should have a democratic form of education.[71] Much has yet to be done to make education really democratic even in countries professedly democratic, and to augment these efforts fresh inspiration can be derived from Dewey's writings.

There were times nevertheless when, in the absence of absolute and universal moral standards and denied any support from historical precedents, he was inclined by reason of his faith in experimentation to sponsor any revolutionary effort no matter what the outcome, but ultimately he returned to the democratic way of life; we had hoped also that as the deficiencies of naturalism and pragmatism declared themselves he might return to an idealism that was yet dynamic and inclusive of all that was valuable in both these schools.

In education we cannot but be grateful to Dewey for his great services in challenging the old 'static cold storage ideal of knowledge'[72] and in bringing education more into accord with the actualities of present-day life. 'The pupil must learn what has meaning, what enlarges his horizon, instead of mere trivialities'.[73] Moreover, he regarded *all* education as taking place in the context of society, as he was bound to do, since for him experience was the constant interaction of man and his environment. The general principle underlying the developments in his philosophy and his applications of these in education appears to be that both philosophy and education should reflect the main currents of contemporary thought and incorporate the techniques that have so signally contributed to modern industrial and social progress.

Dewey's ideas were powerfully influential in the early and middle twentieth century, that is within his own lifetime, in many nations of widely divergent political persuasions. The young Soviet Republic, as we have seen, flirted with his ideas in the twenties and thirties. In Britain the pioneers quoted and followed him in the thirties and forties, but his period of influence really began in the sixties. The emphasis he placed on direct experience and problem-solving resulted in the reshaping of the classical curriculum and the abolition of uncomprehending 'grinding'. He more than anyone displaced the teacher from the centre of his classroom. Dewey's influence was so pervasive that his concepts, especially in reference to the child's need for experience, activity and interest if any meaningful learning is to occur, have become axioms in modern educational thinking.[74]

On the other hand, he has been blamed for some of the more spectacular aberrations in modern education, especially in America. No less a person than President Eisenhower warned the nation in 1959[75] that 'educators, parents and students must be continuously stirred up by the defects in our educational system. They must be induced to abandon the educational path that, rather blindly, they have been following as a result of John Dewey's teaching'. His philosophical doctrines were received only in terms of a narrow instrumentalism, which came in time to be roundly criticised: 'There is no common faith, no common body of principle, no common body of knowledge, no common moral and intellectual discipline. Yet the graduates of these modern schools are expected to form a civilised community'.[76] A counter-attack was led by R. H. Hutchins, with a powerful demand for the restoration of 'basic values'. In 1955 the Progressive Education Association foundered, and two years later its journal died, events which 'marked the end of an era in American pedagogy'.[77]

However, as Dewey's disciple and colleague, Sidney Hook, pointed out,[78] Eisenhower ought to have written about 'the path they have been following as a result of *their misconceptions of* John Dewey's teaching'. Although Dewey stressed the importance of freedom, he was not opposed to authority; on the contrary, for him 'authority is necessary and the supreme one is intelligence'. He had no patience with dictatorships masquerading under the disguise of 'participatory democracy' and distrusted those who 'regarded democracy merely as a means of realising socialism, instead of testing proposed socialist measures as a means of extending and deepening democracy'. Moreover, he regarded democracy as a *political* concept; there was no need, he considered, for all its social agencies, including education, to take the same form of one man, one vote. In short, Dewey's democracy meant concern for all; it encouraged neither mediocrity nor licence.

Nor did he, as the present-day de-schoolers would, equate education with experience. On the contrary, he distinguished educational from non-educational experiences, and laid all his emphasis on the former. Activity, the process most frequently linked with his name, was required to have some intellectual content if it were to have any educational value.[79] In any case, his lifelong devotion to the scientific method as a basis for evaluating learning would have led him to condemn all the more extreme educational nostrums of modern society.

In short, John Dewey has suffered the customary fate of daring innovators, to become the idol of later theorists who mistake rashness for daring, embrace change for its own sake, and regress from innovation into bizarreness and absurdity. His solid influence has been felt in the establishment of education as a university study, in the acceptance of the need for schools to respond to social change, in a continuing (though sometimes wavering) faith in the power of rational inquiry, in emphasis on the child's contribution to his own growth. His philosophy does not immediately appeal in an age in which events often appear to be directed by ponderous forces far beyond human control. Nevertheless, in the late seventies, there is some evidence that, a quarter of a century after his death, the tide is setting again in Dewey's direction.

13

The Twentieth Century

DEWEY was the last of the Great Educators in the classical mode. Perhaps because so many people have become interested in education and acquired a little knowledge of it, there no longer seems to be any place for the towering figure, the seer. This is not to say that prophets are never discovered nor universal nostrums enthusiastically peddled. But the nostrums command no lasting acceptance, and the theories which are accepted are never universal.

The educational problems remain, and allowing for the greater complexity of modern life, they are in general the same questions which occupied the Great Educators. Ours has been a paradoxical century: it has seen increasing assertions of the importance of the individual, but also of the society in which he lives. The interaction of individuals and social groups has come to be the central study of educational theory, not by any means for the first time, though as much of the theorists' time has been devoted to defining terms, 'packing for the journey'. We have also seen, especially in the last quarter of a century, a movement against any kind of determinism, against authoritarianism and, in its extreme form, against authority. Freedom has become a good as absolute as any postulated by Plato. Every experimental assertion has been entertained, every tradition laid open to question. Inevitably, this trend has been succeeded by considerable impatience when the Golden Journey has taken so long to reach Samarkand, or by disillusionment at the uninviting oases it seems to have reached so far.

To each of these problems modern thinkers have contributed solutions, or at least suggestions. This chapter sets out to mention a few. The reader who desires to do these thinkers more justice will find the titles of their books in the bibliography.

Increasing attention to the individual showed itself early in this century in the growth of child study. Arnold Gesell[1] traced the normal pattern of development and shed light on the significance of play and the process whereby children lost, or sublimated, the desire to play. Susan Isaacs,[2] working at the Malting House School in Cambridge, showed how they learn by activity and discovery, and her influence was strong in breaking down the traditional compartmental walls of the primary curriculum. The thirties were the high-water mark of mental testing, most efficiently developed by Sir Cyril Burt,[3] Sir Godfrey Thomson[4] and Sir Fred Schonell,[5] and intended to chart and scale the mental equipment of individual children. The rights of a free man in a democratic community were staunchly defended by Sir Percy Nunn.[6] But the study of the individual in this century has owed most to an Austrian and a Swiss, Sigmund Freud and Jean Piaget.

Freud,[7] a Viennese doctor, found he had small success in diagnosing certain pathological conditions, or indeed in accounting for many normal behaviour patterns until he studied the minds of his patients as well as their bodies. What he found there he could explain only in terms of a theory as revolutionary in its way as Einstein's, a theory succinctly stated in the title of one of his books, *The Psychopathology of Everyday Life*. In his thesis no behaviour is accidental, and if conscious motivation cannot be traced, then the driving force is unconscious. An individual's actions show an attempt to reconcile two warring compulsions, the 'Pleasure Principle', which impels him to satisfy his drives, conscious and unconscious, and the 'Reality Principle', which enforces conformity with the demands of his physical and social environment. The drive which provides the energy to cope with challenges Freud found in emotional, not cognitive effort. This driving force, which motivates all actions, is sexuality, and Freud called it the 'libido'. He postulated three dimensions – the Id, which seeks to gratify emotional needs on the Pleasure Principle; the Ego, which expresses the individual's personality and is controlled by the Reality Principle; and the Super-Ego, which, aspiring towards an ideal, imports a moral element into his conduct. Since these forces are constantly in conflict, his mind develops various mechanisms to defend itself against the attendant distress, notably the unconscious process whereby an intolerable impulse is repressed or sublimated.

Such a theory inevitably attached deep importance to the earliest human relationships, especially those between a child and his parents. Freud discerned sexual impulses of all kinds in the life of an infant, impulses which aroused not only love for both parents, but jealousy and even hatred. This concept above all raised a storm of protest and disbelief. In any case, since he was telling people that what were universally regarded as pathological conditions were in fact part of everyone's daily life, he could hardly expect to be cordially received. More professional critics appraised his ideas on a more professional level. Alfred Adler[8] accepted his concept of a universal drive, but found it in aggressiveness, not sexuality. Carl Jung[9] postulated a general drive, not confined to sexual matters. By some Freud was taxed with undermining the concept of free will and giving everyone an excuse for reprehensible behaviour, the last interpretation of his theories he would have accepted. More recent psychologists regard as over-ambitious his claim that all behaviour, without exception, has a motive, and concentrate their attention on the patterns behaviour forms.

Freud's theories were not new. His concept of the unconscious, for instance, may be found in Herbart,[10] his advocacy of non-repression in Rousseau. But his theory of psycho-analysis, as he worked it out in its entirety, seemed revolutionary, and had the reception generally accorded to successful revolutionary theories, wide disapproval for a time, and equally wide acceptance later, with almost no intermediate stage. In the field of education it spelt the end of compulsion, in intention at least, for every form of repression was seen as dangerous to the health of a child's mind. Educators sought to provide outlets for his drives and energies, stressed the need to foster adaptability, underlined the importance of early relationships. The role of the teacher as a substitute parent was psycho-analysed. 'Freedom methods' of teaching were promoted, and if the ordinary schools stopped short of the liberty required, 'free schools' were established to provide it.

The most radical revolt against the formality of education in the state classrooms was conducted by Alexander S. Neill.[11] Neill, trained as a pupil-teacher in Scotland, began teaching there, but soon came into irreconcilable conflict with the authorities and was dismissed. Deeply influenced by psycho-analytic doctrines, he sought to protect his pupils from the dangers consequent upon repression by encouraging them to express themselves freely: 'One day humanity may trace all its miseries, its hates and its diseases to its particular form of civilization that is essentially anti-life.'[12] 'The question of masturbation is supreme in education. . . . The prohibition of masturbation means miserable, unhappy children. I say that one of the root reasons for the happiness of Summerhill children is the removal of the fear and self-hate that sex prohibitions induce'.[13] 'It is only thwarted power that works for evil. Human beings are good; they want to be good; they want to love and be loved. Hate and rebellion are only thwarted love and thwarted power'.[14] He therefore sought to provide children with the care and affection from which they could draw security. He established a free school at Summerhill, which gained fame far beyond England because of his eloquence in expounding his ideas. He had a number of disciples. Those inside the state system found it virtually impossible to practise his doctrines intact.

Jean Piaget,[15] 'perhaps the only living psychologist whose name is a household word',[16] was born in Neuchâtel in 1896. He was a youthful prodigy, taking his degree in biology in 1915 and his doctorate three years later; he was offered a post in the Geneva museum while he was still at school. A period of research in ecology fostered his interest in the balance of organism and environment, the main theme of his psychological theories. He worked from 1921 to 1971 in the Institut Rousseau at Geneva, the last forty years as Director, and poured out a broad stream of publications, highly original and widely influential, on the cognitive development of children. His Institute attracted scholars from all over the world and a great deal of money from America, notably from the Ford and Rockefeller Foundations. An International Centre was set up in Geneva, and when he retired from the Institute at the age of seventy-five he continued to work in the Centre.

As early as 1923, in *The Language and Thought of the Child*, Piaget laid down the foundations of his developmental theory, specifying three stages of mental life, the *autistic* (the first 18 months), in which the child is ruled by his immediate needs, the *egocentric* (from 18 months to 7 or 8 years), in which he recognises the existence of others but no need to comply or bargain with them, and the *social* (from 7 or 8 to about 16), in which appear the first manifestations of self-criticism and social conformity. The child, in short, travels 'the long road of decentration'.[17] He extends his knowledge by forming patterns based on his experiences, and his ability to do so develops in stages – the sensory-motor (0 to 2), the pre-conceptual (2 to 4 or 5), the intuitive (4 or 5 to 7), the concrete operational (7 to 11) and the formal operational (11 to 16). The most important single factor in the growth of cognitive power is his development of the ability to symbolise.

The motive force for this development Piaget found within the child himself; the governing factor is 'readiness'. There are few, if any, references to the part which may be played by other human beings, teachers for example, in stimulating and promoting development. The foundation of cognitive growth is not perception, but action: the child learns by doing. Above all, Piaget pointed out, echoing Rousseau, a child's modes of thought are fundamentally different from those of an adult.

His method of accumulating evidence was psychological. Showing 'a remarkable flair for empathy with children',[18] he observed their behaviour over lengthy periods and reported his deductions. One of the sharpest criticisms of his work was, and is, that he never gave sufficient attention to measurement, for which observation, however meticulous, cannot be a total substitute.

Nevertheless, a huge volume of research has arisen from his ideas, and the curricula of primary teacher training courses were increasingly indebted to him. In the years after the Second World War he became a cult figure, and although psychologists had never been quite happy with his technique, it was not until the seventies that criticism of his ideas became substantial.[19] His clinical method came under attack, partly because it was held to cut him off from the everyday world of children, but more because he was less than rigorous in following up and confuting alternative hypotheses. His assertion that children learn only by doing was contested, since a number of experiments seemed to indicate that they can learn operational thinking simply by observation, without handling anything,[20] and new research suggested that cognitive structures have their foundations in the processes of perception.

The most persistent criticism concentrated on his theories of moral and emotional development. For both he proposed a progression of stages like those in cognitive growth. Morally, he claimed, the child moves from simple motor behaviour through the egocentric stage to one in which he accepts the rules of the game. His critics held that he underestimated the effect of external (especially parental) precept and example, and to those who traced all morality to the influence of the social environment his theory was totally unacceptable. Emotional development he saw as another facet of the same general process. He leant heavily on Freud and the psycho-analysts, but provided little evidence in support.

As Peters points out,[21] Piaget was influenced by Kant in his concept of the stages by which a child imposes order on the flux of experience. Some psychologists, notably Nathan and Susan Isaacs, proposed alternative stages of their own, and criticised him for separating each too sharply from the next. Moreover, his concentration on the single variable of age passed over the manifest influence of others, such as culture differences.[22] Later research has paid more attention to the actual process of development than to the structure of its stages. But as a description of cognitive growth, Piaget's theories have the ring of truth, and their influence has been profound, especially among teachers of the very young; for them now 'the readiness is all'. Even his critics acknowledge that 'Piaget is obviously one of the giants in the history of psychology'.[23]

With increased attention to the individual has come greater emphasis on the inescapable influence of his environment. From the twenties onward belief steadily decreased in man's ability to withstand the crushing pressures, physical, social and political, to which he is exposed. In the field of intelligence measurement the battle grumbled on between the geneticists and the environmentalists. Concern over the influence of the state, and the need to transform it for the benefit of its citizens had come to the fore after the cataclysm of 1914–18, but there had been a reaction in the twenties against the frightening violence in Russia, Germany and Hungary. The economic recession of the thirties, the fascist adventures, and another world war contributed to a general conviction that society must be converted from the villain to the hero of the educational piece.

The thinker with most influence on education in this period was not a professional educator at all, but a political philosopher. In the view of Karl Marx,[24] man's social existence determines his consciousness; in consequence Marx's conception of philosophy was not contemplative but activist. 'The philosophers', reads his Eleventh Thesis, quoted on his tombstone, 'have only interpreted the world in various ways; the point, however, is to change it.' He was interested only in ideas which would improve the quality of life for ordinary men and women. He believed all history and thought to be products of economic factors, and therefore identified the characteristic feature of Western state systems as their capitalist economy. Unlike Hegel, by whom he was influenced, he emphasised material explanations of historical and social phenomena; mystical and idealist theories of the state as something greater than the sum of its individual citizens he regarded not only as nonsense, but as dangerous to the interests of its citizens. For him capitalism was a thoroughly bad system,[25] harmful to the majority of those who lived under it, for it commandeered without payment a proportion of the labour of each worker, and must constantly force him to increase his productivity in order to preserve itself: 'Capitalist production is in itself indifferent to the particular use-value and distinctive features of any commodity it produces. In every sphere of production it is only concerned with producing surplus value and appropriating a certain quantity of unpaid labour incorporated in the product of labour.'[26]

Moreover, since it was based on exchange-value rather than use-value, capitalism distorted the natural order of things. Here Marx might have been speaking with the voice of Rousseau. However, he believed the days of capitalism to be numbered, and expected some form of socialist state sympathetic to the workers inevitably to take its place. The dynamic political creed which would bring about the change he saw as Communism: 'Between capitalist and communist society lies the period of the revolutionary transformation of the one into the other. There corresponds to this also a political transformation period in which the state can be nothing but the revolutionary dictatorship of the proletariat.'[27]

In fact, Marx did not devote much attention to the mechanism of change. That was left to his followers, notably Lenin, who emphasised and developed the need for discipline in the early years of revolution and the revolutionary state: 'The replacement of the bourgeois state by the proletarian state is impossible without a violent revolution.'[28] 'The overthrow of the bourgeoisie can be achieved only by the proletariat becoming transformed into the ruling class, capable of crushing the inevitable and desperate resistance of the bourgeoisie, and of organising all the labouring and exploited masses for the new economic order.'[29]

Nevertheless Marxism, in one or other of its later versions, became the most powerful political force in the mid twentieth century. With the fading of religion and its promise of felicity hereafter, the Marxist appeal to 'fraternity' offered some prospect of happiness on earth, but not until capitalism which of its nature kills fraternity, was destroyed.[30]

Marx's followers made much of his philosophical method, which they regarded as 'dialectic', developed from the Hegelian series of thesis–antithesis–synthesis. In fact, Marx seldom mentioned this concept, though he did write that 'thinking advances by way of negating'. It might be more accurate, as McBride suggests,[31] to describe the steps of his philosophical process as theory–scrutiny–restatement. Marxists, however, seized on the dialectical method as an ideal instrument for attacking current systems of thought and government. For them opposition became the only method of advance; gradualism and compromise were the tools of ineffectual liberalism and totally unacceptable.

The problem of reconciling the competing claims of the individual and his society is, of course, as old as education. In the middle of the twentieth century, as freedom came to be erected into an absolute good, the problem acquired a new sharpness and urgency. Earlier attempts at a solution, from the twenties to the fifties, concentrated on protecting the individual against the corrupting action of a society he could not control, and training him, by independence of mind, to free himself from social constraints. In the long run, presumably, a race of such men would reorganise society closer to a democratic ideal. Besides John Dewey, the foremost philosopher in this period whose doctrines were of direct impact in education was Alfred North Whitehead.[32] Whitehead's complaint against contemporary metaphysicians was that they mistook abstractions for realities, so his criticism of current education was that it likewise concerned itself with artificialities to the neglect of actualities: 'At present our education combines a thorough study of a few abstractions with a slight study of a larger number of abstractions. We are too exclusively bookish in our scholastic routine.'[33] Like Dewey, he rejected a passive in favour of an active education, and 'in training a child to activity of thought, above all things we must beware of what I will call "inert ideas" – that is to say, ideas that are merely received into the mind without being utilised or tested, or thrown into fresh combinations'.[34] 'From the very beginning of his education the child should experience the joy of discovery.'[35] He summed up by affirming that in all education the main cause of failure is staleness.[36]

He advocated a comprehensive curriculum for all learners, an all-round education. Whereas in *The Aims of Education* he says[37] that there is only one subject-matter for education and that is life in all its manifestations, he later admitted that the curriculum has three aspects: 'There are three main methods which are required in a national system of education, namely the literary curriculum, the scientific curriculum, the technical curriculum. But each of these curricula should include the other two. What I mean is, that every form of education should give the pupil a technique, a science, an assortment of general ideas, and aesthetic appreciation, and that each of these sides of his training should be illuminated by the others.'[38] He rejected utterly a narrow technical education which prepared a man merely to fit into the society in which he lived: 'If in the troubled times which may be before us, you wish appreciably to increase the chance of some savage upheaval, introduce widespread technical education and ignore the Benedictine ideal. Society will then get what it deserves.'[39]

More recently, however, educational thought has concentrated increasingly on altering the terms of the equation by altering society directly. A growing conviction that the existing organisation of Western states could not be allowed to continue acquired urgency in the sixties and seventies, especially in the United States. The heart of many American cities had become a slum, inhabited only by the underprivileged. Protracted poverty had always produced a culture of its own, concentrating strictly on survival, and owing no allegiance to any broader culture in the state. Now there was a growing feeling in the disadvantaged groups that their condition was not hopeless, but capable of improvement, though only by the radical transformation of the old social structure. The problem was to channel this feeling to avoid an explosion: James Bryant Conant warned in 1961 of the 'dynamite' in the situation.

Laissez-faire was dead. From the thirties political and educational observers came to recognise the imperative need for a planned society. Émile Durkheim[40] had regarded all education as deterministic, methodically imposing on its pupils certain modes of behaviour and certain values acceptable in the society operating the educational system. Karl Mannheim[41], a German refugee from the Nazis, sought a middle way between laissez-faire and totalitarianism, a society planned and democratically controlled for the benefit of the individuals living within it. He regarded all thought as socially determined, and postulated certain basic values on which there was wide agreement, an assumption which attracted considerable criticism. Here he touched the central difficulty of a planned society – the sacrifices it calls for in many of its citizens. As Richard Peters points out,[42] democracy is a difficult form of government because the moral principles on which it is founded, fairness, liberty and consideration for the interests of others, have to be imposed on powerful primitive tendencies in other directions. Consequently, education is of prime importance in a planned society. Indeed Mannheim thought education should be society-centred rather than child-centred: home, school and community ought to have a common purpose, and it was impossible to give anyone a full social education in the context of the 'nuclear' family on which Western society is founded. Balance was essential. A child ought to be educated both for originality and for conformity. Stress the first too much and you fostered neuroses; over-emphasise the second, and your society became static and withered. Sociology, the new science, was to be invaluable in producing individuals who understood the society in which they lived and recognised the necessity for sacrifices; this was what Jean Floud called 'the gospel of salvation through sociology'. Like Whitehead, Mannheim demanded a broad education, much wider than a mere technical training, which presumed and promoted conformity.

The curricular reforms of the fifties and early sixties in America and Western Europe were attempts at moderate change, at transforming the system from within. Jerome Bruner[43] described the curricular revolution as 'an effort to start the children younger and more effectively on the way to grasping the more powerful ideas embodied in the learned disciplines . . . inventing for [them] modes of access to the empowering techniques of the culture'. Similarly, organisational expedients were developed inside the system – the community school, for instance, which, it was hoped, would have a beneficial influence on the community. However, from the middle sixties, reformers became impatient and sought more radical solutions: the millennium, they felt, would not wait.

One such solution was the doctrine of equalisation of opportunity, 'compensatory education'. This went beyond impartiality, with which no commentator could take issue, to advocate positive discrimination, providing more attention and assistance for those whose circumstances have handicapped their natural development. This was the rationale of the 'Headstart' programme in America and the 'Educational Priority Areas' established in the United Kingdom, and there were obvious arguments, logical and educational, in its favour. Unfortunately, they were often blurred by supporters who were in reality attacking the social attitudes associated with such inequalities, demonstrating against privilege rather than for equality. A negative statement of the principle proposed by Peters is more helpful: 'No-one should be presumed in advance to have a claim for better treatment than others'; case must be made.[44] However, there remained the question, still unsettled, how far intelligence and power to learn could be increased by altering a child's environment. The debate continued to generate much heat: a statement by A. R. Jensen in 1969[45] that heredity accounted for eighty per cent of IQ differences raised storms of protest, sometimes well-founded but often on humanitarian rather than scientific grounds. P. E. Vernon has suggested[46] that to accept a ratio of two to one for heredity to environment would satisfy all but the extremists and remove most of the arguments, but the debate shows no signs of dying down.

A more radical solution to the problem of the individual's relationship with his society appeared at the beginning of the seventies. Its most convincing proponent was Ivan Illich, who followed Durkheim in stressing the determinism of the educational process. He wrote of the 'hidden curriculum'[47] which persuaded its pupils that schooling in itself was valuable, and made learning a commodity rather than a useful activity, with prizes for those who could memorise facts, all a form of 'knowledge-capitalism'. Not surprisingly the schools were failing to command the respect or even the attention of most of their pupils, and truancy, disobedience and vandalism were common. Attempts to reform the system from within had met no success because the system itself was rotten. Comprehensive education, for example, had never been fairly tried because it did not fit the pattern of the educational establishment. Even the free schools of Neill and his friends produced no more than an illusion of freedom, since they were 'protected gardens', setting their own rules and failing to arm their graduates for the life outside. Schools of any kind limited the teacher's role to the classroom, and made education an artificial enterprise. The teachers themselves added to the distortion by creating a mystique of their trade and branding all uncertificated practitioners as quacks.

Illich's conclusion was inescapable: 'I believe that the disestablishment of the school has become inevitable, and that this end of an illusion should fill us with hope'. The consequence was the movement called 'deschooling',[48] by which schools were to be abolished, and parents given the responsibility of arranging the education of their children; young people would look after their own education by self-motivation and the operation of a free market. All the resources of modern technology would be deployed to offer adequate educational services outside the school system. 'Every man his own teacher.'

Illich was writing originally to meet the problems of the Third World, especially in South America, but his doctrines were taken up by a number of extremists dissatisfied with the capitalist educational system in the West, and they tended to treat him as a new Messiah.[49] On the other hand, equally inevitably, his ideas met stern opposition. Sidney Hook called his *Deschooling Society*[50] 'this smart, silly book . . . a book whose absurd extremism warrants little attention from anyone endowed with a normal portion of common sense'.[51] The most obvious weakness of his doctrine, apart from its vagueness, was the absence of practical alternatives, and it was taken no more seriously by the establishment than Rousseau's proposals two centuries before for the deschooling of Émile. But it was part of a general revolt against the irksome and distorting effects of authority, and no educational theory in the last quarter of the twentieth century would command any credence unless it incorporated proposals for countering these effects and ensuring freedom of growth.

There was evidence in the late seventies that the cult of freedom had overreached itself. Accountability became the watchword in the United States and the practice in the United Kingdom. Compensatory education, it was freely stated, had swallowed vast sums of money without showing any very impressive results. Experimental methods had failed to deliver what they promised. There was a call for a return to firmer control and measurement of results. Statements in such a vein were made by the Prime Minister and the Education Minister in a Labour Government in Britain. In the last analysis, the doctrines promulgated by educators of the left, right or middle ground depended on the view they took of the individual. As Sir Fred Clarke put it, all educational philosophies fall into two groups, according to whether the philosopher does or does not believe in Original Sin. The educational debate is still between the disciples of Rousseau and those of Plato.

Notes and References

1 'The Great Educators'

1. A. N. Whitehead, *Process and Reality: An Essay on Cosmology*.

2 Plato

1. *The Epinomis of Plato*, trans. J. Harward, § 487. On the assumption that the *Epinomis* can be ascribed to Plato, see A. E. Taylor, *Plato: The Man and His Work*, pp. 497–8.

All the succeeding quotations from Plato's writings are from Jowett's 1875 translation, and the references are to the marginal page numbers of that work.

2. For Greek education see Werner Jaeger, *Paideia: The Ideals of Greek Culture*, trans. G. Highet; H. I. Marrou, *A History of Education in Antiquity*, trans. G. Lamb; F. A. G. Beck, *Greek Education, 450–350* B.C.; W. Barclay, *Educational Ideals in the Ancient World*.

3. § 313.

4. *Protagoras*, § 340. Cf. *Euthydemus*, § 277.

5. *Protagoras*, § 309.

6. *Laches*, § 186.

7. Protagoras was the first to accept payment (*Protagoras*, § 348): 'You proclaim in the face of Hellas that you are a Sophist or teacher of virtue or education and are the first that demanded pay in return.'

His method of exacting payment – a form of payment by results – was as follows (*Protagoras*, § 328): 'When a man has been my pupil, if he likes he pays my price, but there is no compulsion; and if he does not like, he has only to go into a temple and take an oath of the value of the instructions, and he pays no more than he declares to be their value.'

The result was, as reported by Socrates in the *Meno*, § 91: 'I know of a single man, Protagoras, who made more out of his craft than the illustrious Pheidias, who created such noble works, or any ten other statuaries.'

The sophists have been designated the founders of educational science: Jaeger, *Paideia*, vol. I, p. 295.

8. *Laches*, § 186.

9. James Bowen, *A History of Western Education*, vol. I, *The Ancient World*, pp. 86–7; J. S. Mill in Barry Gross (ed.), *Great Thinkers on Plato*, pp. 151–2.

10. *Meno*, § 92.

11. § 312.

12. See A. E. Taylor, *Socrates*, and R. W. Livingstone, *Portrait of Socrates*.

13. *Metaphysics*, § 1078, b.

14. § 216.

15. Cf. metaphor of midwife in *Theaetetus*, § 150; also *Symposium*, § 209. Cf. Jaeger, vol. II, p. 27: 'He [Socrates] is the greatest teacher in European history.'

16. *Symposium*, § 204.

17. Ibid., § 217.

18. *Apology*, § 31.

19. Ibid., § 33.

20. § 348.

21. Cf. *Theaetetus*, § 201: 'Knowledge is true opinion accompanied by a reason.'

22. *How Gertrude Teaches her Children*, Eng. trans. (London: Swan Sonnenschein, 1907) p. 46. Cf. p. 57.

23. Cf. for successful examples, J. Adams, *Primer on Teaching* (Edinburgh: T. & T. Clark, 1903) pp. 90–108; also *Exposition and Illustration* (London: Macmillan, 1909) pp. 80–2.

24. See R. S. Black, *Plato's Life and Thought*, or A. E. Taylor, *Plato*.

25. See R. C. Lodge, *Plato's Theory of Education*.

26. § 599.

27. § 644.

28. § 185.

29. § 45.

30. § 50.

31. § 339.

32. § 21.

33. §§ 325–6.

34. For a reconstruction of Plato's own upbringing see Graham Wallas, *The Art of Thought* (London: Jonathan Cape, 1926) p. 230.

35. *The Works of Xenophon*, trans. H. G. Dakyns (London: Macmillan, 1897) vol. III, pt i, pp. 226–7 and note. See also Jaeger, *Paideia*, vol. III, pp. 175–7.

36. The modern name for the work. Plato's was *Politeia*, meaning 'state' or 'constitution', and thus a general treatise on government. See Bowen, *Ancient World*, p. 105.

37. W. Boyd, *Plato's Republic for Today*.

38. *Émile* (Everyman ed.) p. 8.

39. *Evolution of Theology in the Greek Philosophers* (Glasgow: J. MacLehose & Sons, 1904) I 140.

40. Cf. Jaeger, *Paideia, vol.* I, pp. 102–4. 'All virtues are summed up in righteousness.' Also II 202.

41. Cf. Aristotle, *Politics*, III 13: 'Justice has been acknowledged by us to be a social virtue.'
42. Cf. Rousseau, *Émile*, p. 202: 'It is true . . . that we have a very imperfect knowledge of the human heart if we do not also examine it in crowds; but it is none the less true that to judge of men we must study the individual man, and that he who had a perfect knowledge of the inclinations of each individual might foresee all their combined effects in the body of the nation.' Also Jaeger, vol. II, p. 366: 'He [Plato] is founding politics upon ethics . . . For Plato the perfect state is only the ideal frame of a good life.'
43. Robin Barrow, *Plato, Utilitarianism and Education*, p. 1.
44. *Republic*, § 369.
45. K. R. Popper, *The Open Society and Its Enemies*, p. 171; Barrow, *Plato*, p. 50.
46. Note that Plato presupposes an initial inequality. Cf. Aristotle, *Politics*, II: 'Similars do not constitute a state.'
47. *Politics*, I 2.
48. *Republic*, §§ 369–72.
49. Ibid., § 373.
50. Ibid., § 372.
51. Lewis Campbell, *Plato's Republic* (London: John Murray, 1902) p. 54.
52. Greek *pseudos*, a fable or myth, introduced to elucidate an argument, not as a deliberate lie. See Barrow, *Plato*, p. 130.
53. *Republic*, § 415.
54. Ibid., § 423.
55. Cf. Aristotle, *Politics*, II 5, 23: 'What will be the education, form of government, laws of the lower class Socrates has nowhere determined.' Cf., however, *Republic*, § 467.
56. Campbell, *Plato's Republic*, p. 65.
57. Ibid., p. 54. Plato refers to the workers as 'those whose natural talents were defective from the first, and whose souls have since been so grievously marred and enervated by their life of drudgery as their bodies have been disfigured by their crafts and trades'. *Republic*, § 495.
58. Barrow, *Plato*, p. 151.
59. *Politics*, I 3.
60. Cf. *Protagoras*, § 322: 'For cities cannot exist, if a few only share in the virtues as in the arts.' Also Aristotle, *Politics*, III 15, and II 2.
61. *Prolegomena to Ethics* (OUP, 1899) § 207.
62. *Republic*, §§ 376–412.
63. Almost equivalent to the term Arts in a university curriculum.
64. *Republic*, § 410. Cf. passage from *Protagoras* quoted above.
65. *Republic*, § 376: cf. and contrast Aristotle, *Politics*, VII 15. 'The care of the body ought to precede that of the soul, and the training of the appetitive part should follow: none the less the care of it must be for the sake of the reason, and our care of the body for the sake of the soul.'
66. *Republic*, § 377.
67. Cf. Aristotle, *Politics*, , VII 17.
68. *Republic*, § 376.

69. Ibid., § 378.
70. Ibid.,
71. Barrow, *Plato*, p. 110.
72. *Republic*, § 380.
73. § 383.
74. § 386.
75. *Republic*, §§ 386–8.
76. § 389. Cf. the international morality in More's *Utopia*.
77. *Republic*, § 392.
78. Ibid., §§ 392–403.
79. § 395.
80. § 401.
81. § 401. Cf. Aristotle, *Politics,* VII 17: 'All that is mean and low should be banished from their sight.' Also B. Bosanquet, *The Education of the Young in the Republic of Plato* (CUP, 1904) p. 102, fn.
82. *Republic*, § 522.
83. Ibid., §§ 403–12.
84. § 404.
85. § 411.
86. § 412.
87. § 522.
88. § 536.
89. *Republic*, § 376. Here we have the beginnings of vocational selection and of selection board procedures.
90. Ibid., § 413. Not quite 'an education through perfect circumstances', as Lewis Campbell supposed, *Plato's Republic,* p. 73.
91. *Republic*, §§ 521–41.
92. Ibid., § 535.
93. § 487.
94. § 490.
95. § 521.
96. § 518.
97. See Jaeger vol. II, pp. 267–8 for description of Plato's philosopher.
98. *Republic*, § 523.
99. § 522.
100. § 525.
101. *Republic*, § 527.
102. Ibid., § 526. This argument is repeated in almost identical terms in the *Laws,* § 747: 'Arithmetic stirs up him who is by nature sleepy and dull, and makes him quick to learn, retentive, shrewd, and aided by art divine he makes progress quite beyond his natural powers.'
103. *Republic*, § 527.
104. Ibid., § 531.
105. E. C. Moore, *What Is Education?* (Boston and London: Ginn, 1915) ch. 3. It must be put to Plato's credit that in interpreting a faculty as a function (*Republic,* § 477) he avoided the 'faculty' doctrine which long retarded the development of psychology.
106. *Republic*, § 526. The idea of good, or 'the Form of the Good', is the

ultimate principle in Plato's philosophy, at once the source of all being and of all knowledge. Cf. ibid., § 509.

107. Ibid., § 527.

108. Ibid.

109. § 530. In accordance with this principle the calculation of Neptune into existence by Adams and Leverrier would have been commended by Plato; the verification of its existence by actual observation would have merited his contempt.

110. Marrou, p. 371, translates music here by 'acoustics' – 'the science of mathematics introduced by Pythagoras, the study of the numerical structure of intervals and rhythms'.

111. *Republic*, § 531.

112. Ibid., § 533. In the *Cratylus* Plato defined the dialectician as 'he who knows how to ask questions and how to answer them'. In the *Phaedrus* he identifies dialectic with the process of division and generalisation, and he adds, *Republic*, § 537, 'For according as a man can survey a subject as a whole or not, he is or is not a dialectician.'

113. *Republic*, § 534.

114. Ibid., §§ 537–41.

115. § 536. The tests for philosophers include intelligence tests. The tests for the guardians are mainly temperament tests.

116. § 539. Cf. Aristotle, *Ethics*, I 3: 'The young man is not a fit student of Politics.'

117. *Republic*, § 540.

118. Ibid. Cf. §§ 451–7.

119. Ibid., § 457. The great waves or paradoxes in the construction of Plato's ideal state are: (1) the community of goods and of pursuits; (2) the community of wives and children; (3) summarised in the statement, 'Until kings are philosophers or philosophers are kings, cities will never cease from ill.'

120. *Politics*, II 3.

121. *Émile*, Everyman's Library (1911) p. 236.

122. *Laws*, §§ 739, 753.

123. Ibid., §§ 643–4.

124. § 804. Cf. Aristotle, *Politics*, VIII 1.

125. *Laws*, §§ 804–6.

126. Ibid., § 814.

127. *Laws*, § 795. Cf. ibid. §§ 814–16.

128. Ibid., § 796.

129. Ibid., § 814.

130. Cf. ibid., §§ 659–70, 800–4, 811.

131. Ibid., § 664.

132. Ibid., § 643.

133. *Laws*, § 788.

134. Ibid., §§ 788–92.

135. Ibid., § 653.

136. Ibid., § 794.

137. Cf. *Republic*, § 424.

138. *Laws*, § 794.
139. Ibid.
140. *Laws*, § 810.
141. Ibid., §§ 817–18.
142. Ibid., § 819.
143. § 967.
144. §§ 765–6; § 809.
145. § 641.
146. Gross, *Thinkers on Plato*, introd. p. xx.
147. See Karl Popper, *The Open Society and Its Enemies*.
148. Barrow, *Plato*, p. 14.
149. Ibid., p. 24.
150. *The Aims of Education* (London: Williams & Norgate, 1929) p. 77.
151. Ibid., p. 71.
152. *Contemporary American Philosophy*, vol. II (London: George Allen & Unwin, 1930) p. 21.
153. R. H. Crossman, *Plato Today*, p. 84; Bertrand Russell, 'Philosophy and Politics', in *Unpopular Essays*; Barrow, *Plato*, pp. 2, 123.

3 Quintilian

1. *Institutio Oratoria*, III i 19. All references in this chapter not otherwise indicated are to the *Institutio Oratoria* in the Loeb Classical Library text and translation by H. E. Butler.
2. For Roman education see A. S. Wilkins, *Roman Education*; A. Gwynn, *Roman Education from Cicero to Quintilian*; James Bowen, *History of Western Education*, vol. 1, *The Ancient World*.
3. Bowen, *Ancient World*, p. 199. For Quintilian's life, see F. H. Colson, *M. Fabii Quintiliani Institutionis Oratoriae, Liber* I (CUP, 1924) pp. ix–xx; M. L. Clarke, 'Quintilian: A Biographical Sketch', *Greece and Rome*, 2nd ser., XIV (April 1967).
4. Tacitus had a low opinion of Afer's moral character, but Quintilian makes no mention of the subject, saying only that his master's powers waned as he grew old. See Clarke, 'Quintilian', pp. 28–9.
5. George Kennedy, *Quintilian*, p. 111.
6. I introd. 1.
7. Cf. Quintilian's reference to 'the only professors of wisdom', a characterisation of the sophists employed by Plato in the *Laches*, § 186.
8. I x 4: 'I am not describing any orator who actually exists or has existed, but have in my mind's eye an ideal orator, perfect down to the smallest detail.'
9. Kennedy, *Quintilian*, p. 13.
10. I introd. 9–18.
11. *Vir bonus, dicendi peritus;* XII i 1. Cf. II, xv 1. Quintilian restricts the name of orators and the art itself to those who are good. Also II xv 33. Gwynn (p. 40) claims that this definition was designedly opposed to Greek ideals.
12. I introd.

13. 'It is plain from the outset that he is writing for the children of the rich. Not a word is said about the elementary schoolmaster (*ludi magister*) and his classes.'–Gwynn, p. 189.

14. Typically Roman and in striking contrast to Greek sentiment.

15. I i, 2.

16. § 4.

17. In his chapter on memory, xi ii, some of Quintilian's statements are surprisingly in accordance with experimental results.

18. *Politics*, viii 2. Cf. J. Burnet, *Aristotle on Education* (CUP, 1903) p. 97.

19. I ii.

20. Quintilian on corporal punishment is quoted in Addison's *The Spectator* (Everyman, vol. I, bk ii, p. 313), where schoolmasters are referred to as licensed tyrants.

21. I iv.

22. See Wilkins's *Roman Education*, pp. 19 ff.

23. I iv. Cf. I i.

24. Quintilian, II i, 4, defines grammar as 'the science of letters'. Colson, p. xxxiv: 'Grammar was then a living study. . . . It held in fact in the mental outlook of the student of the time much the same position as science does today.'

25. I vi.

26. I vii.

27. I viii.

28. I x, and xi iii.

29. Cf. xi iii.

30. I ix.

31. I xii.

32. II i.

33. II ii. Probably the first rating scale for teachers. Cf. the modern version: 'All that a teacher requires is a knowledge of his subject and a sense of humour.' Quoted by J. Adams, *The Herbartian Psychology Applied to Education* (London: D. C. Heath, n.d.).

34. Bowen, *Ancient World*, p. 200.

35. Cf. A. T. Quiller-Couch, *On the Art of Writing* (CUP, 1916) pp. 138–9.

36. Bk x.

37. Cf. Colson, p. xxv: 'While Quintilian's book is the great representative of the rhetorical school of educational thought and indeed of ancient pedagogy in general, it must be remembered that it is not as a whole a treatise on education, not even indeed a treatise on how to *teach* rhetoric. The great part of it, Book II. 14–xi, is a treatise *on* rhetoric.'

38. Kennedy, *Quintilian*, pp. 139–40.

39. See Colson, ch. 4, 'Knowledge and Use of Quintilian after 1416'; also John F. Downes, 'Quintilian Today',
Milton mentions the first few books of the *Institutes* for moral edification.

40. W. H. Woodward, *Studies in Education during the Age of the Renaissance* (CUP, 1906) p. 272.

4 Loyola

1. A gradual movement, not a sudden rebirth, as the traditional view assumed. See L. E. Elliot-Binns, *England and the New Learning* p. 10; E. M. W. Tillyard, *The English Renaissance: Fact or Fiction*.

2. For the life of Ignatius Loyola see Francis Thompson, *Saint Ignatius Loyola*; Paul Van Dyke, *Ignatius Loyola: The Founder of the Jesuits*; Leonard von Matt and Hugo Rahner, *St Ignatius of Loyola: A Pictorial Biography*, trans. John Murray; James Brodrick, *Saint Ignatius Loyola: The Pilgrim Years. The Autobiography of St Ignatius Loyola, with related documents*, ed. John C. Olin; trans. Joseph O'Callaghan.

3. James Bowen, *History of Western Education*, vol. 2, *Civilization of Europe* p. 423.

For origin and history of the Society of Jesus see James Brodwick, *The Origin of the Jesuits* and *The Progress of the Jesuits*. Also T. Corcoran, 'Jesuit Education', in *The Encyclopaedia and Dictionary of Education*, ed. F. Watson (London: Sir Isaac Pitman, 1921) vol. II, pp. 913–16.

4. Francis Thompson, *Saint Ignatius Loyola*, pp. 171–2.

5. It is unhistorical to assume that the Society was founded to combat Protestantism. It represents rather an original development within the Church itself. The Jesuit educational system is likewise a phase of the Renaissance movement, and the general practice of the Jesuit schools corresponded with the practice of all Western and Central Europe of whatever religion. See R. Schwickerath, *Jesuit Education: Its History and Principles*, p. 77; also F. Charmot, *La Pédagogie des Jésuites* (Paris: Spes, 1943) pp. 32–47.

6. The official publications of the Society of Jesus are *The Spiritual Exercises, The Constitutions of the Society* and the *Ratio Studiorum*.

Various translations of *The Spiritual Exercises* are available: *Spiritual Exercises of St Ignatius of Loyola*, ed. O. Shipley (London, 1870); W. H. Longridge, *The Spiritual Exercises of St Ignatius of Loyola* (London: A. R. Mowbray, 1930); *The Text of the Spiritual Exercises of St Ignatius* (London: Burns & Oates, 1880); *Manresa or the Spiritual Exercises of St Ignatius,* new ed. (London: Burns & Oates, 1881).

The *Constitutiones Societatis Jesu. Romae, in aedibus Societatis Jesu* 1558. *Reprinted from the Original Edition: with an Appendix containing A Translation, and Several Important Documents* (London: J. G. & F. Rivington, 1838) does not include the Declarations or Clarifications. The appendix contains The First Approbation of the Society of Jesus by Paul III, 1540, A Translation of the Bull for the Effectual Suppression of the Order of Jesuits by Clement XIV, 1773, A Translation of the Bull for the Restoration of the Order of Jesuits by Pius VII, 1814. *Saint Ignatius' Idea of a Jesuit University* by George E. Ganss includes part IV of the *Constitutions* of the Society of Jesus translated from the Spanish of Saint Ignatius of Loyola, together with an account of the origin of the *Constitutions* and titles of the ten parts. E. A. Fitzpatrick also included part IV of the *Constitutions* in *St Ignatius and the Ratio Studiorum*.

The *Ratio Studiorum et Institutiones Scholasticae Societatis Jesu* in G. M.

Pachtler, *Monumenta Germaniae Paedagogica*, vol. v, contains the Latin text of the 1586 *Ratio*, and Latin texts and German translations of the 1599 and 1832 versions. The 1591 version was evidently not known to Pachtler (see Alan P. Farrell, *The Jesuit Code of Liberal Education: Development and Scope of the Ratio Studiorum*, p. 308). T. Corcoran issued for academic use in University College, Dublin, the *Renatae Litterae saeculo a Chr. XVI in Scholis Societatis Jesu Stabilitae* containing portions of the three versions of the *Ratio* in Latin which he designated *Ratio Studiorum Prima* (1586), *Ratio Studiorum Intermedia* (1591), *Ratio Studiorum Definitiva* (1599). Farrell's book (see above) traces the development of the *Ratio* and includes the 1832 version prepared after the Restoration of the Society.

7. In the 1832 revision of the *Ratio Studiorum*, Reg. Praef, Stud. Inf. 8, § 12, reference is made to elementary schools.

8. Ganss, ch. 12, Clarification C, p. 332.

9. Cf. Pachtler, *Monumenta Germaniae Paedagogica*, vol. ii, p. 311.

10. *Ratio Studiorum, Reg. Provincialis, 21,* § 4. Cf. Pachtler, vol. ii, p. 258.

11. *Constitutions*, iv xv 4: 'Just as the Society teaches free.' In the *Constitutions*, iv vii 3, Ignatius decrees that gifts to which special conditions are attached are not to be accepted by the Society. On the principle of gratuity in Jesuit education see Farrell, pp. 436–40.

12. T. Hughes, *Loyola and the Educational System of the Jesuits* (London: William Heinemann, 1892) pp. 67, 117. Cf. also *Constitutions*, iv vii 3; iv xv 4. The *Ratio Studiorum*, Reg. Praef. Stud. Infer. 9, enacts that no one shall be excluded because he is poor or of lowly station. The Reg. Com. Prof. Class. Infer. 50 declares that the professor is to slight no one, to care as much for the progress of the poor pupil as of the rich. Cf. Fitzpatrick, p. 155.

13. Hughes, *Loyola*, p. 99.

14. *Saint Ignatius Loyola*, p. 179. Cf. Ganss, p. 117: 'he [Ignatius] seems to have been the first founder of a religious order to make the education of youths in both secular and sacred subjects one of the major works prescribed by the Constitutions of the order'.

15. Thompson, *Loyola*, p. 136.

16. *Constitutions*, v, iii 3.

17. A table of contents is provided by Ganss, p. 287.

All the quotations from part iv of the *Constitutions* are taken, by permission, from the translation from the Spanish by G. Ganss, *St Ignatius' Idea of a Jesuit University*, pp. 281–345.

18. *Constitutions*, i ii 6–13. Cf. qualifications in First Papal Approbation: 'prudent in Christ and conspicuous in learning'.

19. Cf. Thompson, *Loyola*, p. 282. Borgia became the third General of the order.

20. iii ii. Also iv iv 1. Cf. Ganss, p. 303.

21. *Constitutions*, iv v 1. Ganss, pp. 306–7.

22. *Constitutions*, iv vi 4. Ganss, p. 310.

23. *Constitutions*, iv vi 8. Ganss, p. 312.

24. Ibid., § 13. Repeated in *Ratio Studiorum*, Reg. Com. Prof. Class. Infer. 18, and modified slightly in 1832 *Ratio*.

25. *Constitutions,* IV vi 10–12.
26. Ibid., § 7.
27. Ch. viii.
28. Ibid., § 3.
29. Ch. xvii, § 5.
30. Ch. xii, § 4.
31. Ch. xii, § 3.
32. Cf. IV vii 2; also IV xiii 2. In the *Ratio Studiorum* the same freedom is retained. Cf. Regulae Praepositi Provincialis, 39.
33. Jouvancy's *Ratio Discendi et Docendi,* first published in 1692, was reissued in 1703 – revised and adapted to meet the requirements of a decree passed by the General Assembly of the Order in 1696–7. French and German editions of Jouvancy's *Ratio* exist, but no English translation. Hughes's *Loyola,* pp. 163–6, gives an outline. For account of Joseph de Jouvancy, 1643–1719, see F. Charmot, *La Pédagogie des Jésuites* (Paris: Spes, 1943) pp. 559–63.
34. Bowen, *Civilization of Europe*, p. 423.
35. No great originality was claimed for the *Ratio,* but it did claim to embody the best practice of the day and to have systematised this.
36. In these on specified days the pupils hold lectures, debates, etc., among themselves.
37. Regulae Praepositi Provincialis. Cf. Fitzpatrick, pp. 121–37.
38. Regulae Rectoris. Cf. Fitzpatrick, pp. 137–43.
39. Reg. 9. The same view was expressed in a criticism of the 1586 *Ratio.* See Hughes, *Loyola,* pp. 160–1.
40. Rules for Rector, 2. Fitzpatrick, p. 138.
41. Rules for Prefect of Studies. Fitzpatrick, pp. 143–50.
42. Rules for Prefect of Lower Studies. Fitzpatrick, pp. 176–90.
43. Rule 22. Fitzpatrick, p. 142.
44. Regulae Communes Omnibus Professoribus Superiorum Facultatum. Cf. Fitzpatrick, pp. 150–5.
45. Cf. Reg. 9.
46. Reg. 11.
47. Reg. 13, 1599 *Ratio.* No definite time is specified in the 1832 *Ratio.*
48. Reg. 20.
49. *Monumenta Germaniae Paedagogica*, vol. v, pp. 346–51.
50. Regulae Praefecti Studiorum Inferiorum. Cf. Fitzpatrick, pp. 176–90.
51. Reg. 4.
52. Reg. 6.
53. Reg. 8, § 3.
54. Reg. 8, § 4.
55. Reg. 13.
56. Reg. 23.
57. Reg. 26.
58. Reg. 37.
59. Reg. 38. Cf. Ganss, p. 319.
60. Reg. 40.

61. Regulae Communes Professoribus Classium Inferiorum. Cf. Fitz-patrick, pp. 195–208.
62. Reg. 27.
63. Cf. Farrell, *The Jesuit Code of Liberal Education*, pp. 292–6.
64. Reg. 31, 32, 34, 35.
65. T. Gomperz, *Greek Thinkers*, Eng. trans. (London; John Murray, 1901) vol. I, p. 43.
66. Pachtler, vol. v, p. 27.
67. Cf. Hughes, *Loyola*, chs X, XII. Schwickerath, *Jesuit Education*, ch. xv.
68. Pachtler, vol. v, p. 154; Schwickerath, pp. 432–3.
69. Cf. Reg. Rectoris, 73: 'The subject of tragedies and comedies, which would be in Latin and but rarely performed, must be pious and edifying.'
70. Bacon would have the art of acting (*actio theatralis*) made a part of the education of youth. The Jesuits, he says, do not despise it; and he thinks they are right; for though it be of ill repute as a profession, yet as a part of discipline it is of excellent use.
71. In one of his *Aphorisms* Herbart declared: 'The old pedagogy be-trayed its weakness in nothing as much as its dependence on compulsion; the modern in nothing so much as in the emphatic value it places on supervision. Great perplexity can alone be the motive for exclusively recommending a measure at once so prejudicial, insufficient and costly. The hindrance of offences is only good when a new activity continually takes the place of that which is restrained.' In his *Outlines of Educational Doctrine*, § 178, he says, however, 'Gambling must be forbidden, and in case compliance with this prohibition is doubtful, obedience must be secured by watchful supervision.'
72. Rules for Prefects of Lower Studies, 38. Cf. Fitzpatrick, p. 187, and Rules Common to Professors of Lower Studies, 40. Cf. Fitzpatrick, p. 206.
73. Cf. Thompson, *Loyola*, p. 295.
74. Cf. Schwickerath, pp. 553–5.
75. See Chap. 9 of this work for incompleteness of Herbart's conception of the end of education as morality.
76. See *The Times*, 2 Jan 1958, 'Jesuit Fathers: Training and Functions in the Modern World'.
77. *Loyola*, p. 181.

5 Comenius

1. John E. Sadler, *J. A. Comenius and the Concept of Universal Education*, is the best and most comprehensive book on Comenius as an educator.
2. For life see Matthew Spinka, *John Amos Comenius: That Incomparable Moravian*. See also Eduard Beneš *et al.*, *The Teacher of Nations: Addresses and Essays in Commemoration of the Visit to England of Jan Amos Komensky, Comenius, 1641–1941*, ed. Joseph Needham.
   For visit to England see *The Times Educational Supplement*, 10 March 1928, and R. F. Young, *Comenius in England*. Also G. H. Turnbull, 'Plans of Comenius for his Stay in England', *Acta Comeniana*, II i 7–23, and *Hartlib, Dury and Comenius* pp. 349–70.

3. *Utopia*, §§ 182, 183.

4. See Dagmar Capkova, 'The Significance of Comenius's Ideas on the Theory and Practice of Pre-school Education', *Durham Research Review*, VI 22 (Spring 1969) 334.

5. Cf. Spinka, *Comenius*, p. 32: 'He became an educational reformer more by accident than by primary design; and it would be doing him less than justice if we were to fail to recognise his primary and dominant life-motive.' See also Mark Williamson, 'Innovation and Realism: A Study in Comenius' School of Infancy', *Education for Development*, III (April 1974) 39.

6. Capkova, 'Comenius's ideas', p. 334.

7. John Amos Komensky, *The Labyrinth of the World and the Paradise of the Heart* (1623), ed. and trans. Count Lutzow (London: Swan, Sonnenschein, 1901). Or J. A. Comenius, *The Labyrinth of the World and the Paradise of the Heart*. There is also a translation by Matthew Spinka (Chicago, 1942).

8. Spinka, *Comenius*.

9. Count Lutzow's translation, pp. 116–17.

10. *The Labyrinth*, pp. 335–6.

11. London: Constable, 1917, p. 36.

12. S. S. Laurie, *John Amos Comenius*, p. 20.

13. John Amos Comenius, *The Way of Light* (1668), trans. and introd. E. T. Campagnac (University Press of Liverpool, 1938) pp. 148–51.

14. R. F. Young (*Times Educational Supplement*, 10 Mar 1928) traced the development of a great college for scientific research from the Accademia Platonica at Florence in the fifteenth century, the Accademia Secretorum Naturae founded at Naples in 1560, the Accademia dei Lincei established at Rome in 1603, and similar Italian scientific societies of the sixteenth and early seventeenth centuries.

15. Written in Czech between 1628 and 1632, published in Latin 1657–8. The Czech version was not published till 1849. Eng. trans. by M. W. Keatinge, *The Great Didactic of John Amos Comenius*. Cf. V. Jelinek, *The Analytical Didactic of Comenius* (University of Chicago Press, 1954).

16. J. W. Adamson, *Pioneers of Modern Education* (CUP, 1905) p. 149. Bacon, for example, took all knowledge for his province.

17. Quoted Laurie, *John Amos Comenius*, p. 55.

18. *The Great Didactic*, ch. IX.

19. Ibid., ch. VIII, § 7.

20. Ch. XXIX, § 2.

21. Ch. XXVIII. Also *The School of Infancy*, trans. D. Benham (London: W. Mallalieu, 1858). Or *The School of Infancy*, ed. E. M. Eller (University of North Carolina Press, 1957).

22. 'I am unwilling to advise that children should be kept at home beyond the six years.'

23. *The Great Didactic*, ch. XXIX, § 2.

24. Ibid., ch. XXI, § 4.

25. *Essays*: 'Of the Institution and Education of Children' (1580). From a manuscript emendation (cf. S. S. Laurie, *Studies in the History of Educational Opinion from the Renaissance* (CUP, 1903) p. 105) it appears that

Montaigne would give such pupils even shorter shrift, as he there advises the masters to 'strangle such youths if they can do it without witnesses'.

26. *The Great Didactic*, ch. xix, §§ 7, 8.
27. Ibid., ch. xix, § 14.
28. Ch. xvi, § 56 (ii).
29. Ch. xvii, § 17.
30. Cf. ibid., § 42.
31. Ch. xvi, § 19.
32. Ch. xvii, § 2 (viii). Cf. § 38 (iii).
33. Ch. xviii, § 28. Cf. ch. xx.
34. *The Great Didactic*, cf. ch. xvii, §§ 27, 28.
35. Ibid., ch. xxix, §§ 3–4. For the teaching of the vernacular see whole chapter.
36. *Essays* (1580): 'Of the Institution and Education of Children': 'I would first know my own tongue perfectly, then my neighbours with whom I have most commerce.'
37. *The Great Didactic*, ch. xii, § 2.
38. Ibid., ch. x, § 1.
39. See nevertheless the significance assigned to the teacher in the *Pampaedia* below, p.73.
40. *The Great Didactic*, ch. xxx, § 15. Cf. ch. xix, §§ 16–29.
41. Ibid., ch. xvi, §§ 7–10.
42. Ibid., ch. xvi, § 25; xvii, § 2.
43. Ibid., ch. xvii, § 2.
44. Ch. xviii, § 4.
45. Ch. xix, § 14.
46. *Exposition and Illustration*, p. 31.
47. *The Great Didactic*, ch. xvi, § 19.
48. Ibid., ch. xvii, § 13.
49. Ch. xviii, § 16. Cf. ch. xix, § 20 (ii).
50. Ch. xvii, § 38. Cf. § 35.
51. Cf. Spinka, *Comenius*, pp. 129–30.
52. *The Great Didactic*, ch. xvii, § 62 (ii).
53. Ibid., ch. ix, § 6. Cf. ch. xix, § 52.
54. Reg. Provincialis, 34.
55. Reg. Com. Prof. Class. Inf. 8.
56. *The Great Didactic*, ch. xxi.
57. Cf. A. P. Farrell, *The Jesuit Code of Liberal Education*, pp. 248–51.
58. *The Great Didactic*, ch. xvii, §§ 19–20. For further references to contests see ch. xix, § 25; xxvi, § 5; to public debates or dissertations, ch. xxxi, § 5.
59. Ibid., ch. xix, § 16.
60. See above, Chap. 3.
61. *The Great Didactic*, ch. xvii, § 41 (i).
62. Ibid., ch. xxvi.
63. John E. Sadler, 'Comenius as a Great Educator', *History of Education Society Bulletin*, vi (Autumn 1970) 32.
64. For comparison of the *Janua* of Comenius with that published earlier

by Bathe, a Jesuit priest of the Irish College at Salamanca, see T. Corcoran, *Studies in the History of Classical Teaching*, pp. 1–130.

If Comenius's *Janua* was not original, he must be given credit for preparing a series of textbooks in a graded manner – Janua, Vestibulum, Atrium and Palladium. It was not until more than a century later that it became common to write textbooks in series – John A. Nietz, 'Some Findings from Analyses of Old Textbooks', *History of Education*, III 3 (Spring 1952) p. 81.

On picture books see *The Great Didactic*, ch. xxviii, §§ 25–6. The *Orbis Pictus* was not the first illustrated textbook. See letter on 'Early Textbooks' by W. Brickman, *Journal of Education* (London, June 1947). Comenius evidently derived the suggestion of a school book with pictures from Eilhard Lubinus (1565–1621), Professor of Theology at Rostock. For origin of *Orbis Pictus* and photograph of an early incomplete version see G. H. Turnbull, 'An Incomplete Orbis Pictus of Comenius. Printed in 1653', *Acta Comeniana* (Prague, 1957) I i 35–54.

The boys of G. W. Leibniz's time (1646–1716) appear to have been brought up on 'the picture book of Comenius and the little catechism [Luther's]' – R. Latta, *Leibniz: The Monadology* (1898) p. 1. Kant in his lectures on education also mentions the *Orbis Pictus*.

65. An account of the discovery of the manuscript is given in the German edition of the *Pampaedia*, pp. 490–5, also in an article 'Schools in the *Pampaedia* of J. A. Comenius' by A. Turek, *Research Review*, The Research Publications of the Institute of Education, University of Durham, II (Sep 1951) 29–39 (University of London Press).

66. Quelle Meyer.

67. *Pampaedia*, ch. 3, § 19.

68. Pp. 507–11.

69. *Pampaedia*, ch. 5, § 6.

70. Ibid., ch. 5, § 7.

71. Ch. 5, schools; ch. 6, books; ch. 7, teachers.

72. Sadler, 'Comenius as a Great Educator', p. 33.

73. Ch. 7, §§ 3–5.

74. Ch. 7, § 16.

75. Cf. Shakespeare's seven ages of man in *As You Like It*, III vii: (1) infant, (2) schoolboy, (3) lover, (4) soldier, (5) justice, (6) pantaloon, (7) second childishness.

76. *Pampaedia*, ch. 8.

77. See John Bowlby, *Child Care and the Growth of Love* (Harmondsworth: Penguin Books, 1965); Mark Williamson, 'Innovation and Realism', pp. 40–3.

78. *Pampaedia*, ch. 9.

79. Ch. 28.

80. *School of Infancy*, ch. 12.

81. *Pampaedia*, ch. 10.

82. A fuller account of the activities at the elementary-school stage appears in Turek's article, 'Schools in the *Pampaedia* of J. A. Comenius'.

83. *Pampaedia*, ch. 12.

84. *Pampaedia*, ch. 1, §§ 1–8.
85. I. L. Kandel in 'National Education in an International World', *N.E.A. Journal* (Apr 1946) p. 175.
86. R. Ulich, *Professional Education as a Humane Study* (New York: The Macmillan Co., 1956) p. 115.
87. Mark Williamson, 'Innovation and Realism', p. 47.

6 Locke

1. See Maurice Cranston, *John Locke: A Biography*; Peter Laslett, *John Locke: Two Treatises of Government*, ch. 2, 'Locke the Man and Locke the Writer'; D. J. O'Connor, *John Locke*; James L. Axtell, *The Educational Writings of John Locke*.
2. Published 1690.
3. The *Second Treatise* was first in time, 1679; amended and extended 1689.
4. 1693. See. R. H. Quick, *Some Thoughts Concerning Education by John Locke* or Axtell, *Educational Writings of Locke*.
5. See Laslett, p. 38.
6. M. G. Mason, 'John Locke's Experience of Education and Its Bearing on His Educational Thought', *Journal of Educational Administration and History*, III 2 (June 1971).
7. Ch. 2, § 4; Laslett, p. 287; ch. 2, § 6, Laslett, p. 289; ch. 8, § 95, Laslett, p. 348. Cf. also *The Prose Works of John Milton* (London: Henry G. Bohn, 1848–53) vol. II p. 8: 'No man, who knows aright can be so stupid to deny that all men naturally were born free, being the image and semblance of God Himself, and were, by privilege above all creatures, born to command and not to obey.'
8. Treatise I, ch. ix, § 101; Laslett, p. 233. Cf. J. Milton, *A Defence of the People of England, Prose Works*, I 108: 'I am of opinion that the law of God does exactly agree with the law of nature'; also IV 211–12. Cranston, pp. 64–5, says of the law of nature: 'It is a notion as old as Stoic philosophy. It had an important place in the theory, if not in the practice, of Roman jurisprudence. In mediaeval Christendom it was identified with the law of God, and the Church assumed the duty of upholding it over the heads of temporal rulers.'
9. *Second Treatise*, ch. 2, § 4; Laslett, p. 287.
10. *Second Treatise*, ch. 6, § 54; Laslett, p. 322.
11. T. Fowler, *Locke's Conduct of the Understanding* (Oxford: Clarendon Press, 1901) p. 5, scct. 2, 'Parts'. Also, *Essay*, The Epistle to the Reader: 'We have our understandings no less different than our palates.'
12. *Second Treatise*, ch. 6, § 55; Laslett, p. 322.
13. *Second Treatise*, ch. 6, §§ 57–8; Laslett, pp. 323–5.
14. § 61; Laslett, p. 326.
15. Laslett, pp. 321–6.
16. This distinction Locke had elaborated in the *First Treatise of Government* by citing numerous texts from the Scriptures where both father

and mother are included, his aim being to controvert the arguments adduced by Sir R. Filmer in defence of absolute monarchy and the divine right of kings.

17. *Second Treatise*, ch. 15, § 170; Laslett, p. 399.

18. *First Discourse*, ch. 9, § 93; Laslett, p. 228.

19. Epistle to the Reader–'Having been begun by chance, was continued by entreaty, written by incoherent parcels, and, after long intervals of neglect, resumed again, as my humour or occasions permitted, and at last in a retirement where an attendance of my health gave me leisure, it was brought into that order thou now seest it.' Published 1689.

20. Laslett, p. 86, says: 'Even between the *Essay* and the work on education, where the barrier of anonymity is absent on both sides and the connection is intimate, Locke makes no cross-references. It is pointless to look upon his work as an integrated body of speculation and generalisation, with a general philosophy at its centre and as its architectural framework.'

21. Epistle to the Reader.

22. Essay, bk I, ch. i, note.

23. Ibid., I iv 25.

24. I i 8, I i note.

25. I ii 1. Cf. I iv 12.

26. I iii 1.

27. I iii 14. Cf. ibid., § 22.

28. I iii 13; also § 3.

29. Ch. 2, § 11; Laslett, p. 292.

30. *Essay*, II xxi 6.

31. Ibid., II xxii 17.

32. II xxi 20.

33. Note the use of this term in the title of the *Essay*, where it is equated to Mind.

34. *Essay*, II vii 1; II xx 1.

35. Ibid., II i 4.

36. II xxi 29.

37. Ibid., § 48.

38. II xx 6. Cf. ibid., xxi 40.

39. *Essay*, II i 8.

40. Ibid., II xx 1.

41. Cf. Gilbert Ryle, 'Locke on the Human Understanding', in *John Locke: Tercentenary Addresses* (OUP, 1933) pp. 26, 34.

42. *Psychological Principles* (CUP, 1918) p. 143.

43. *Thoughts*, §§ 217, 139, 133.

44. Ibid., § 217, The Epistle Dedicatory.

45. Cranston, p. 427.

46. *Thoughts*, § 217. For Locke's project for the maintenance and upbringing of pauper children see Quick, appendix A.

47. Pp. 4, 51.

48. *Thoughts*, § 66.

49. See Axtell, p. 52.

50. *Essay*, introduction.

51. *Discourses on University Education*, VIII, 'Philosophical Knowledge Viewed in Relation to Professional' (Dublin, 1852).

52. *Essay*, I 1: cf. 'out of an affectation of an universal knowledge'.

53. § 195.

54. R. H. Quick, appendix B.

55. *Thoughts*, § 94.

56. Ibid., § 70.

57. Cranston, pp. 25, 349–50.

58. Ibid., p. 355.

59. Laslett explains (p. 28): 'What had begun as a medical undertaking, turned itself into an educational experiment, and the third earl [of Shaftesbury] tells us that he and his five brothers and sisters were all educated by Locke "according to his own principles (since published by him)".'

60. See K. Dewhurst, *John Locke, Physician and Philosopher: A Medical Biography*; 'An Oxford Medical Quartet', *British Medical Journal*, 5 Oct 1963, also 'John Locke's Medical Notes', *British Medical Journal*, 4 Apr 1964.

61. Cf. J. Adams, *Modern Developments in Educational Practice* (London: University of London Press, 1922) p. 30. For the slogan 'from the gutter to the university' see S. S. Laurie, *The Training of Teachers and Methods of Instruction* (CUP, 1902) pp. 194–5; cf. pp. 149–50.

62. *Thoughts*, § 7.

63. Ibid., § 30.

64. Locke's *Thoughts* was among the books heading Spencer's article in *The British Quarterly Reviews* for Jan and Apr 1858.

65. *Thoughts*, § 134.

66. *Thoughts*, § 140.

67. Ibid., § 145.

68. § 94.

69. § 70.

70. § 147.

71. R. Quick, appendix B.

72. *Thoughts*, § 195. Cf. F. Bacon, *Advancement of Learning*, bk II. 'For pedantical knowledge . . . whereunto appertain divers considerations of great fruits. As first, the turning and seasoning of knowledges as with what to initiate them, and from what for a time to refrain them. Secondly, the consideration where to begin with the easiest and so proceed to the more difficult, and on what courses to press the more difficult and then to turn them to the more easy. . . . A third is the application of learning according to the propriety of the wits for there is no defect in the faculties intellectual but seemeth to have a proper cure contained in some studies.'

73. *Thoughts*, § 46.

74. Ibid., § 149.

75. Ibid., § 74.

76. § 108.

77. § 167.

78. Ibid.

79. § 72.

80. § 54.

81. § 81.

82. § 43. Cf. § 52.

83. § 47.

84. § 49.

85. §§ 83–7.

86. § 66.

87. This exhortation has also been cited in support of the contention that Locke was one of the first to express the guidance point of view. See *Introduction to Testing and to the Use of Test Results*, by Margaret Selover, Agatha Townsend, Robert Jacobs, Arthur E. Traxler (New York: Educational Records Bureau, 1950) p. 1. Cf., however, F. Bacon, *Of the Advancement of Learning*, bk II: with regard to the 'application of learning according unto the propriety of the wits', Bacon observes that masters ought to attend to it for the guidance of the parents in choosing their son's course of life, and also because a man will advance so much faster in studies for which he has a natural aptitude than in any others.

88. *Thoughts*, § 155.

89. Ibid., § 160.

90. § 161. Locke himself used a form of shorthand. Cf. Cranston, p. 80. For shorthand in Roman times, see Marrou, pp. 312–13.

91. Cranston, pp. 241–2, note.

92. *Thoughts*, § 163.

93. *Thoughts*, § 189.

94. Ibid., § 162.

95. § 195. He evidently thought it was impossible to train both a scholar and a gentleman!

96. §§ 201, 204.

97. § 210.

98. § 32.

99. *Thoughts*, § 66. Laslett notes (p. 82): 'Locke is, perhaps, the least consistent of all great philosophers, and pointing out the contradictions either within any of his works or between them is no difficult task.' Also (p. 89): 'A great deal, perhaps too much, has been made of Locke's inconsistencies. But it must be remembered that all thinkers are inconsistent.'

100. Oscar Browning, *Milton's Tractate on Education* (CUP, 1897) p. 17.

101. *Thoughts*, § 38. In reply to Molyneux's objection to the severity of his educational method Locke suggested that Molyneux had taken his method to be more severe than it was. Cf. Cranston, p. 321.

102. § 94.

103. P. 15.

104. *Conduct of the Understanding*, p. 20.

105. *Thoughts*, § 172.

106. *Thoughts*, § 188.

107. British Museum, Add. MS. 38777. See Rand, p. 25 note 1.

108. *Thoughts*, § 6.

109. J. W. Adamson, *A Short History of Education* (CUP 1919) p. 204.

110. CUP (1922) p. 11.

111. J. Adams, *Herbartian Psychology Applied to Education* (London: Isbister, 1909) p. 33.

112. Axtell, p. 17.

113. He was one of those men who, in John Aubrey's words, 'would not beleeve till he had seen and putt his fingers into the holes'.

7 Rousseau

1. F. C. Green, *Jean-Jacques Rousseau: A Critical Study of his Life and Writings*.
For psychosomatic study of Rousseau see R. Grimsley, *Jean-Jacques Rousseau: A Study in Self-awareness*.

2. Frederika Macdonald, *Jean-Jacques Rousseau: A New Criticism*, vol. I, p. 156. Grimsley nevertheless accepts the traditional view that Rousseau abandoned his children. See his *Jean-Jacques Rousseau*, pp. 77, 109, 154, 282, 306–7, 325. Also Green, pp. 37–8, but see p. 178, Mme de Luxembourg's search proved fruitless to trace the elder child through the records of the Foundlings Hospital.

3. Translation from Macdonald, *Rousseau* pp. 225–7.

4. References throughout to *Émile* are to the Everyman translation by B. Foxley.

5. Ibid., p. 58.

6. Locke, *Two Treatises of Government*, I vi 58; Laslett, p. 201: 'He that will impartially survey the nations of the world will find so much of their governments, religions and manners brought in and continued amongst them by these means (Fashion, Custom) that he will have but little reverence for the practices which are in use and credit amongst men, and will have reason to think that the woods and forests where the irrational, untaught inhabitants keep right by following nature, are fitter to give us rules than cities and palaces where those that call themselves civil and rational, go out of their way, by the authority of example.'
Cf. also references to Locke in *Émile*, author's preface, also p. 53 of *Émile*, and elsewhere.

7. Jean-Jacques Rousseau, *A Discourse on the Arts and Sciences*, in *The Social Contract and Discourses* (Everyman) pp. 125–54.

8. See R. Grimsley, *The Philosophy of Rousseau*, pp. 20–5.

9. See the writer's *The Philosophical Bases of Education*, pp. 121–3.

10. 1755. *The Social Contract and Discourses*, Everyman, pp. 155–238.

11. Cf. *Émile*, bk I: 'If all human knowledge were divided into two parts, one common to all, the other peculiar to the learned, the latter would seem small compared with the former.'

12. 'The Biology of Children in Relation to Education', in *Suggestions of Modern Science Concerning Education* (New York: The Macmillan Co., 1925) p. 6.

13. 1755. *The Social Contract and Discourses*, Everyman, pp. 247–87.

14. Bk v.

15. *Politics*, VIII 3.

16. *Discourse*, p. 269.

17. Ed. G. Kudler (London: The Scholartis Press, 1928) p. 34.

18. 1772. See *The Minor Educational Writings of Jean-Jacques Rousseau*, sel. and trans. W. Boyd (London: Blackie & Son, 1911) pp. 137–49.

19. Cf. C. E. Vaughan, *The Political Writings of Jean-Jacques Rousseau* (CUP, 1915) vol. I, p. 1: 'Strike out the *Discours sur l'inégalité* with the first few pages of the *Contrat Social* and the "individualism" of Rousseau will be seen to be nothing better than a myth.' Also p. 2: 'Rousseau, so far from supporting the individualistic theory, is its most powerful assailant.'

20. See Vaughan, *Political Writings of Rousseau*, vol. I, p. 234, and vol. II, p. 142.

21. 1761.

22. *Émile*, p. 46, also Grimsley, *Jean-Jacques Rousseau*, p. 264. Cf. *Émile*, p. 39: 'Brought up in all the rusticity of the country'.

23. *Émile*, p. 49.

24. Ibid., p. 6.

25. P. 7.

26. Aristotle, *Ethics*, bk x.

27. *Emile*, p. 5.

28. Ibid., p. 217.

29. P. 167.

30. Cf. p. 298: 'We are not concerned with a savage of this sort.'

31. *Émile*, p. 6.

32. Nettleship, in *The Theory of Education in Plato's 'Republic'* (OUP, 1969) p. 61, explains that for Plato 'the rational self in man is his most real self, and that life in accordance with the rational order of the world is his truest life.' For Locke the law of nature is also the law of reason: see above, p. 82.

33. *Émile*, p. 250.

34. Ibid., pp. 236, 237.

35. Everyman, p. 184.

36. *The Social Contract*, Everyman, p. 18.

37. *Émile*, p. 299. Cf. for same view Pestalozzi's *Letters to Greaves on Early Education* (London: Sherwood, Gilbert & Piper, 1827) p. 47.

38. Kant's formulation of the moral law follows Rousseau's statement: 'every man is virtuous when his particular will is in all things comformable to the general will, and we voluntarily will what is willed by those whom we love' – *Discourse on Political Economy*, in *The Social Contract and Discourses* (Everyman) p. 262. Rousseau's 'general will', both in *The Social Contract* and here, is equivalent to a universal moral principle or law. Cf. Vaughan, *The Political Writings of Jean-Jacques Rousseau*, vol. II, pp. 19–20.

39. *Émile*, p. 8.

40. P. 9.

41. Cf. E. Caird, *The Critical Philosophy of Immanuel Kant* (Glasgow: James MacLehose & Sons, 1889) vol. II, p. 356. 'Rousseau's primary conception of man is, in a sense, individualistic, that is, it is individualistic in the

sense of the Stoics in which the claims of the individual are based on the fact that he is in himself a *universal*.'

42. *Émile*, p. 18.
43. Ibid., p. 10.
44. P. 217.
45. P. 19.
46. P. 19. Cf. p. 356: 'I cannot repeat too often that I am not dealing with prodigies.'
47. P. 321.
48. *Politics*, § 1253.
49. Ibid., § 1333.
50. *Émile*, p. 7.
51. J. Plamenatz, 'Rousseau: the Education of Émile', *Proceedings of the Philosophy of Education Society of Great Britain*, vi 2 (July 1972).
52. *Émile*, p. 175.
53. Ibid., p. 278.
54. For criticism of the stratification view of human development as contrasted with the theory of concomitant development of the mental powers, see appendix iii by Cyril Burt, to the report of the Consultative Committee on *The Primary School* (H.M. Stationery Office, 1931):
'The traditional descriptions of mental growth divide the whole period from birth to maturity into a series of sharply demarcated stages . . . But the one fact that modern investigations reveal most clearly is the marked continuity of mental life. There are no sudden breaks . . . The mental growth of the child is a fairly steady advance up an inclined plane, not a jerky ascent from one level to another by a series of sudden steps; and the lines drawn between the successive stages of mental growth are more or less artificial.'
55. *Émile*, p. 61.
56. In his *Philosophy of Right*, § 153, note, Hegel adds his criticism of Rousseau's proposal: 'The attempts of speculative education to withdraw people from their present social life and bring them up in the country, a proposal made by Rousseau in *Émile*, have been vain because no one can succeed in alienating man from the laws of the world. Although the education of young men must take place in solitude, we cannot believe that the odour of the world of spirits does not in the end penetrate their seclusion, or that the power of the spirit of the world is too feeble to take possession of even the remotest corner.'
57. *Émile*, p. 155.
58. *Émile*, p. 293.
59. Ibid., p. 122.
60. P. 54.
61. *Émile*, author's preface. See also Plamenatz, 'The Education of Emile', pp. 185, 187.
62. *Émile*, p. 212.
63. P. 165.
64. P. 76.
65. P. 141.

66. Leslie F. Claydon, *Rousseau on Education*, p. 26.

67. There are three views:

	Recapitulation	Participation	Preparation
represented by	Stanley Hall	John Dewey	Herbert Spencer
denoting	past experience	present needs	future adult requirements

They might be combined in the statement that education is a rehearsal for life.

68. *Émile*, p. 42.

69. Ibid., p. 43.

70. In *Virginibus Puerisque* R. L. Stevenson writes in similar terms in defence of youth.

71. *Émile*, p. 41. 'Present interest, that is the motive power, the only motive power that takes us far and safely.'

72. Ibid., p. 126.

73. P. 19.

74. P. 210.

75. P. 209.

76. P. 85.

77. P. 44.

78. *Rousseau* (London: Macmillan & Co., 1886, repr. 1888) vol. II, p. 250.

79. *Jean-Jacques Rousseau: A New Criticism*, vol. I, p. 181.

80. *Émile*, p. 43.

81. Ibid., p. 48. Cf. *Letters from the Mountain*: 'One must not confound independence and liberty; the two things are so different that they mutually exclude each other. When every one does what pleases himself, he often does what consists less in doing one's own will than in remaining uncompelled to obey the will of others; *it also consists* in being unable to compel others to do our will. . . . Whoever is a master is not free; to reign is to obey. . . . There is no liberty without laws, and no liberty when anyone is above the law.' Trans. from Macdonald, vol. II, p. 141.

82. *Émile*, p. 56.

83. *Ibid.*, p. 43. 'A more valid criticism is that he pays too little attention to a child's need of affection and praise.' See Plamenatz, 'The Education of Émile', p. 182.

84. *Émile*, p. 16.

85. P. 198.

86. P. 5.

87. P. 334.

88. P. 256.

89. P. 56.

90. P. 334.

91. Kant maintains that in man there are only germs of good. Providence has not placed goodness ready formed in him.

92. Ernest Jones, *Papers on Psycho-Analysis*, 5th ed. (London: Baillière, Tindall & Cox, 1913, 1950) p. 24.

93. *Émile*, p. 14.

94. Ibid., p. 333. Cf. Bacon, *Essays*, 'Of Custom and Education'. Education 'is, in effect, but an early custom'.

95. *Émile*, p. 7. Cf. p. 271: 'The habit of the bath, once established, should never be broken off.'

96. Ibid., p. 30.

97. P. 94.

98. P. 72, note.

99. In like manner he defends his use of paradox, preferring rather to fall into paradox than into prejudice (p. 57), and he does not hesitate to acknowledge exceptions to his own rules (p. 207).

100. *Émile*, p. 163.

101. Ibid., p. 130. All habits are, however, socially initiated.

102. P. 125, note.

103. P. 49.

104. P. 56.

105. P. 80.

106. P. 147.

107. P. 81.

108. P. 73.

109. P. 74.

110. P. 143.

111. Cf. Locke, *On the Human Understanding*, III, x 14: 'Another great abuse of words is the taking them for things.' Also cf. the *Conduct of the Understanding*, § xxix.

112. *Émile*, p. 133.

113. Ibid., p. 57.

114. P. 65.

115. P. 53. Herbert Spencer, ignorant of Rousseau's treatment, reiterated the same argument in his chapter on 'Moral Education' in his *Education: Intellectual, Moral and Physical* (1861).

116. Cf. *Democracy and Education* (New York: The Macmillan Co., 1916) pp. 32–3. For fuller discussion of the discipline by natural consequences see R. R. Rusk, *The Philosophical Bases of Education* (The University of London Press, 1956) pp. 55–9.

117. *Émile*, p. 77.

118. Ibid., p. 210.

119. P. 57.

120. Pp. 82–97.

121. Pp. 97–122.

122. *Émile*, p. 84.

123. Ibid., pp. 21, 33, 21, 82, 84.

124. Cf. Plato, *Timaeus*, § 86. 'No man is voluntarily bad; but the bad become bad by reason of an ill disposition of the body, and bad education.'

125. *Émile*, p. 90.

126. *Critique of Pure Reason*, preface to 2nd ed., 1787.

127. T. P. Nunn, *Education: Its Data and First Principles*, rev. ed. (London: Edward Arnold, 1930) p. 242.

128. Board of Education, H.M. Stationery Office, 1931, p. 93.

129. *Émile*, p. 297.
130. Ibid., p. 106.
131. P. 71.
132. Pp. 124–5, 126.
133. P. 134.
134. P. 142.
135. P. 140.
136. P. 135.
137. P. 139.
138. *Émile*, pp. 131, 168.
139. Ibid., pp. 131–4.
140. *Thoughts*, § 204.
141. For a full discussion of this prescription, see Claydon, *Rousseau on Education*, pp. 94–107.
142. *Émile*, p. 158.
143. Ibid., p. 159.
144. P. 163.
145. Pp. 140, 165.
146. Pp. 144, 214.
147. P. 147.
148. *Émile*, p. 170.
149. Ibid., p. 278.
150. P. 172.
151. P. 175.
152. P. 292.
153. P. 196.
154. P. 206.
155. Asked what he did when he got into the water he laconically replied: 'Sank'.
156. Cf. A. N. Whitehead, *Adventures of Ideas* (Pelican Books, 1948). 'The deepest definition of Youth is, Life as yet untouched by tragedy. And the finest flower of youth is to know the lesson in advance of the experience.'
157. *Émile*, p. 198.
158. Ibid., p. 193.
159. P. 199.
160. Pp. 199–200.
161. P. 202. Cf. Thackeray's introduction to *Henry Esmond*.
162. *Émile*, p. 201.
163. Ibid., p. 202.
164. P. 205.
165. Ibid.
166. P. 210.
167. P. 216.
168. P. 220.
169. A. T. Quiller-Couch, *On the Art of Writing* (CUP, 1916) p.15.
170. Rousseau refers to the materialist as one 'who prefers to say that stones have feelings rather than that men have souls' (*Émile*, p. 242). He

likewise rejects the naturalist's contention that there is no difference between intelligent behaviour on the perceptual level and the abstract reasoning of which only men are capable: 'It is not in my power to believe that passive and dead matter can have brought forth living and feeling beings, that blind chance has brought forth intelligent beings, that that which does not think has brought forth thinking beings' (ibid., p. 239). For relation of Rousseau's theology to Christianity see Grimsley, *Jean-Jacques Rousseau*, pp. 324–30.

171. *Émile*, p. 236.
172. Ibid., p. 237.
173. P. 239.
174. P. 243. Rousseau adds that it is not the word 'freedom' that is meaningless, but the word 'necessity'. Kant assigned necessity to the phenomenal or scientific sphere and freedom to the moral order. Hegel regards freedom as 'the truth of necessity'.

Kant's *Critique of Practical Reason* might be regarded as little more than a metaphysical formulation of Rousseau's 'Creed of a Savoyard Priest'.

175. *Émile*, p. 245. Rousseau does not derive these rules from the principles of the higher philosophy; he finds them in the depth of his heart (p. 249).

176. In the *Critique of Practical Reason* Kant employs the same argument to equate happiness to virtue.

177. *Émile*, p. 252.
178. Ibid., p. 254.
179. P. 278, note.
180. P. 270.
181. P. 278.
182. See Grimsley, *The Philosophy of Rousseau*, p. 126.
183. *Émile*, p. 309.
184. Ibid., p. 285.
185. P. 289.
186. Rousseau's ideas on love and its place in life may be found in *Julie, or the New Héloïse*, than which 'no more sententious novel was ever written.' See Plamenatz, 'The Education of Émile', § iv.

187. Mabel and William Sahakian, *Rousseau as Educator*, pp. 39–40.
188. *Émile*, p. 415.
189. See. p. 98.
190. Rousseau adopts Aristotle's view of woman rather than Plato's. Cf. *Politics*, i 13 § 9: 'The courage of a man is shown in commanding, of a woman in obeying. And this holds of all other virtues.' Hegel, *Philosophy of Right*, § 166, addition, repeats Rousseau's later views. M. Fénelon in his *Instructions for the Education of Daughters* (1687) advises: 'Begin early thus to harden her for disappointments, to moderate her desires and affections, and to render her easy to bear refusals.'

191. Letters XLVI and CXXIX.
192. P. 339.
193. *Émile*, p. 332.
194. Ibid., p. 333.

195. P. 326.
196. P. 328.
197. P. 340.
198. P. 349.
199. P. 329.
200. P. 332.
201. P. 340.
202. P. 341.
203. *Émile*, p. 359.
204. *Fragmente aus dem Nachlasse,* quoted by N. Kemp Smith: *A Commentary to Kant's Critique of Pure Reason* (London: Macmillan, 1918) p. lvii.
205. E. Cassirer, *Rousseau, Kant, Goethe* (Princeton University Press, 1945). H. Heine, *Religion and Philosophy in Germany: a fragment*, trans. J. Snodgrass (London: English and Foreign Philosophical Library, vol. 18, 1882) p. 108, gives the following account of Kant's routine: 'The history of Immanuel Kant's life is difficult to portray, for he had neither life nor history. He led a mechanical, regular, almost abstract bachelor existence in a little retired street of Königsberg. I do not believe that the great clock of the cathedral performed in a more passionless and methodical manner its daily routine than did its townsman, Immanuel Kant. Rising in the morning, coffee-drinking, writing, reading lectures, dining, walking, everything had its appointed time, and the neighbours knew that it was exactly half-past three o'clock when Immanuel Kant stepped forth from his house in his grey tight-fitting coat, with his Spanish cane in his hand, and betook himself to the little linden avenue called after him to this day, the Philosopher's Walk.'
206. *Social Contract*, ch. 4.
207. There is a brief but useful discussion of Rousseau's influence in M. and W. Sahakian, *Rousseau as Educator,* chs. 7 and 8.
208. By John Dewey and Evelyn Dewey (London: J. M. Dent, 1915).

8 Pestalozzi

1. Kate Silber, *Pestalozzi: The Man and His Work*, is the definitive work on this Great Educator.
2. To keep a deathbed promise to Pestalozzi's father, she stayed with his widow till death, forty years in all.
3. M. R. Heafford, *Pestalozzi*, p. 43.
4. Heafford, *Pestalozzi*, p. vii.
5. His reputation benefited much more than his pocket.
6. Heafford, *Pestalozzi*, p. 21.
7. *Pestalozzi's Educational Writings*, ed., J. A. Green, p. 228.
8. Herbart, *ABC of Sense Perception and Minor Pedagogical Works*, trans. W. J. Eckoff (New York: D. Appleton, 1903) p. 52. Hereafter referred to as Herbart's *Minor Pedagogical Works*.
9. Visited at Richterswil on Lake Zürich by Fichte (1793).
Visited at Burgdorf by Herbart twice (1797–9).

Visited at Yverdon by Froebel (1805, 1808). Visitors from Britain and Ireland included Dr Mayo Greaves – to whom *Hints to Mothers on Early Infant Education* was addressed – Mrs. Hamilton, Miss Edgeworth, Synge, Pullen, Owen, Dr Andrew Bell, Lord Brougham. See also Silber, *Pestalozzi: The Man and his Work*, appendix I, pp. 278–315, 'Pestalozzianism in Britain and the United States'.

10. Herbart, *Minor Pedagogical Works*, pp. 36–7.

11. Ibid., p. 36.

12. *Letters on Early Education*. Addressed to J. P. Greaves, Esq., by Pestalozzi. Translated from the German manuscript (London: Sherwood, Gilbert & Piper, 1827) p. 88. Cf. *Evening Hours of a Hermit*: 'All mankind are fundamentally alike, and for the satisfaction of their needs there is one and the same way.'

13. *Émile*, Everyman; p. 9.

14. *Letters to Greaves*, p. 85.

15. *How Gertrude Teaches Her Children*, by J. H. Pestalozzi, trans. Lucy E. Holland and Francis C. Turner, p. 178. Also J. A. Green, *Pestalozzi's Educational Writings* (London: Edward Arnold, 1912) pp. 85–153.

16. *Ansichten und Erfahrungen* (Views and Experiences Concerning the Idea of Elementary Training), pub. 1807.

17. Translated by his son Hermann Krüsi in *Studies in Education*, ed. Earl Barnes, 2nd ed. (Philadelphia, 1903) vol. I, p. 273. Cf. *How Gertrude Teaches Her Children*, Second Letter. Green, *Pestalozzi's Educational Writings*, p. 94.

18. Cf. *Kant on Education*, trans. Annette Churton (London: Kegan Paul, 1899) p. 81: 'In the culture of *reason* we must proceed according to the Socratic method. . . . The Socratic method should form, then, the rule for the catechetical method. True, it is somewhat slow, and it is difficult to manage so that in drawing ideas out of the child, the others shall also learn something.'

19. Cf. *Leonard and Gertrude*: 'The school ought really to stand in closest connection with the life of the home.' *Evening Hours of a Hermit*: 'The home should be the foundation of any natural scheme of education. Home is the great school of character and of citizenship.'

20. *Minor Pedagogical Works*, pp. 74–6.

21. A personal impression of Pestalozzi at this stage by one of his collaborators, Hermann Krüsi, is given in *My Educational Recollections* (see above).

22. *Minor Pedagogical Works*, pp. 37–8. Cf. p. 183. Also *How Gertrude Teaches Her Children*, p. 41: 'I believe it is not possible for common popular instruction to advance a step, so long as formulas of instruction are not found which make the teacher, at least in the elementary stages of knowledge, merely the mechanical tool of a method, the result of which springs from the nature of the formulas and not from the skill of the man who uses it.'

23. *How Gertrude Teaches Her Children*, pp. 139, 19, 25.

24. Pestalozzi, *Writings 1805–26*, I 174.

25. *Minor Pedagogical Works*, p. 61.

26. Cf. title of pamphlet published in Dublin in 1815, 'A Sketch of

Pestalozzi's Intuitive System'. See also the analysis of *Anschauung* in Silber, pp. 138–41.

27. *Critique of Pure Reason*, 'The Elements of Transcendentalism'.
28. Herbart, *Minor Pedagogical Works*, p. 46.
29. P. 134.
30. *How Gertrude Teaches Her Children*, pp. 86–8. Cf. pp. 33, 51–2.
31. Pestalozzi's language, number and form foreshadow the modern concepts of verbal, numerical and spatial ability, which intelligence tests try to measure. See *Heafford, Pestalozzi*, p. 54.
32. Dealing with Locke's conception of 'substance', D. J. O'Connor (*John Locke*, Penguin Books, 1952, pp. 84–5) enumerates as follows the conditions which determine the application of the term: 'Qualities should be (*i*) manifested in the same spatio-temporal neighbourhood, (*ii*) associated in this way during a certain minimum of time, (*iii*) should change when they do so, jointly and in coordination, (*iv*) physical objects must be public and neutral, (*v*) should contain both visual and tactual components.'
33. See Herbart, *Minor Pedagogical Works*, pp. 28–49, 57–61.
34. J. G. Fichte, *Reden an die deutsche Nation*. A translation by R. F. Jones and G. H. Turnbull, *Addresses to the German Nation*, was published by The Open Court Publishing Company, Chicago and London, 1922.
35. *Minor Pedagogical Works, p. 135.*
36. *How Gertrude Teaches Her Children*, p. 35. Cf. p. 84: 'I found in the effort to teach writing, the need of subordinating this art to that of drawing, and in the efforts to teach drawing the combination with, and subordination of this art to, that of measurement.'
37. P. 60.
38. P. 51.
39. P. 69.
40. Ibid.
41. Cf. p. 129: 'As writing, considered as form, appears in connection with measuring and drawing, so it appears again as a special kind of learning to talk.'
42. Heafford, *Pestalozzi*, p. 57.
43. *How Gertrude Teaches Her Children*, p. 54.
44. Ibid., 51. Vertical strokes were usually adopted by Pestalozzi to represent the units.
45. Catherine Stern, *Children Discover Arithmetic* (New York: Harper & Brothers, 1949) p. 19.
46. Cf. *How Gertrude Teaches Her Children*, p. 150.
47. *Addresses to the German Nation*, Eng. trans. p. 166.
48. *Minor Pedagogical Writings*, p. 38. Froebel in *The Education of Man* repeats that the word and the thing are to the child one and the same.
49. *How Gertrude Teaches Her Children*, p. 36: 'The child must learn to talk before he can be reasonably taught to read'; p. 84: 'Thus I found, in teaching to read, the necessity of its subordination to the power of talking.'
50. Ibid., p. 33. Cf. p. 51: 'Through a well-arranged nomenclature, indelibly impressed, a general foundation for all kinds of knowledge can be laid, by which children and teacher, together, as well as separately, may rise

gradually, but with safe steps, to clear ideas in all branches of knowledge.'
51. *How Gertrude Teaches Her Children*, p. 113.
52. Ibid., p. 55.
53. *Minor Pedagogical Works*, pp. 43–4.
54. *Addresses to the German Nation*, Eng. trans. p. 164.
55. *Minor Pedagogical Works*, pp. 54, 60.
56. See *How Gertrude Teaches Her Children*, pp. 231–3.
57. *Critique of Pure Reason*, 'The Transcendental Logic', introd.
58. P. 123.
59. *Minor Pedagogical Works*, pp. 34–5. Programmed learning is based on this principle.
60. *How Gertrude Teaches Her Children*, p. 173.
61. *Addresses to the German Nation*, Eng. trans. p. 169.
62. *Minor Pedagogical Works*, p. 36.
63. *Addresses to the German Nation*, Eng. trans. p. 167.
64. Pp. 177–8. Cf. *Letters to Greaves*, pp. 89–98.
65. The reason is probably to be found in the fact that there was no expert in physical education at Yverdon, as there was for example in mathematics. See Heafford, p. 68.
66. Theodor Wiget, *Grundlinien der Erziehungslehre Pestalozzis* (Leipzig: K. F. Koehler, 1914) pp. 94–5.
67. *How Gertrude Teaches Her Children*, p. 173.
68. Ibid., p. 75.
69. P. 160. 'Man can only become man through his inner and spiritual nature. He becomes through it independent, free and contented. Mere physical nature leads him not hither. She is in her very nature blind; her ways are ways of darkness and death. Therefore, the education and training of our race must be taken out of the hands of blind sensuous Nature and the influence of her darkness and death, and put into the hands of our moral and spiritual being and its divine, eternal, inner light and truth.'
70. P. 187.
71. *Letters to Greaves*, p. 19.
72. *How Gertrude Teaches Her Children*, p. 184.
73. Ibid., p. 189.
74. Heafford, p. 64.
75. Ibid., p. 71.
76. Green, *Pestalozzi's Educational Writings*, p. 281.
77. P. 18.
78. Pp. 156–7. Also in *Views and Experiences*: 'The sole aim of education is the harmonious development of the powers and dispositions which make up personality.'
79. Silber, *Pestalozzi: The Man and his Work*, p. 219.
80. Herbart's visit to Burgdorf took place in 1797–9.
81. Froebel in his *Autobiography* admits: 'There was no educational problem whose resolution I did not firmly expect to find there.'
82. The first visit lasted a fortnight, Froebel leaving Yverdon mid-October 1805.
83. 1808–10.

84. Pestalozzi frequently referred to his own methods as experimental. Cf. *How Gertrude Teaches Her Children*, pp. 154, 166, 172.
85. Cf. *How Gertrude Teaches Her Children*, p. 83: 'Since my twentieth year, I have been incapable of philosophic thought, in the true sense of the word.'
86. Ibid., p. 18.
87. Silber, p. xi.
88. Heafford, p. 49.

9 Herbart

1. The most recent work on Herbart is Harold B. Dunkel's *Herbart and Herbartianism: An Educational Ghost Story*.
2. Dunkel, *Herbart and Herbartianism*, p. 50.
3. Margaret K. Smith, *Textbook of Psychology* (1891), translating Herbart's *Lehrbuch zur Psychologie* (1816).
4. H. M. and E. Felkin, *The Science of Education* (London and Boston 1892), translating Herbart's *Allgemeine Pädagogik aus dem Zweck der Erziehung abgeleitet* (1835).
5. J. F. Herbart, trans. A. F. Lange, *Outlines of Educational Doctrine*, § 2.
6. *Briefe über die Anwendung der Psychologie auf die Pädagogik*, trans. B. C. Mullinger (London: Swan Sonnenschein, 1898) Letter I (hereafter referred to as *Application of Psychology*).
7. *Bemerkungen über einen pädagogischen Aufsatz* (1814). J. F. Herbart's *Kleinere philosophischen Schriften* (Leipzig: G. Hartenstein, 1842) vol. I pp. 15–28. Included in *ABC of Sense Perception and Minor Pedagogical Works*, trans. W. J. Eckoff (hereafter referred to as *Minor Pedagogical Works*) p. 72.
8. G. F. Stout, *Mind*, XIII (1888) 321–8, 473–98, 'The Herbartian Psychology'; XIV (1889) 1–26, 'Herbart compared with the English Psychologists and with Beneke'; pp. 353–68, 'The Psychological Work of Herbart's Disciples'.
9. *Textbook of Psychology* (1st ed. 1816). Vol. IV of Herbart's *Collected Works* in German (Langensala, 1891) pp. 205–436, contains the fuller 2nd ed. with sections differently numbered.
10. *Outlines of Educational Doctrine*, § 20.
11. *Kurze Encyclopädie der Philosophie*, § 107.
12. § 93. Cf also § 122.
13. Herbart's term *Vorstellung* is rendered throughout by 'presentation' and is virtually equivalent to Locke's term 'idea'; it includes percepts as well as concepts. 'Just as physiology builds the body out of fibres, so psychology builds the mind out of a series of presentations.'
14. *Textbook of Psychology*, § 62.
15. Ibid.
16. *Mind*, vol. XIV, p. 363.
17. R. Ulich, *History of Educational Thought* (New York: The American Book Co., 1945) p. 275.

18. §§ 95–106.

19. *Application of Psychology*, Letter xvi, also *Textbook*, §§ 32, 36, 37.

20. Cf. Sir W. Le Gros Clark, 'The Humanity of Man', Presidential Address to the British Association, 1961: 'The conception at one time current in psychology that mental experience can be separated into the rather sharply contrasted categories termed "cognitive" and "affective" has long since been recognised as misleading, for intellectual and emotional factors are so closely interlocked in any form of behaviour that they cannot be dissociated – even arbitrarily.' See, nevertheless, p. 85 above.

21. *Textbook of Psychology*, § 33.

22. In a reply to the author.

23. See Stout, *Mind*, vol. xiii.

24. *Textbook of Psychology*, 1st ed., § 89, 2nd ed., § 47.

25. *Textbook of Psychology*, 2nd ed., §§ 124, 125.

26. The term 'repression' plays a prominent role in psycho-analysis. Ernest Jones in *Sigmund Freud: Life and Work* (London: The Hogarth Press, 1953) pp. 309, 408, acknowledges its prior use by Herbart. Note that 'repression' with Herbart as with Freud results from conflict. It may be added that in his *Textbook of Psychology* Herbart has a section on dreams (2nd ed., § 216 – German ed. of Collected Works, vol. iv, pp. 411–12).

27. The title of the second part of the *Textbook of Psychology* is: Von den Vorstellungen als Kräften.

28. *Textbook of Psychology*, 1st ed., § 127, 2nd ed., § 87.

29. *Mind*, vol. xiv (1889) p. 3.

30. *Textbook of Psychology*, 1st ed., § 127.

31. Jones, *Sigmund Freud*, p. 442: 'Freud took care never to use the term *unterbewusst*, subconscious, which he regarded as misleading; it suggests merely something that is slightly less conscious.'

32. *Mind*, vol. xvi, p. 23.

33. J. McV. Hunt, *Intelligence and Experience* (New York: The Ronald Press, 1961) p. 357.

34. An alternative term for 'apperception mass' is 'mental background', J. Adams, *Exposition and Illustration* (London: Macmillan & Co, 1909) ch. iv (the whole chapter deals with 'Mental Backgrounds'); in *The Humanities Chart Their Course* (Stanford University Press, California, 1945) p. 19, Max Radin in 'The Search for the Major Premise' says: 'I have preferred the metaphor of a cultural "matrix" to the more usual one of a background, because we think of a background as something fixed and dead and we picture living reality moving in front of it, to be sure, but quite detachable.' 'The concept "frame of reference" has been substituted and defined as the functionally related factors, both past and present, which operate at the moment to determine perception, judgment and affectivity.' *The Journal of Personality*, xviii (June 1949) 370, quoting M. Sherif and H. Cantril, *The Psychology of Ego Involvement* (New York: John Wiley & Son).

35. *Lehrbuch*, § 213.

36. *Analytic Psychology*, (London: Sonnenschein & Co., 1896) vol. ii, pp. 137–8.

37. *Talks to Teachers on Psychology: and to Students on Some of Life's Ideals* (London: Longmans Green, 1903) p. 157.

38. See Dunkel, *Herbart and Herbartianism*, p. 148.

39. *Minor Pedagogical Works*, pp. 285–6.

40. *The Science of Education*, p. 108.

41. P. 195.

42. *Minor Pedagogical Works*, p. 151.

43. Translated by Eckoff in Herbart, *ABC of Sense Perception and Minor Pedagogical Works*, pp. 92–120, under the title 'The Aesthetic Presentation of the Universe, the Chief Office of Education', and by H. M. and E. Felkin in *The Science of Education*, pp. 57–77, under the title 'On the Aesthetic Revelation of the World as the Chief Work of Education'.

44. *The Science of Education*, p. 108.

45. *Minor Pedagogical Works*, p. 16. In early Greek thought there was no separation between ethics and aesthetics. Ward in his *Encyclopaedia Britannica* article on 'Herbart' (11th ed., 1911, p. 337; 14th ed., 1929, p. 447) explains the relationship between aesthetics and ethics thus: 'Aesthetics elaborates the "ideas" involved in the expression of taste called forth by those relations of objects which acquire for them the attribute of beauty or the reverse. The beautiful is predicated absolutely and involuntarily by all who have attained the right standpoint. Ethics, the chief branch of Aesthetics deals with such relations among volitions as thus unconditionally please or displease.'

C. Burt in *The Young Delinquent* (University of London Press, 1925) p. 480, regards the relationship thus: 'The so-called moral sense is in part an aesthetic sense, a nice fastidious taste in matters of social behaviour.'

46. § 60.

47. P. 181.

48. *The Science of Education*, p. 142.

49. *Education: Its Data and First Principles* (London: Edward Arnold, 1930).

50. *The Science of Education*, p. 111.

51. *Umriss*, § 65.

52. *The Science of Education*, p. 111; also p. 119.

53. Ibid., p. 133. Cf. *Minor Works*, p. 39. 'What is needful to us is needful either to our physical or our moral nature. We need it either as sensuous beings to enable us to live or we need it as beings in the social relations of citizenship, family life and so forth, in order that we may know and do our duty.'

54. *Umriss*, § 36.

55. *The Science of Education*, p. 138.

56. Ibid., p. 120.

57. Ibid., p. 141.

58. Ibid., p. 84.

59. *Aphorismen*, XXI.

60. *Umriss*, § 126.

61. In the *Textbook of Psychology* Herbart explains the distinction between analytic and synthetic instruction thus: 'The former occurs through

reproduction for a purpose; the latter seeks to produce a combination of new concepts in conformity with a purpose.'

62. *The Science of Education*, p. 155.

63. Ibid., p. 187.

64. W. Rein, in his *Outlines of Pedagogics*, trans. C. C. and Ida Liew (London: Swan Sonnenschein, 1899) p. 153, distinguishes narrative presentation (*erzählend darstèllend*) from progressively developing presentation (*entwickelnd darstellend*) which would include both Herbart's purely synthetic and analytic forms. J. Adams, *Exposition and Illustration*, pp. 57–63, follows Herbart more closely.

65. *The Science of Education*, pp. 170–86.

66. Ibid., p. 165. For 'recapitulation', see the writer's *Philosophical Bases of Education*, pp. 49–53.

67. P. 132.

68. W. H. Kilpatrick, *Remaking the Curriculum* (New York and Chicago: Newson & Co., 1936) p. 48.

69. See above, p. 20.

70. xxx.

71. *The Science of Education*, p. 138.

72. *Umriss*, § 62.

73. Ibid., § 71.

74. *The Science of Education*, pp. 128–9.

75. Ibid., p. 192.

76. *Umriss*, § 77, note.

77. *The Science of Education*, p. 238.

78. Adams, *Herbartian Psychology*, pp. 262, 263.

79. *Umriss*, § 125.

80. Ibid., § 72.

81. London: Ernest Benn, 1962, p. 1.

82. *Umriss*, § 71.

83. Ibid., § 268.

84. *The Aims of Education*, p. 2.

85. *Umriss*, § 58, note.

86. *The Science of Education*, pp. 123–8. Also *Textbook of Psychology*, § 210.

87. *Aphorismen*, I.

88. *The Science of Education*, p. 126; *Umriss*, §§ 68–9.

89. *The Science of Education*, pp. 144–5.

90. *Umriss*, § 69.

91. Ibid., § 69.

92. Ibid., § 68.

93. Ibid. Cf. § 70.

94. E.g. J. J. Findlay, *Principles of Class Teaching* (London: Macmillan, 1907).

95. *The Science of Education*, p. 129. G. F. Stout, *Mind*, vol. XIII, p. 490: 'Desire is, according to Herbart, a composite mode of consciousness belonging on the one hand to the region of feeling, on the other to that of presented content. It has no unique character by which it can be marked off from both.'

96. Cf. Descartes, *Meditations*, IV: 'It is accordingly a dictate of the natural light that the knowledge of the understanding ought always to precede the determination of the will.'
97. *The Science of Education*, pp. 209–10.
98. *Replik gegen Jackmanns Recension der Allgemeinen Pädagogik*.
99. *The Science of Education*, pp. 220, 214.
100. *Umriss*, § 150.
101. *Replik gegen Jackmanns Recension*.
102. *The Science of Education*, p. 92.
103. Also in *Application of Psychology*, Letter II.
104. *The Science of Education*, p. 108.
105. *Umriss*, § 58.
106. *Replik gegen Jackmanns Recension*.
107. *The Science of Education*, p. 94.
108. Ibid., § 189.
109. Ibid., p. 99.
110. Pp. 230–1.
111. *Umriss*, § 43.
112. *The Science of Education*, pp. 238, 239.
113. Ibid., p. 111.
114. P. 233.
115. P. 234.
116. *Umriss*, § 42. Cf. § 126.
117. *The Science of Education*, p. 101.
118. § 46.
119. *Berichte an Herrn von Steiger*, III.
120. Dunkel (pp. 156–9) suggests that Herbart himself claims no great novelty for what he has to say about discipline. He is much more interested in instruction, for which 'government' merely clears the way.
121. 'Aesthetische Darstellung,' *The Science of Education*, pp. 63–4.
122. *The Science of Education*, p. 206.
123. 'Aesthetische Darstellung', *The Science of Education*, p. 54.
124. *Minor Pedagogical Works*, p. 99.
125. Ibid., p. 96.
126. *Umriss*, § 152.
127. *Berichte an Herrn von Steiger*, I.
128. *The Science of Education*, p. 263, note.
129. *Aphorismen*, XIX.
130. 'Aesthetische Darstellung', *The Science of Education*, p. 77.
131. F. Boutroux, *Education and Ethics*, trans. F. Rothwell (London: Williams & Norgate, 1913) p. x.
132. *The Science of Education*, p. 209.
133. P. 263 note.
134. *Outlines of Educational Doctrine*, § 10.
135. Dunkel, pp. 93–4.
136. *The Science of Education*, p. 260. J. Ruskin in *Unto This Last* interprets Justice by Righteousness, and distinguishes Justice from Equity as follows: The word 'righteousness' properly refers to the justice of rule, or

right, as distinguished from 'equity' which refers to the justice of balance. More broadly Righteousness is King's justice; and Equity Judge's justice: the King guiding or ruling all, the Judge dividing or discerning between opposites (therefore, the double question 'Man, who made me a ruler [δικαστής] or a divider [μεριστής] over you?'). (Kent: George Allen, 1877, p. 72, footnote.)

137. Dunkel, p. 99.

138. Herbart presents as alternatives to these verbs a series of adjectives, just as to the nouns signifying the four formal steps he offers as alternatives a series of verbs. The scheme with translations of the terms is as follows:

Klarheit (clearness) – *zeigen* (cognise)

Merken (register) – *anschaulich* (appearing)

Association (association) – *verknüpfen* (assimilate)

Erwarten (expect) – *continuierlich* (mediating)

System (system) – *lehren* (reflect)

Fordern (desire) – *erhebend* (enhancing)

Methode (method) – *philosophieren* (generalise)

Handeln (act) – *in die Wirklichkeit eingreifend* (objectifying)

139. *The Science of Education*, p. 200.

140. *Umriss*, § 58.

141. *The Science of Education*, p. 212.

142. *Lehrbuch*, § 223. Cf. § 107.

143. *Manual of Psychology* (London: University Correspondence College Tutorial Series, 1899) p. 711.

144. *Umriss*, § 152.

145. *Umriss*, § 58.

146. *The Science of Education*, p. 213.

147. *Replik gegen Jackmanns Recension*.

148. *The Science of Education*, p. 226 note.

149. Although it contradicts his general position that 'Knowledge is one thing, virtue is another' (*Discourses on University Education* (Dublin, 1852), *Discourse* VI) Newman expresses Herbart's view in referring to 'that moral persuasiveness which attends on tried and sustained conviction' (*Discourse* I, introductory).

150. *Grundlegung zur Lehre von erziehenden Unterricht* (Leipzig: L. Prenitzsch, 1865).

151. One member of its Executive Council was John Dewey.

152. His book stood second only to DeGarmo's in the American publisher's list.

153. It is interesting that both Adams and another Herbartian author, A. M. Williams, worked in church training colleges in Aberdeen.

10 Froebel

1. For life, see *Autobiography of Friedrich Froebel*, trans. E. Michaelis and H. K. Moore (London: Swan Sonnenschein, 1886); *Reminiscences of Friedrich Froebel*, by Baroness B. von Marenholz-Bülow, trans. Mrs

Horace Mann (Boston: Lee & Shepherd, 1895); Irene M. Lilley, *Friedrich Froebel: A Selection from His Writing*.

2. In a letter written at Dresden, 20 January 1839, he says: 'You, my dear wife, could have told this man that, as this system of education, as he said, is clear and palpable to the youngest child, it also contains in itself all philosophy.' Friedrich Froebel, *Letters on the Kindergarten*, trans. E. Michaelis and H. K. Moore (London: Swan Sonnenschein, 1891).

3. *Reminiscences*, pp. 199–200.

4. Cf. *Autobiography*, p. 29: 'I studied nothing purely theoretical except mathematics; and of philosophical teaching and thought I learnt only so much as the intercourse of university life brought with it; but it was precisely through this intercourse that I received in various ways a many-sided intellectual impulse.'

5. *Autobiography*, p. 107.

6. Of Kant, even more than of Locke, it can be said that his philosophy was more influential than his education. Fichte has remarked (*The Educational Theory of J. G. Fichte*, by G. H. Turnbull (University of Liverpool Press, 1926) pp. 8–9, 16) that Kant had no influence on Pestalozzi's development. That may be so, and any similarity in their views may be explained by the fact that both were disciples of Rousseau.

7. Froebel in his *Autobiography* (p. 93) states that even in military exercises 'I could see freedom beneath their recognised necessity'!

8. P. 40

9. J. Watson, *Schelling's Transcendental Idealism* (Chicago: S. C. Griggs & Co., 1882) pp. 95–6.

10. *The Education of Man*, p. 153.

11. 1770–1831. J. N. Findlay, *Hegel: A Re-examination* (London: George Allen & Unwin Ltd, 1958).

12. *Hegel's Philosophy of Right*, trans. S. W. Dyde (London: George Bell & Sons, 1896) author's preface, p. xxvii.

13. *Hegel's Philosophy of Mind*, by W. Wallace (OUP, 1894) p. 7.

14. Ibid., p. 11: 'The sphere of education is the individual's only; and its aim is to bring the universal mind to exist in them.' For Hegel's views on education see F. L. Luqueer, *Hegel as Educator* (London: Macmillan, 1896).

15. F. Froebel, *The Education of Man*, trans. W. N. Hailman (New York: D. Appleton, 1909).

16. Bertrand Russell in *History of Western Philosophy* (London: Allen & Unwin, 1946) p. 456, enumerates the defects of the scholastic dialectic: indifference to facts and science, belief in reasoning in matters which only observation can decide, and an undue emphasis on verbal distinctions and subtleties.

17. Cf. Findlay, *Hegel* pp. 68–71.

18. *The Philosophy of Right*, § 211, addition.

Karl Marx adopted the Hegelian dialectic but applied it in the economic field, hence the dialectical materialism of modern communism. The dialectical method supports a revolutionary view of human progress, one extreme inviting another. It was abandoned by later idealists in favour of evolutionary development under the influence of Darwin's *The Origin of Species* (1859).

The dialectical method has apparently an attraction for some modern writers on education who would not care to be aligned with Hegel or Karl Marx. Cf. Sir Richard Livingstone, *Education for a World Adrift* (CUP, 1943) p. 118; Basil A. Fletcher, *Education and Crisis* (University of London Press, 1946).

Other conceptions of development of which education has availed itself are the 'cyclical' and 'recapitulation'.

19. *The Education of Man*, p. 42.
20. *The Pedagogics of the Kindergarten*, p. 11.
21. *The Education of Man*, ch. I.
22. *Education by Development*, p. 204. Cf. p. 286.
23. *Reminiscences*, p. 225.
24. 24 Mar 1828. See *Autobiography*, pp. 104–26.
25. *Reminiscences*, p. 248.
26. *The Education of Man*, p. 68.
27. Pp. 5, 6. This is a biological formulation of predetermined development, the psychological equivalent of which is maturation; for criticism of predetermined development see J. McV. Hunt, *Intelligence and Experience* (New York: The Ronald Press, 1961).
28. *The Education of Man*, p. 27.
29. P. 120.
30. Pp. 7–8.
31. P. 9.
32. P. 10.
33. P. 13.
34. Ibid.
35. *The Education of Man*, p. 50.
36. Ibid., p. 54.
37. P. 91.
38. P. 176.
39. P. 55. Cf. Montaigne, *Essays*, bk I, ch. 22: 'We must take note that the games of children are not games in their eyes; and we must regard these are their most serious actions.'

Also Locke, *Thoughts*, § 130: 'All the plays and diversions of childhood should be directed towards good and useful habits, or else they will introduce ill ones.'

Moreover children, especially the younger ones, find play situations even where they are not intended: two Cardiff researchers in 1969, investigating the use of linear programmes with young children, found that 'they tended to insist on treating the situation as an unstructured game, an excuse to exercise their unbridled inventiveness and powers of emotional identification' (M. J. Apter and D. Boorer, 'Skinner, Piaget and Froebel: a Study of Programmed Instruction with Young Children', *Programmed Learning and Educational Technology*, July 1969).

40. *Reminiscences*, pp. 67–8.
41. For the distinction between playing at teaching and teaching by play

see Herbert Read, *Education through Art* (London: Faber & Faber, 1943) p. 219; also J. Dewey, *Democracy and Education* (New York: The Macmillan Co., 1916) p. 230.

42. *The Education of Man*, p. 94.

43. Ibid., p. 174.

44. P. 99.

45. P. 102.

46. P. 112. Cf., however, Hunt, *Intelligence and Experience*, p. 176. 'When the child, instead of playfully using a chip of wood to represent a boat in his play, makes something approximating a boat by hollowing out the wood and putting on a sail, he is moving from the realm of playful assimilation towards that of imitation and work.'

47. *The Education of Man*, p. 32.

48. For the fallacies in the sharp opposition of play and work see J. Dewey, *How We Think* (London: D. C. Heath & Co., 1909) pp. 213–14.

49. *The Education of Man*, pp. 101, 106, 113.

50. *The Philosophy of John Dewey*, edited by Paul Schlipp (Evanston: Northwestern University Press, 1939) p. 453.

51. *The Education of Man*, pp. 94–5.

52. Ibid., pp. 34–5. Cf. pp. 236–7.

53. *The Education of Man*, p. 210.

54. Ibid., p. 228.

55. The name 'Kindergarten' came to Froebel one spring day in 1840 as with some friends he was proceeding from Keilhau to Blankenburg when from a hill he saw the valley of the Rinne, a tributary of the Saale, stretching out before him like a great garden and exclaimed, 'I have found it. Kindergarten shall the name be.' J. Prüfer, *Friedrich Fröbel: sein Leben und Schaffen* (Leipzig, 1927) p. 92. Prüfer also argues that it was not till 1843 that the institution of the Kindergarten, as we now know it, was founded, the date usually given – 1840 – being '*durchaus unrichtig*' (p. 89)

56. *The Pedagogics of the Kindergarten*, p. 95.

57. P. 143.

58. For criticism of Froebel's use of symbolism see W. H. Kilpatrick, *Froebel's Kindergarten Principles Critically Examined*.

59. *The Pedagogics of the Kindergarten*, p. 92.

60. Ibid., p. 98.

61. P. 105.

62. Cf. *The Pedagogics of the Kindergarten*, pp. 233–4: 'A want of classification is the bane of all combination plays for children which have till now been known to me, and the said plays lose by this their formative influence for spirit and mind, as well as their applicability for life.'

63. *Democracy and Education*, pp. 67–8.

11 Montessori

1. E. M. Standing, *Maria Montessori: Her Life and Work*.

2. M. Montessori, *The Secret of Childhood*, trans. and ed. Barbara B. Carter (London: Longmans, Green, 1936) pp. 69, 137.

3. M. Montessori, *The Montessori Method*, trans. Anne E. George (London: William Heinemann, 1912) p. 56.

4. *The Montessori Method*, p. 43.

5. The first House of Childhood was opened on 6 Jan 1907.

6. Cf. M. Montessori, *The Advanced Montessori Method*, trans. Florence Simmonds and Lily Hutchinson (London: William Heinemann, 1917) vol. I, ch. 3.

7. *Montessori Method*, p. 45.

8. E. Séguin, *Idiocy: and its Treatment by the Physiological Method* (Columbia University Teachers College Educational Reprints) pp 10–11.

9. *Idiocy*, p. 24. Cf. H. Holman, *Séguin and his Physiological Method* (London: Sir Isaac Pitman, 1914).

10. Cf. *Advanced Montessori Method*, vol. I, p. 81. 'The long, occult experiment – suggested to me by Itard and Séguin – is, in fact, my initial contribution to education.'

11. *Montessori Method*, p. 104.

12. M. Montessori, *The Absorbent Mind*, p. 97.

13. See R. C. Orem, *Montessori Today* (New York: Putnam, 1971) pp. 32–4.

14. *Montessori Method*, p. 358.

15. Paula P. Lillard, *Montessori: a Modern Approach*.

16. Quoted by Orem, *Montessori Today*, p. 36.

17. *Montessori Method*, p. 356.

18. Ibid., p. 371.

19. Ibid., p. 80.

20. Ibid., p. 346.

21. *Allgemeine Pädagogik*, bk I, ch. 1, § 2.

22. *Advanced Montessori Method*, vol. I, pp. 19–20.

23. Ibid., vol. I, p. 72.

24. Ibid.

25. Montessori, *The Absorbent Mind*, p. 140.

26. Lillard, *Montessori*, p. 120.

27. Josephine Tozier, *An Educational Wonder-Worker: The Methods of Maria Montessori* (New York: The House of Childhood Inc., 1912).

28. *Montessori Method*, pp. 139–40.

29. Cf. ibid., p. 143.

30. Cf. *Advanced Montessori Method*, vol. I, p. 44. 'The technique of our lessons is governed by experimental psychology.'

31. Ibid., p. 73. 'This does not penetrate into the ancient ambit of pedagogy as a science that *measures* the personality, as the experimental psychology introduced into schools has hitherto done, but as a science that *transforms* the personality.'

32. *Montessori Method*, p. 169.

33. Vol. I, p. 75.

34. *Montessori Method*, p. 190.

35. *Montessori Method*, p. 236. For the teaching of geometry see ibid., p. 243; also *Advanced Montessori Method*, vol. II, pt 4.

36. *Montessori Method*, p. 221. See P. A. Dennis, 'Lévi-Strauss in the

Kindergarten: The Montessori Pre-Schooler as Bricoleur', International Review of Education, XXI (1974).

37. For evaluation of the criticisms of the Montessori system, see the writer's *History of Infant Education* (University of London Press, 1941).

38. *Montessori Method*, pp. 226–7.

39. Ibid., p. 256.

40. Ibid., p. 261.

41. Ibid., p. 288.

42. Ibid., pp. 287–8, 289.

43. Ibid., p. 294.

44. Ibid., p. 296. Cf. *Advanced Montessori Method*, vol. II, ch. 15.

45. The child passes from the reading of script to the reading of print without guidance (*Montessori Method*, p. 301), a point which has been noted by other experimenters in the teaching of reading.

46. Montessori Method, p. 301.

47. Ibid., p. 298.

48. Ibid., p. 301–2.

49. E. Holmes, *The Montessori System of Education*, p. 16.

50. Tozier, *Educational Wonder-Worker*, p. 13.

51. Catherine Stern, *Children Discover Arithmetic: An Introduction to Structural Arithmetic* (New York: Harper & Bro, 1949).

That the Montessori exercises are not inconsistent with the Gestalt psychology has been shown by the writer in his *History of Infant Education* pp. 78–80.

52. *Advanced Montessori Method*, pt 3.

53. William Kilpatrick, *The Montessori System Examined*, pp. 28–9.

54. *Montessori Method*, p. 160.

55. Cf. Herbart, *Textbook of Psychology*, p. 73: 'Quite as much imagination belongs to original scientific thinking as to poetic creation, and it is very doubtful whether Newton or Shakespeare possessed the more imagination.'

56. Vol. I, pp. 241–55. See also whole ch. 9.

57. In *Advanced Montessori Method*, vol. II, p. 191, the readings used are said to be numerous and of great variety, and include: 'fairly tales, short stories, anecdotes, novels, historical episodes.' For the child's preference for facts over fiction see, however, vol. ii, p. 195.

58. *Montessori Method*, p. 89.

59. Ibid., p. 107.

60. Ibid., p. 176. Cf. Ibid., p. 224.

61. *Advanced Montessori Method*, vol. I, p. 128. See same work, vol. I, 'The Preparation of the Teacher'.

62. Dennis, 'Lévi-Strauss in the Kindergarten', p. 13.

63. *Modern Developments in Educational Practice* (University of London Press, 1922) ch. 6.

64. Kilpatrick, *Montessori System Examined*, pp. 65–6.

65. Nancy Rambusch, *Learning How to Learn: An American Approach to Montessori*.

66. Paula P. Lillard, *Montessori: A Modern Approach* (New York: Schocken Books, 1972).

67. R. C. Orem, *Montessori Today*.
68. Nathan Isaacs, in the *Froebel Journal*, 12 (1968) 22–7.
69. *Montessori Method*, p. 167.
70. Susan Isaacs, *Intellectual Growth in Young Children* (1930) p. 21.
71. Nathan Isaacs, p. 27.
72. R. C. Orem, *Montessori Today*, p. 16.

12 Dewey

1. A biography of John Dewey edited by his daughter is prefixed to *The Philosophy of John Dewey*, ed. Paul Arthur Schlipp, being vol. I of The Library of Living Philosophers. See also *John Dewey: Master Educator*, ed. W. W. Brickman and S. Lehrer.
2. For a comprehensive study of the laboratory school see Arthur G. Wirth, *John Dewey as Educator*.
3. Malcolm Skilbeck, *Dewey*, p. 33.
4. *Democracy and Education*, p. 386.
5. John Dewey, 'From Absolutism to Experimentalism', in *Contemporary American Philosophy*, vol. II, ed. C. P. Adams and W. P. Montague (London: George Allen & Unwin; New York: The Macmillan Co., 1930) p. 22.
6. Cf. Morton G. White, *The Origin of Dewey's Instrumentalism*.
7. Dewey, *The Study of Ethics: A Syllabus* (1894); White, *Dewey's Instrumentalism*, pp. 83, 111; Wirth, *Dewey as Educator*, p. 22; Skilbeck, *Dewey*, p. 2.
8. Cf. *Contemporary American Philosophy*, vol. II, p. 22: 'Upon the whole, the forces that have influenced me have come from persons and from situations more than from books.'
9. Cf. W. B. Gallie, *Peirce and Pragmatism* (Penguin Books, 1952). James K. Feibleman, *An Introduction to Peirce's Philosophy* (London: George Allen & Unwin, 1960).
10. *Contemporary American Philosophy*, vol. II, p. 24.
11. *Human Nature and Conduct* (London: George Allen & Unwin, 1922) pp. 34, 36.
12. Cf. Dewey's *The Quest for Certainty*, p. 295: 'It [knowing] marks a transitional redirection and rearrangement of the real. It is intermediate and instrumental.' And p. 298: 'Knowledge is instrumental. But the purport of our whole discussion has been in praise of tools, instrumentalities, means, putting them on a level equal in value to ends and consequences, since without them, the latter are merely accidental, sporadic and unstable.' See also Maxine Greene, 'John Dewey and Moral Education', *Contemporary Education*, XLVIII 1 (Fall 1976) 18.
13. Cf. T. Gomperz, *Greek Thinkers*, Eng. trans. (London: John Murray, 1901) vol. I, ch. 1.
14. *The Quest for Certainty*, p. 229.
15. *The School and Society*, p. 71; Wirth, ch. 15.
16. R. H. S. Crossman, *Plato To-day* (London: George Allen & Unwin, 1937) p. 225.

17. *Addresses to the German Nation*, trans. R. F. Jones and G. H. Turnbull, ed. and introd. George A. Kelly (New York: Harper Torchbooks, 1968) p. 122.

18. P. 228.

19. A. N. Whitehead *Science and the Modern World* CUP, 1926, pp. 6, 40, 250.

20. Dewey, *How We Think*, pp. 95, 151.

21. Dewey, *Freedom and Culture*, p. 157.

22. P. 87.

23. New York: The Macmillan Co., 1926, p. 12.

24. *Kant on Education*, trans. Annette Churton (London: Kegan Paul, 1899) p. 14.

25. *Social Statics: Or The Conditions Essential to Human Happiness* (London: John Chapman, 1851) p. 341.

26. *The Quest for Certainty*, p. 37 note.

27. P. 393.

28. Pp. 30, 120.

29. *The Quest for Certainty*, pp. 36, 129, 136. Cf. p. 166: 'thought is a mode of directed overt action'; p. 167: 'knowing is itself a kind of action'; p. 207: knowing 'a form of doing'; p. 245: knowing 'an existential overt action'.

30. *The Aims of Education*, p. 155.

31. *Freedom and Culture*, p. 58.

32. The fallacy of both hedonism and pragmatism was succinctly formulated in another connection by Lord Justice Donovan when, on delivering judgement in the Soblen case, he said: 'otherwise the quality of an act would be determined by its consequences, which was obviously untrue, because cause and effect were not the same thing.' – *The Times* Law Report, 31 Aug 1962.

John Milton, *Prose Works* (London: Henry G. Bohn, 1848–53) vol. I, *The Second Defence of the People of England*, p. 276. 'On the nature of success I will say a few words. Success neither proves a cause to be good, nor indicates it to be bad; and we demand that our cause should not be judged by the event, but the event by the cause.' Also, 'Whether it is lawful to rise against a tyrant', Milton (vol. II, p. 23) answers: 'that the vulgar judge of it according to the event, and the learned according to the purpose of them that do it.'

33. *The Roots of Honour* (Kent: George Allen, 1877) p. 8.

34. *Sources of a Science of Education* (New York: H. Liveright, 1929) pp. 55–60.

35. *Human Nature and Conduct*, p. 119.

36. *Of the Advancement of Learning*, in *Philosophical Works* (London: Routledge, 1905) p. 60.

37. *Democracy and Education*, p. 384.

38. By K. C. Mayhew and A. C. Edwards, p. vi.

39. *School and Society*, p. 17.

40. The original article appeared in *The Westminster Review*, July and Oct 1895.

41. Cf. Irwin Edman, 'The Arts of Liberation', in *The Authoritarian Attempt to Capture Education* (New York: King's Crown Press, 1945) p. 29. 'Science is popularly often conceived to be a palace of mechanical wonders or a chamber of mechanical horrors. But the fruits of science are spiritual and educative as well, and these are only beginning to be realised or broached in modern study and teachings. They have scarcely affected the imagination of the general educated public, or even the basic forms and assumptions of thought of scientists themselves. The very method of scientific inquiry is a moral lesson in objectivity, disinterestedness and detachment. Its careful, patient procedure is a lesson in devotion and responsibility, respect for the facts as they are found to be, and faith in the infinite resources which understanding might make of nature for human uses. There is a whole making of a whole religion in the landscape of experience as inquiry discloses it, and the prospects for mankind that that landscape suggests.'

42. *Sources of a Science of Education*, pp. 65–6.

43. *Democracy and Education*, p. 281.

44. Quoted by Jacques Maritain in *Education at the Cross Roads* (Yale University Press, 1943) p. 55.

45. *The New Republic*, 9 July 1930.

46. *Democracy and Education*, p. 223.

47. British Association Address to Section L (Educational Science), 1923.

48. *The Quest for Certainty*, p. 79.

49. P. 188.

50. Wirth, *Dewey as Educator*, p. 172.

51. Bk II.

52. Pp. 91–4.

53. *The Aims of Education*, p. 80.

54. E. Meyerson, *Identity and Reality*, Eng. trans. (New York, The Macmillan Co., 1930) p. 396.

55. *The Quest for Certainty*, p. 84.

56. Meyerson, p. 398: 'The principle of kinetic theories . . . must be attributed to a deduction.'

57. *Science and the Modern World*: The Lowell Lectures 1925 (CUP, 1926) p. 41.

58. Cf. also D. B. Klein, 'Psychology's Progress and the Armchair Taboo', in *Twentieth Century Psychology* (New York: The Philosophical Library, 1946).

59. *Freedom and Culture*, p. 65.

60. Cf. *Democracy and Education*, p. 204, where claims advanced for it are: directness, open-mindedness, single-mindedness, responsibility.

61. H. E. Armstrong, *The Teaching of Scientific Method* (New York: The Macmillan Co., 1925) 'The Heuristic Method'.

62. *Problems of Men* (New York: The Philosophical Library, 1946) pp. 137–8.

63. Wirth, *Dewey as Educator*, p. 210.

64. *Democracy and Education*, p. 192.

65. Cf. Max Wertheimer, *Productive Thinking* (New York and London: Harper & Brothers, 1943) pp. 190–1.

66. Dewey was not the originator of the term. Personal letter to present author, 9 Feb 1933: 'The term project was not original with me.' It was widely publicised by W. H. Kilpatrick (*Teachers' College Record*, XIX, 1918), but came to be widely misconstrued, being applied to almost any activity by pupils loosely clustered round a 'centre of interest' they might or might not have formed for themselves.

67. P. 231.

68. Harvard University Press, 1931, p. 31.

69. See biography prefixed to Schlipp's *Philosophy of John Dewey*.

70. *Politics*, v, §§ 9, 11.

71. Nevertheless, unlike his followers, he stopped short of indulging individual whims. The first statement in his 'Plan of Organisation of the University Primary School' (unpublished) reads: 'The ultimate problem of all education is to co-ordinate the psychological and social factors'. See Wirth, *Dewey as Educator*, p. 121.

72. *Democracy and Education*, p. 186.

73. *School and Society*, p. 71.

74. See A. K. Thomas, 'A Consideration of John Dewey's Relevance Today', *Swansea College Faculty of Education Journal* (1970) 21–5.

75. In a letter to *Life*, 15 Mar 1959.

76. Walter Lippmann, 'Education without Culture', *Commonweal*, XXXIII (1940–1).

77. L. A. Cremin, *The Transformation of the School* (New York, 1961) foreword. See also Leonhard Frosse, 'Die Uberwindung des Deweyismus in den USA', *International Review of Education* v 12 (Mar 1966) 24–37.

78. Sidney Hook, *Education and the Taming of Power*.

79. See A. K. Thomas, 'Dewey's Relevance Today', pp. 23, 24.

13 The Twentieth Century

1. 1880–1961. *The Normal Child and Primary Education*; (ed.), *The First Five Years of Life*; (with Frances Ilg), *The Child From Five to Ten*; (with Frances Ilg and Louise Bates Ames), *Youth: The Years from Ten to Sixteen*.

2. 1885–1948. *The Children We Teach*; *The Intellectual Growth of Young Children*; *The Social Growth of Young Children*.

3. 1883–1971. *The Young Delinquent; The Backward Child*.

4. 1881–1955. Thomson's most influential work resulted in the long series of 'Moray House' tests, named after the Training Centre in Edinburgh of which he was Director of Studies.

5. 1900–69. *Backwardness in the Basic Subjects*.

6. 1870–1944. *Education: Its Data and First Principles*.

7. 1856–1939. The standard edition of Freud's works is published by the Hogarth Press. See especially: vols 4 and 5, *The Interpretation of Dreams* (1900); vol. 6, *The Psychopathology of Everyday Life* (1901); vol. 13, *Totem and Taboo* (1913); vol. 18, *Beyond the Pleasure Principle* (1920).

Works on Freud include: Ernest Jones, *The Life and Work of Sigmund*

Freud; J. A. C. Brown, *Freud and the Post-Freudians*; Frank Cioffi (ed.), *Freud* (Modern Judgements series).
8. 1870–1937. *The Practice and Theory of Individual Psychology*. See Lewis Way, *Alfred Adler: An Introduction to his Psychology*.
9. 1875–1961. *Psychology of the Unconscious*; *Modern Man in Search of a Soul* (London: Kegan Paul, 1933); *The Integration of the Personality* (London: Kegan Paul, 1940). See Jolande Jacobi, *The Psychology of C. G. Jung* (London: Routledge & Kegan Paul, 6th ed., 1962).
10. See. pp. 160–61.
11. 1883–1973. *A Dominie's Log* (London: Herbert Jenkins, n.d.); *A Dominie Dismissed* (London: Herbert Jenkins, n.d.); *Summerhill: a Radical Approach to Education*. See Leslie R. Perry (ed.), *Four Progressive Educators*.
12. *Summerhill*, p. 100.
13. Ibid., p. 224–5.
14. Ibid., p. 316.
15. Born 1896. *The Language and Thought of the Child*; *The Moral Judgment of the Child*; *The Psychology of Intelligence*; *The Growth of Logical Thinking*. Piaget has also produced a long series of books on the child's conception of various phenomena.
16. Ved P. Varma and Philip Williams (eds), *Piaget, Psychology and Education: Papers in Honour of Jean Piaget*, p. xi.
17. Jerome Bruner, *The Relevance of Education*, p. 13.
18. Varma, *Piaget*, p. 10.
19. Piaget contributed to his own protection by the vagueness of some of his language and by modifying his theories continuously over half a century.
20. W. S. Anthony, 'Activity in the Learning of Piagetian Operational Thinking', *British Journal of Educational Psychology*, XLVII 1 (Feb 1977) 18–23.
21. Richard Peters, *Ethics and Education*, p. 49.
22. Bruner, *Relevance of Education*, p. 24.
23. Jan Smedlund, quoted in an article by Nicholas Bagnall, *Times Educational Supplement*, 18 Mar 1977. Works on Piaget include: Ruth M. Beard, *An Outline of Piaget's Developmental Psychology for Students and Teachers*; Mildred Hardeman (ed.), *Children's Ways of Knowing: Nathan Isaacs on Education, Psychology and Piaget*.
24. 1818–83. *Capital*, 6 vols (London: Lawrence & Wishart, 1974); *Selected Works*, 2 vols (Moscow: Foreign Languages Publishing House, 1950). See David McLellan, *Karl Marx: His Life and Thought*.
25. Of its nature. It was the theory of capitalism that Marx attacked, not its historical manifestation in Western Europe and America.
26. *Capital*, III 191.
27. *Critique of the Gotha Programme (Selected Works*, II 30).
28. *State and Revolution* (1918).
29. *Ibid*.
30. See Peters, *Ethics and Education* pp. 218.–21.
31. William Leon McBride, *The Philosophy of Marx*, p. 56.

32. 1861–1947. *Adventures of Ideas*; *The Aims of Education*. See W. Mays, *The Philosophy of Whitehead*; Harold B. Dunkel, *Whitehead on Education*.

33. *Science and the Modern World* (New York: New American Library, Mentor Books, 1964) p. 177.

34. *Aims of Education*, pp. 1–2.

35. Ibid., p. 3.

36. Ibid., p. 86.

37. P. 10.

38. P. 75.

39. Pp. 68–9.

40. 1858–1917. *Rules of Sociological Method*.

41. 1893–1947. *Diagnosis of Our Time*; (with W. A. C. Stewart), *An Introduction to the Sociology of Education*.

42. *Ethics and Education*, p. 319.

43. *Relevance of Education*, pp. 17–19.

44. *Ethics and Education*, p. 121.

45. A. R. Jensen, 'How Much Can We Boost I.Q. and Scholastic Achievement,' *Harvard Educational Review*, xxxix (1969) 1–123.

46. Varma, *Piaget*, p. 40.

47. Illich, 'The Alternative to Schooling', *Saturday Review*, 19 June 1971, pp. 44–8.

48. The name was given by John Holt in a letter in *Reformulations*, 1971.

49. See Peter Lund, 'Illich', *Times Educational Supplement*, 21 Jan 1977.

50. Ivan Illich, *Deschooling Society*.

51. Sidney Hook, *Education and the Taming of Power* (New York: Alcove Press, 1974) pp. 90, 166.

Bibliography

Chapter 1 'The Great Educators'

Whitehead, A. N., *Process and Reality: An Essay on Cosmology* (New York: Harper & Row, 1957).

Chapter 2 Plato

Bambrough, Renford, *Plato, Popper and Politics: Some Contributions to a Modern Controversy* (Cambridge: Heffer, 1967).

Barclay, W., *Educational Ideals in the Ancient World* (London: Collins, 1959).

Barrow, Robin, *Plato, Utilitarianism and Education* (London: Routledge & Kegan Paul, 1975).

Beck, F. A. G., *Greek Education, 450–350 B.C.* (London: Methuen, 1964).

Black, R. S., *Plato's Life and Thought* (London: Routledge & Kegan Paul, 1949).

Bowen, James, *A History of Western Education*, vol. I, *The Ancient World* (London: Methuen, 1972).

Boyd, W., *Plato's Republic for Today* (London: Heinemann, 1962).

Crossman, R. H., *Plato Today* (London: Allen & Unwin, 1963).

Gross, Barry (ed.), *Great Thinkers on Plato* (New York: Capricorn Books, 1969).

Jaeger, Werner, *Paideia: The Ideals of Greek Culture*, trans. G. Highet (Oxford: Basil Blackwell, vol. I, 1939; vol. II, 1944; vol. III, 1945).

Livingstone, R. W., *Portrait of Socrates* (OUP, 1938).

——, *Plato and Modern Education* (CUP, 1944).

Lodge, R. C., *Plato's Theory of Education* (London: Routledge & Kegan Paul, 1947).

Marrou, H. I., *A History of Education in Antiquity*, trans. G. Lamb (London: Sheed & Ward, 1956).

Nettleship, R. L., *The Theory of Education in the Republic of Plato* (OUP, 1935).

——, *Lectures on the Republic of Plato*, 2nd ed. (London: Macmillan, 1958).

Plato, *The Epinomis of Plato*, trans. J. Harward (OUP, 1928).

——, *The Laws*, trans. Trevor J. Saunders (Harmondsworth: Penguin Books, 1970).

——, *The Republic*, trans. H. D. P. Lee (Harmondsworth: Penguin Books, 1955).

——, *Works*, trans. Benjamin Jowett (OUP, 1875).

Popper, K. R., *The Open Society and Its Enemies*, vol. I, *The Spell of Plato* (London: Routledge & Kegan Paul, 1966).

Russell, Bertrand, *Unpopular Essays* (London: Allen & Unwin, 1950).

Taylor, A. E., *Socrates* (London: Peter Davies, 1933).

——, *Plato: The Man and His Work* (London: Methuen, University Paperbacks, 1960).

Chapter 3   Quintilian

Bowen, James, *History of Western Education*, vol. I, *The Ancient World* (London: Methuen, 1972).

Clarke, M. L., 'Quintilian: A Biographical Sketch', in *Greece and Rome*, 2nd ser., XIV (April 1967).

Colson, F. H., *M. Fabii Quintiliani Institutionis Oratoriae, Liber I* (CUP, 1924).

Downes, John F., 'Quintilian Today', in *School and Society*, LXXIII (March 1951).

Gwynn, A., *Roman Education from Cicero to Quintilian* (Oxford: Clarendon Press, 1926).

Kennedy, George, *Quintilian* (New York: Twayne, 1969).

Quintilian, *Institutio Oratoria*, trans. H. E. Butler (Loeb Classical Library) 4 vols (London: Heinemann, 1921).

Wilkins, A. S., *Roman Education* (CUP, 1905).

Chapter 4　Loyola

Bowen, James, *History of Western Education*, vol. II, *Civilization of Europe* (London: Methuen, 1975).

Brodrick, James, *The Origin of the Jesuits* (London: Longmans Green, 1940).

——, *The Progress of the Jesuits* (London: Longmans Green, 1947).

——, *Saint Ignatius Loyola: The Pilgrim Years* (London: Burns & Oates, 1956).

Elliot-Binns, L. E., *England and the New Learning* (London: Lutterworth Press, 1937).

Farrell, Alan P., *The Jesuit Code of Liberal Education: Development and Scope of the Ratio Studiorum* (Milwaukee: Bruce Publishing Co., 1938).

Fitzpatrick, E. A., *St Ignatius and the Ratio Studiorum* (New York and London: McGraw-Hill, 1933).

Ganss, George E., *Saint Ignatius' Idea of a Jesuit University* (Milwaukee: Marquette University Press, 1956).

Hughes, T., *Loyola and the Educational System of the Jesuits* (London: William Heinemann, 1892).

Loyola, Ignatius of, *The Autobiography of St Ignatius Loyola, with Related Documents*, ed. John C. Olin, trans. Joseph O'Callaghan (New York: Harper Torchbooks, 1974).

Matt, Leonard von, and Rahner, Hugo, *St Ignatius of Loyola: A Pictorial Biography*, trans. John Murray (London: Longmans Green, 1956).

Pachtler, G. M., *Monumenta Germaniae Paedagogica* (Berlin, 1887–94).

Schwickerath, R., *Jesuit Education: Its History and Principles* (St Louis: B. Herder, 1903).

Thompson, Francis, *Saint Ignatius Loyola* (London: Burns & Oates, 1909).

Tillyard, E. M. W., *The English Renaissance: Fact or Fiction* (London: Hogarth Press, 1952).

Van Dyke, Paul, *Ignatius Loyola: The Founder of the Jesuits* (New York and London: Charles Scribner's Sons, 1927).

Chapter 5   Comenius

Beneš, E., *et al.*, *The Teacher of Nations: Addresses and Essays in Commemoration of the Visit to England of Jan Amos Komensky, Comenius, 1641–1941*, ed. Joseph Needham (CUP, 1942).

Bowen, J., *Orbis Sensualium Pictus by Joannes Amos Comenius* (New York: International School Book Service, 1967).

Comenius, J. A., *The Labyrinth of the World and the Paradise of the Heart* (London: Dent's Temple Classics, 1905).

——, *The School of Infancy*, ed. E. M. Eller (University of North Carolina Press, 1957).

Corcoran, T., *Studies in the History of Classical Teaching* (London: Longmans Green & Co., 1911).

Jelinek, V., *The Analytical Didactic of Comenius* (University of Chicago Press, 1954).

Keatinge, M. W., *The Great Didactic of John Amos Comenius* (London: A. & C. Black, 1910).

Laurie, S. S., *John Amos Comenius* (CUP, 1899).

Sadler, John E., *J. A. Comenius and the Concept of Universal Education* (London: Allen & Unwin, 1966).

Spinka, Matthew, *John Amos Comenius: That Incomparable Moravian* (University of Chicago Press, 1943; repr. 1973).

Turnbull, G. H., *Hartlib, Dury and Comenius* (University Press of Liverpool, 1947).

Young, R. F., *Comenius in England* (OUP, 1932).

Chapter 6   Locke

Axtell, James L., *The Educational Writings of John Locke* (CUP, 1968).

Cranston, Maurice, *John Locke: A Biography* (London: Longmans Green, 1957).

Dewhurst, K., *John Locke, Physician and Philosopher: A Medical Biography* (London: Wellcome Historical Medical Library, 1963).

Gay, Peter (ed.), *John Locke on Education* (New York: Teachers' College, 1964).

Laslett, Peter, *John Locke: Two Treatises of Government* (CUP, 1960).

O'Connor, D. J., *John Locke* (Harmondsworth: Penguin Books, 1952).

Quick, R. H., *Some Thoughts Concerning Education by John Locke* (CUP, 1895).

Stocks, J. L. *et al.*, *John Locke: Tercentenary Addresses Delivered in the Hall at Christchurch* (OUP, 1933).

Yolton, John W., *John Locke: Problems and Perspectives* (Philadelphia Book Co., 1971).

——, *John Locke and Education* (Philadelphia Book Co., 1971).

Chapter 7   Rousseau

Boyd, W., *Émile for Today* (London: Heinemann, 1956).

——, *Educational Theory of Jean-Jacques Rousseau* (London: Longmans, 1911; repr. 1963).

Claydon, Leslie F., *Rousseau on Education* (London: Macmillan, 1969).

Compayre, Gabriel, *Jean-Jacques Rousseau and Education from Nature* (New York: B. Franklin, 1907; repr. 1972).

Green, F. C., *Jean-Jacques Rousseau: A Critical Study of His Life and Writings* (CUP, 1955).

Grimsley, R., *Jean-Jacques Rousseau: A Study in Self-awareness*, 2nd ed. (Cardiff: University of Wales Press, 1970).

——, *The Philosophy of Rousseau* (OUP, 1973).

Macdonald, Frederika, *Jean-Jacques Rousseau: A New Criticism* (London: Chapman & Hall, 1906).

Rousseau, Jean-Jacques, *Émile*, trans. Barbara Foxley (Everyman ed., London: Dent, 1911).

Sahakian, M. and W., *Rousseau as Educator* (New York: Twayne, 1974).

Chapter 8   Pestalozzi

Green, J. A. (ed.), *Pestalozzi's Educational Writings* (London: Edward Arnold, 1912).

Heafford, M. R., *Pestalozzi* (London: Methuen, 1967).

Herbart, J. F., *ABC of Sense Perception and Minor Pedagogical Works*, trans. W. J. Eckoff (New York: D. Appleton, 1903).

Pestalozzi, J. H., *How Gertrude Teaches Her Children*, trans. Lucy E. Holland and Francis C. Turner (London: Swan Sonnenschein, 1907).

Silber, Kate, *Pestalozzi: The Man and His Work*, 3rd ed. (London: Routledge & Kegan Paul, 1973).

Chapter 9   Herbart

Adams, J., *The Herbartian Psychology Applied to Education* (London: Isbister, 1909).

Dunkel, Harold B., *Herbart and Herbartianism: An Educational Ghost Story* (University of Chicago Press, 1970).

Herbart, J. F., *Textbook of Psychology*, trans. Margaret K. Smith (New York: D. Appleton, 1891).

——, *ABC of Sense Perception and Minor Pedagogical Works*, trans. W. J. Eckoff (New York: D. Appleton, 1903).

——, *Outlines of Educational Doctrine*, trans. A. F. Lange (New York: The Macmillan Co., 1904).

——, *The Science of Education*, trans. H. M. and E. Felkin (London: Swan Sonnenschein, 1904).

Chapter 10   Froebel

Froebel, Friedrich, *Autobiography of Friedrich Froebel*, trans. E. Michaelis and H. K. Moore (London: Swan Sonnenschein, 1886).

——, *Letters on the Kindergarten*, trans. E. Michaelis and H. K. Moore (London: Swan Sonnenschein, 1891).

——, *The Pedagogics of the Kindergarten*, trans. Josephine Jarvis (London: Edward Arnold, 1900).

——, *Education by Development*, 2nd part of *The Pedagogics of the Kindergarten*, trans. Josephine Jarvis (New York: D. Appleton, 1905).

——, *The Education of Man*, trans. W. N. Hailman (New York: D. Appleton, 1909).

Kilpatrick, W. H., *Froebel's Kindergarten Principles Critically Examined* (New York: The Macmillan Co., 1916).

Lawrence, Evelyn (ed.), *Friedrich Froebel and English Education* (London: Routledge & Kegan Paul, 1952; repr. 1969).

Lilley, Irene M., *Friedrich Froebel: A Selection from His Writing* (CUP, 1967).

Marenholz-Bülow, Baroness B. von, *Reminiscences of Friedrich Froebel*, trans. Mrs Horace Mann (Boston: Lee & Shepherd, 1895).

Chapter 11   Montessori

Kilpatrick, W. H., *The Montessori System Examined* (Boston: Houghton Mifflin, 1914).

Lillard, Paula P., *Montessori: A Modern Approach* (New York: Schocken Books, 1972).

Montessori, M., *The Montessori Method*, trans. Anne E. George (London: William Heinemann, 1912).

——, *The Advanced Montessori Method*, trans. Florence Simmonds and Lily Hutchinson (London: William Heinemann, 1917).

——, *The Secret of Childhood*, trans. and ed. Barbara B. Carter (London: Longmans Green, 1936).

——, *The Absorbent Mind* (Wheaton, Ill.: Theosophical Press, 1964).

Orem, R. C., *Montessori Today* (New York: Putnam, 1971).

Rambusch, Nancy, *Learning How to Learn: An American Approach to Montessori* (New York: Taplinger Publishing Co., 1962).

Standing, E. M., *Maria Montessori: Her Life and Work* (London: Hollis & Carter, 1957).

Chapter 12   Dewey

Brickman, W. W., and Lehrer, S. (eds), *John Dewey: Master Educator* (New York: Society for the Advancement of Education, 1959).

Dewey, John, *The School and Society* (University of Chicago Press, 1900).

——, *How We Think* (London: D. C. Heath & Co., 1909).

Dewey, John, *Democracy and Education* (New York: The Macmillan Co., 1916).

——, *The Quest for Certainty* (New York: Minton, Balch & Co., 1929).

——, *A Common Faith* (New Haven: Yale Univ. Press, 1934).

——, *Freedom and Culture* (London: Allen & Unwin, 1940).

Hook, Sidney, *Education and the Taming of Power* (London: Alcove Press, 1974).

Mayhew, K. C., and Edwards, A. C., *The Dewey School* (New York: D. Appleton–Century Co., 1936).

Schlipp, Paul Arthur (ed.), *The Philosophy of John Dewey* (Evanston and Chicago: Northwestern University Press, 1939).

Skilbeck, Malcolm, *Dewey* (London: Macmillan, 1970).

White, Morton G., *The Origin of Dewey's Instrumentalism* (New York: Columbia University Press, 1943).

Wirth, Arthur G., *John Dewey as Educator* (New York: Wiley, 1966).

Chapter 13   The Twentieth Century

Adler, Alfred, *The Practice and Theory of Individual Psychology*, trans. P. Radin (London: Kegan Paul & Co., 1924).

Beard, Ruth M., *An Outline of Piaget's Developmental Psychology for Students and Teachers* (London: Routledge & Kegan Paul, 1969).

Brearley, M., and Hitchfield, E., *A Teacher's Guide to Reading Piaget* (London: Routledge & Kegan Paul, 1966).

Brown, J. A. C., *Freud and the Post-Freudians* (Harmondsworth, Penguin Books, 1964).

Bruner, Jerome, *The Relevance of Education* (London: Allen & Unwin, 1971).

Burt, Cyril, *The Backward Child*, 5th ed. (University of London Press, 1961).

——, *The Young Delinquent*, 4th ed. (University of London Press, 1969).

Cioffi, Frank (ed.), *Freud* (Modern Judgements series; London: Macmillan, 1973).

Clarke, Fred, *Freedom in the Educative Society* (University of London Press, 1948).

Curtis, S. J., and Boultwood, M. E. A., *A Short History of Educa-*

tional Ideas, 3rd ed. (London: University Tutorial Press, 1961).

Dunkel, Harold B., *Whitehead on Education* (Ohio State University Press, 1965).

Durkheim, Émile, *Rules of Sociological method* (London: Collier-Macmillan, 1964).

Freud, Sigmund, *The Psychopathology of Everyday Life* (London: Hogarth Press, 1953).

——, *Beyond the Pleasure Principle* (London: Hogarth Press, 1920).

Gesell, Arnold, *The Normal Child and Primary Education* (London: Ginn, 1912).

——, (ed.), *The First Five Years of Life* (London: Methuen, 1966).

——, and Frances Ilg, *The Child from Five to Ten* (London: Hamish Hamilton, 1965).

——, Frances Ilg and Louise Bates Ames, *Youth: The Years from Ten to Sixteen* (London: Hamish Hamilton, 1965).

Hardeman, Mildred (ed.), *Children's Ways of Knowing: Nathan Isaacs on Education, Psychology and Piaget* (USA Teachers' College Press, 1974).

Illich, Ivan, *Deschooling Society* (Harmondsworth: Penguin Books, 1973).

Isaacs, Susan, *The Intellectual Growth of Young Children* (London: Routledge & Kegan Paul, 1930).

——, *The Children We Teach* (University of London Press, 1932).

——, *The Social Growth of Young Children* (London: Routledge & Kegan Paul, 1937).

Jacobi, Jolande, *The Psychology of C. G. Jung,* 6th ed. (London: Routledge & Kegan Paul, 1962).

Jones, Ernest, *Life and Work of Sigmund Freud*, 3 vols (London: Hogarth Press, 1958).

Jung, C. G., *Psychology of the Unconscious* (London: Kegan Paul, 1916).

Lawrence, Elizabeth, *The Origins and Growth of Modern Education* (Harmondsworth: Penguin Books, 1972).

Lister, Ian, *Deschooling: A Reader* (CUP, 1974).

McBride, William Leon, *The Philosophy of Marx* (London: Hutchinson, 1977).

McLellan, David, *Karl Marx: His Life and Thought* (London: Macmillan, 1973).

Mannheim, Karl, *Diagnosis of Our Time* (London: Routledge & Kegan Paul, 1943).

Mannheim, Karl, and Stewart, W. A. C., *An Introduction to the Sociology of Education* (London: Routledge & Kegan Paul, 1962).

Mays, W., *The Philosophy of Whitehead* (London: Allen & Unwin, 1959).

Morrish, Ivor, *The Disciplines of Education* (London: Allen & Unwin, 1968).

Neill, A. S., *Summerhill: A Radical Approach to Education* (London: Gollancz, 1962).

Nisbet. R. A., *Émile Durkheim* (New York: Prentice-Hall, 1965).

Nunn, Percy, *Education: Its Data and First Principles*, 2nd ed. (London: Edward Arnold, 1930).

Perry, Leslie R., *Four Progressive Educators* (London: Collier-Macmillan, 1967).

Peters, Richard, *Ethics and Education* (London: Allen & Unwin, 1970).

Piaget, Jean, *The Moral Judgment of the Child* (London: Kegan Paul, 1932).

——, *The Psychology of Intelligence* (London: Routledge & Kegan Paul, 1950).

——, *The Growth of Logical Thinking* (London: Routledge & Kegan Paul, 1958).

——, *The Language and Thought of the Child*, 3rd ed. (London: Routledge & Kegan Paul, 1960).

Schonell, Fred, *Backwardness in the Basic Subjects* (Edinburgh: Oliver & Boyd, 1942).

Varma, Ved P., and Williams, Philip (eds), *Piaget, Psychology and Education: Papers in Honour of Jean Piaget* (London: Hodder & Stoughton, 1976).

Way, Lewis, *Alfred Adler: An Introduction to His Psychology* (Harmondsworth: Penguin Books, 1956).

Whitehead, Alfred N., *Adventures of Ideas* (Harmondsworth: Pelican Books, 1948).

——, *The Aims of Education* (London: Ernest Benn, 1962).

INDEX